Y OF KILLING RUSSIA'S POLICE CHIEF

The Funeral Procession of the Murdered Minister.

E. S. Sazonov, Who Threw the Bomb,
Photographed in the Hospital.

Gregor, Dulebov, One of the Watch
Who Disguised Himself as a Cabr

returned his bomb to Schweitzer. In
evening we met at the Zoological Ga
Sazonov was depressed. He consi
himself the cause of the failure and r
tained silence. The others were
silent. It was painful to all of us to t
upon the incident of that meeting.
no one dared speak of it. U. was
first to break the silence.

"We haven't a single man with a bo
It is therefore not surprising that we
with failure."

"What do you mean?"

U. answered sternly.

"I say, we are all young people.
don't know how to do things."

Sazonov stared up, but controlled
self. It was evident that he was suf
ing terribly. Sikorsky blushed, but
maintained silence. Kalyaev could
restrain himself.

"Who is to blame?" he asked.

"Who? Do I know who is to blam

"Yes. You are to blame. If you
not gone away with Sikorsky, if you
waited for Schweitzer, I would not
been the only one to get the bomb,
would have been three of us, and
Please, wl

1911.

ELLS OF HIS DEED

The Carriage of the Grand Duke After t

passports. They had left them with
their things at the railway station. I
had the checks. They could not go to
the station for their passports, and without passports they had to pass the night
in the street. They were dressed as peasants, while I was dressed as a well-to-do
Englishman. They were frozen and exhausted, hardly able to walk. I decided
to take them to a restaurant, notwithstanding that our clothes were so different. The taverns were closed.

We entered a restaurant known as
the Alpian Rose. The porter would
not admit us at first. I asked for the
manager, and we were finally admitted.
It was warm, there; Kalyaev soon became animated, and with emotion in his
voice again told us about the scene at the
City Hall. He said that he was afraid
of committing a crime against the Organization and that he felt happy that his
comrades did not censure his action. Alexandrovich was silent. He was pale and
mask

"There will
His firm se
tinued:
"If the G
I'll kill him.
Opanas tu
"Decide s
I decided.
We got o
Square. T
Kreml str
"Good-b
"Good-b
He kisse
to the Ni
I stopp
der 11. I
palace of
stood in
nixed th
the Gra
his offi
I wait
riage a
arrange
Is master of the sar

POLICE AND REDS BOTH HUNT AZEFF

Only Question Seems to be at Whose Hands He Will Die.

PLANNED MANY MASSACRES

While Streets of Russian Cities Ran
with Blood He Lived In Comparative
Luxury with Family In Paris.

Special Cable to THE NEW YORK TIMES.

LONDON, Feb. 6.—Where Is Azeff?
Who will get to him first? Who will
be his executioner, the Russian police
or the revolutionists? These questions
all Europe is asking.

The career of this double traitor and
arch agent provocateur, vile and bloody
as it is, has struck the imagination of
the Continent. The general expectation
is that he will be found and killed, but
if so, regret for him will be felt even
in Russia, because Russia knows and
admires the artistic intrigue, and

is Prince Obolensky, form
of the Holy Synod, he wa
arrested.

Bewildering Mass of

It is a bewildering mas
and corruption. Is Lopuk
scapegoat for the unspeak
ity of the Russian secret po
Was Azeff spirited away
for further use, or is he
flight from both the pol
former Terrorist accomplice
cumstantially reported tha
caped to Japan by way of
One of the four Terrorist
on his track declares that he
ed him in Switzerland. He h
ported in Finland, and is so
been seen in London, on t
and again at Shepherd's Bus

Lopukhin came to this c
teen months ago under myst
cumstances. His daughter,
here, disappeared from a par
the Aldwych Theatre. Two
a letter came from her declar
she was confined in a cellar.
hastened to London and in a
his daughter came back, but
tery of her disappearance and
was never solved.

Azeff's wife resides in Paris
two children. She seems to h
kept in ignorance of her dou
They lived in comparative
while, it is declared, 10,000 Te
ists were executed or imprise
Azeff's instigation and while in
of Moscow, Kieff, Odessa, an
stadt ran with blood during up
organized by Azeff with polico

a Photograph
Had Hurled
Bomb.

Alexander Park
aid:
Have we

another word for
god what a great
allowing such a
tp. He took upon
mask

COMRADE
VALENTINE

COMRADE VALENTINE

Richard E. Rubenstein

Harcourt Brace and Company

New York   San Diego   London

Grateful acknowledgment is made to Doubleday to quote from *Aseff the Spy:
Russian Terrorist and Police Stool* by Boris Nikolajewsky (Trans. by George Reavey.
Copyright Trans. 1934 by Doubleday.) and from *Azef* by Roman Goul (Trans. by
Mirra Ginsburg. Copyright Trans. 1962 by Roman Goul.). Used by permission of
Doubleday, a division of Bantam Doubleday Dell Publishing Group, Inc.

Library of Congress Cataloging-in-Publication Data
Rubenstein, Richard E.
Comrade Valentine/Richard E. Rubenstein.—1st ed.
p. cm.
Includes bibliographical references and index.
ISBN 0-15-152895-0
1. Azef, Evno Fishelevich, 1869–1918. 2. Revolutionaries—
Russia—Biography. 3. Informers—Russia—Biography. 4. Partiĩa
sotsĩalistov-revolĩutsionerov—Biography. 5. Russia—History—Nicholas II,
1894–1917. I. Title.
DK254.A8R77 1994
947.08′092—dc20 93-37988

Designed by Lydia D'moch

Printed in the United States of America
First edition
A B C D E

This book is dedicated to the memory of

BRENDA RUBENSTEIN
EDITH LIBMAN
JOSEPHINE RUBENSTEIN

CONTENTS

Preface

Yevno Azef is not a figure familiar to most modern readers, but there was a time when his name was on everyone's lips. Readers opening the *New York Times* on the morning of February 7, 1909, would have discovered the following headline: "POLICE AND REDS BOTH HUNT AZEFF. Only Question Seems to Be at Whose Hands He Will Die."

"Where is Azeff?" the story began. "Who will get to him first? Who will be his executioner, the Russian police or the revolutionists? These questions all Europe is asking." According to the news report, Russian terrorists had sentenced the fugitive to death on the grounds that he had been a spy for the Secret Police, while the police were convinced that he was a revolutionary terrorist! "It is a bewildering mass of intrigue and corruption," complained the *Times* reporter. "Was Azeff spirited away by the police for further use, or is he actually in flight from both the police and his former Terrorist accomplices?"

For three years the hunt continued, providing a rich feast of rumors and speculation for the European and North American press. Photos and drawings of Azef appeared in newspapers and magazines around the globe. He was reported to have escaped to Japan. He was "located" in Switzerland. He was spotted in Finland, on the Strand in London, and on the streets of New York. Then, in 1912, another sensation: the object of all this attention surfaced long enough to be interviewed in Frankfurt by a well-known Russian journalist. Apparently, he *was* in flight both from the police and the terrorists, having earlier worked in some capacity or other for both sides. As abruptly as he had reappeared, however, the hunted man vanished, leaving behind a smoky trail of unanswered questions.

More pressing matters soon intervened; Europe was engulfed by war and Russia by revolution. Finally, on March 21, 1925, with Calvin Coolidge in the White House and Joseph Stalin beginning his rise to absolute power in the Soviet Union, the *New York Times* wrote finis to its story. "REVEAL MASTER SPY DIED 7 YEARS AGO," announced the headline. "Russians, Seeking Azeff for Sixteen Years, Get Proofs of His Death in Berlin in 1918."

I first came across references to this enigmatic figure while writing a book on the causes and nature of terrorism. Although every expert on political violence had something to say about Azef, his character and motives seemed as obscure in the mid-1980s as they had been in 1909. In the decades after his death, articles about him appeared in numerous journals, accounts of his life were published in at least six languages, and several novels were based wholly or in part on his career. Even so, as Harvard historian Walter Laqueur put it, "the personality of Azef remained an impenetrable mystery." Moreover, the period in which his career flowered—the years of savage underground combat between Russian terrorists and the czar's Secret Police—had virtually disappeared both from Western consciousness and from Russian (i.e., Soviet) history. The Azef Affair had become a mere footnote—another curious relic of Russia's pre-Communist past.

I completed my general study of terrorism only to find myself obsessed by the "impenetrable mystery." Was Azef, as some alleged,

Russia's most deadly terrorist in the turbulent years before the Russian Revolution? Had he also served as a top-ranking agent of the Secret Police? And if he had somehow functioned both as revolutionary and police agent, terrorist and spy, why would anyone play such a strange double game? My research had convinced me that most terrorists, as well as their opposite numbers on the police side, are not incomprehensible monsters, but people like us: relatively normal men and women driven by unusual circumstances to perform extraordinary deeds. But what of Yevno Azef? Could he, by any stretch of the imagination, be considered a person like us?

Answering these questions took almost seven years. Even now, I am not sure that I have plumbed the mystery to its bottom, but it has been an effort well worth making. Azef's story is a rich source of information about the personalities and motives of violent political activists, the social conditions that spawn them, and the shadowy milieux in which they operate. It represents a lost chapter of Russian history, one whose recovery may contribute in some way to that nation's quest for identity and self-understanding. Above all, however, it is a fascinating story in its own right: a tale so filled with dangerous adventures and moral crises, narrow escapes and reversals of fortune, as to seem almost too dramatic for a work of nonfiction.

Had I written a novel about Azef and his contemporaries, I would have omitted much of the "action" described in this biography. Life is less credible than art. Nevertheless, I have tried to keep the work focused on its subject: a Russian Jew, born in poverty, whose search for freedom, security, and power led him to the dark heart of an underground civil war. Enough historical context has been provided to make the period accessible to those unfamiliar with Russian history. It will be for the reader to decide if I have succeeded in making "Comrade Valentine" comprehensible as a human being.

Acknowledgments

I am greatly indebted to a number of experts in Russian language, history, and culture who assisted in the research for this biography.

Dr. Delano Dugarm of Stanford University explored the Boris I. Nikolaevsky Collection of the Hoover Institution Archives at the Hoover Institution on War, Peace, and Revolution, and translated several documents. Dr. Karl Crosby combed through relevant materials at the U.S. Library of Congress and provided valuable advice. Ms. R. Sheila Penners translated Boris Nikolaevsky's monograph, *The Last Days of Azef,* as well as assisted in the translation and interpretation of other materials. Dr. Svetlana Chervonnaya of the Russian Academy of Sciences researched materials available in Moscow, and her colleague, Dr. Vladimir S. Vasiliev, explored the newly declassified police files of the Russian State Archive, uncovering a previously undisclosed letter from Azef to his wife. Naomi Baden undertook numerous research tasks, including the selection of the maps and photographs included in this volume. Karl Payne assisted with research into journalistic sources. Matthew Rubenstein did important bibliographic research. And Judith Paar helped prepare the manuscript for publication. I am most grateful to all these talented and dedicated helpers.

I also want to acknowledge the warm and helpful assistance provided by Dr. Sadi Mase of Washington, D.C., and his wife, Mira Mase. Dr. Mase's father, the famous Rabbi Simon Mase of Moscow, knew Azef and his family quite well. Rabbi and Mrs. Mase shared a *dacha* with the Azefs during one vacation, and it is to their son that I owe the information that Yevno and Lubov Azef had two children, a son and a daughter, who were known by their French nicknames. In addition, Sadi and Mira Mase provided important insights about the period, as well as about Russian politics and culture generally.

My efforts to understand Azef's psychological development and motives were aided by several colleagues and friends. Dr. John W. Burton, my colleague at the Institute for Conflict Analysis and Resolution, drew my attention to the crucial role played by the basic human need for identity in motivating political violence. Dr. Joseph Tarantolo of Washington, D.C., and Dr. Peter Breggin of the Center for the Study of Psychiatry also provided important psychological insights, for which I am most grateful. And I must acknowledge the assistance rendered by an unexpected (and unknowing) source: John le Carré, whose novel *A Perfect Spy* brilliantly illuminated the personal development of a double agent. Naturally, none of these experts is responsible for my own interpretation of Azef's personality.

John Radziewicz, my editor at Harcourt Brace & Company, guided my progress with unfailing patience, good taste, enthusiasm, and wit, as well as sharing his considerable knowledge of Russian language and culture. Thank you, John. Thanks also to Ronald Goldfarb, my friend and literary agent, and to the faculty, students, and staff of the Institute for Conflict Analysis and Resolution at George Mason University, who did so much to support this lengthy project. I am particularly grateful to Christopher R. Mitchell, the institute's director, and to Mary Lynn Boland, its office manager.

This book would not have been completed were it not for the personal support furnished by colleagues, friends, and family following the death of my beloved wife, Brenda Rubenstein, in 1991. I am grateful to Peter Bloom, whose insight helped me to work creatively during a period of grief and personal reconstruction, and to a community of gracious friends including (but not limited to) Ann and Larry Ribstein, Sheila and Kevin Avruch, Lois and Chris Mitchell, and Buzz and Alice Palmer. Most of all, I have been sustained each day by the love of Nicki and Shana Rubenstein, Matthew and Alec Rubenstein, DeAnn Trucano, Ellen and Michael Schwartz, Ludwig Libman, and Judie Paar. My wife, Beth Rubenstein, knows how much her unfailing courage and devotion contributed to the completion of this work.

R. E. R.

Pronunciation and Method

To pronounce Azef's name correctly, one accents the first syllable of his first name and the second syllable of his surname, pronouncing the *A* as in *Ah*. Thus: YEV-no Ah-ZEF. The reader will already have noticed that the surname is spelled "Azeff" by the *New York Times*. Those inspired to read earlier books about him will also find him called "Asef," "Aseff," "Asew," and "Azev"—the inevitable result of transliterating Cyrillic names into languages using the Roman alphabet. I have adhered generally to the transliteration system of the United States Board of Geographic Names, and have used Russian names rather than their English equivalents, except where the English equivalent of a well-known name is in common use (for example, Catherine the Great, Moscow).

Russians' names ordinarily come in three parts: first name, patronymic, and family name. Since Azef's father was called Fischel, the son would have been named Yevno Fischelevich Azef, and he would have been addressed as "Yevno Fischelevich." For the sake of simplicity and ease of reading, however, I have dropped all patronymics, except where full names are used in direct quotations. The participants in this story are referred to, as they would be in American English, by their first and family names.

Some may wonder about the derivation of Azef's first name. Evidently, Yevno (which may also be found spelled "Evno" and "Ievno") has no English equivalent and is not a common name either in Russian, Yiddish, Lithuanian, or Polish. It may simply be a case of the sort of parental inventiveness that one often finds today, especially among impoverished families seeking to give their children some ineffaceable stamp of individuality. Several writers, considering Yevno a shortened form of Yevgeny, took it upon themselves to call Azef "Eugene," but I have seen no evidence that he was ever called Yevgeny.

So far as dates are concerned, I have used the modern Western (Gregorian) calendar exclusively, except when referring to an event whose accepted designation is based on the Julian calendar in effect in Russia from 1699 until 1918, for example, the "October Revolution." During most of the period covered by this book, Russians would have dated events according to their old calendar, which after 1900 ran thirteen days behind ours.

In several places in the text, I have also given the modern dollar equivalents of Russian rubles. These conversions were accomplished by taking into account the exchange rate in 1909 (1 dollar = 2.1 rubles) and multiplying by an inflation factor (based on the percentage increase in Gross Domestic Product) of 18. Thus a 1909 ruble is considered to have been worth about nine 1993 U.S. dollars—a very rough equivalence, to be sure, since the old Russian economy more closely resembled that of a modern Third World nation than that of the United States.

Finally, I should say a brief word about my biographical method. The interpretation of character, we understand, calls for the exercise of imagination as well as scholarly judgment—a task made more complex when the subject, like Azef, "speaks" more through actions than words. Nevertheless, this is a biography, *not* a historical novel. I have not invented facts, altered them, or reversed their order in time, nor have I pretended to know what participants in the story were thinking or feeling in the absence of compelling documentary evidence of their states of mind. Where I speculate about such matters, I do so openly, with notice to the reader. Where conflicting versions of certain events exist, I have chosen the version that makes most sense to me, giving my reasons in the *Notes on Sources* appended to the text. On occasion, I have taken the liberty of reconstructing conversations, based on the available evidence. The *Notes on Sources* indicate where this technique has been employed. Quotation marks are never used in the text, however, except where the remark quoted is documented by a reliable source.

Azef and Hedy at the Seashore

Prologue

THERE IS THIS PECULIARITY about charismatic figures: no one seems quite able to describe them. Or perhaps I should say that although everybody tries to describe them, the descriptions overlap without coinciding. They leave us with a blurred image, as if the subject were moving too fast to be caught by the camera.

Boris Savinkov, the terrorist, novelist, and *bon vivant,* first met Azef in 1903. His impression was that of "a man about thirty years old, very stout, with a broad, calm face which seemed to have been hewn from stone, and big, gray eyes." To friends and followers Azef *was* a rock: powerful, steadfast, obdurate, and impenetrable. They speak of his quiet authority, his mastery of detail, his patience, determination, and warm concern for their welfare. Men were prepared to die at his command; women found him strangely attractive. But others, no less knowledgeable, declare him a repulsive personality. Their Azef is a cold and menacing figure feared for his cruel tongue and distrusted for his inscrutability—a man in whom some essential human characteristic seemed always to be missing.

Was Yevno Azef a mere schemer or a master of scientific planning? A disciplined person with a taste for pleasure or an addict of money and sex? While his closest comrade in the revolutionary movement praises his "cool courage as a terrorist," a knowledgeable biographer labels him "a coward at heart." Even descriptions of his voice vary with the onlooker's perspective. According to one former colleague, it was "deep and melodious," but another heard it as "a harsh rumble." Canceling out the conflicting adjectives leaves us in the company of one whose gift—or curse—was to be perceived in radically different ways by different observers.

On one fact, at least, all witnesses agree: Azef was not a handsome man. Photographic evidence confirms the ovoid skull, surmounted by a short crop of dark, woolly hair; the pronounced occipital ridge and dark brows overhanging surprisingly large, protuberant eyes; the large, flat nose, fleshy lips, and round, jutting jaw that make one think of unlikely combinations such as a black Mussolini or a Jewish Tatar. A short man, surely no more than five feet six inches tall, Azef weighed at least 180 pounds. One of his party pseudonyms was "The Fat One," and fat he was, although he carried a good deal of that weight in his chest and powerful shoulders.

Examine the photograph entitled "Azef and Hedy at the Seashore" at the beginning of the prologue. A small, heavyset man stands almost up to his navel in the surf, staring directly into the camera with something like a smile. His companion stands a foot or two behind him. She stoops slightly as if to minimize the difference in their heights, but she cannot help overtopping him. The water barely covers her knees.

Beauty and the Beast! Both are dressed in Edwardian bathing costumes. Azef's striped shirt is comical, emphasizing his bulk, while Hedy's dark gown and cloche are charmingly suggestive. One can understand how, dressed in a low-cut gown with those long white arms gesturing dramatically, she could have become the toast of the St. Petersburg nightclub circuit, "*la belle* Hedy de Hero." Yet Azef dominates the photo. He stands like a rock in the foaming surf, supporting his beloved with a firm hand while the sunlit world evaporates all around him.

We do not know when or where this snapshot was taken, but the very fact that Azef allowed it to be taken suggests that the year was 1910 or 1911, and the place a resort on the Greek or Italian coast. Before that time, the man in the striped bathing suit had every reason to be camera-shy, for he was the leader of the most feared terrorist group in Russia: the Fighting Organization of the Socialist Revolutionary party.

The Organization was a name to be whispered, not spoken aloud, in St. Petersburg's richly furnished ministries and salons. At its hands, more than two hundred czarist officials, including Russia's most powerful grand duke, two ministers of the interior, several governors of provinces, and numerous generals, admirals, police chiefs, prison officials, and lower-level bureaucrats, not to mention several important police spies, had met their deaths. Reason enough to have avoided staring into any camera's eye—but Azef had another motive for avoiding photographs like the one taken at the seashore. The woman in the picture, photos of whom were reproduced on postcards and sold wherever she performed, was not his wife. Shortly after he posed as if on honeymoon with Hedy, Azef's wife and two children were on their way to the United States, part of the great tide of Russian immigrants seeking new lives (and, in their cases, new identities) in a new land.

By 1910, "The Fat One" was a former family man and a retired terrorist. Even so, to allow this photograph to be taken required a certain courage (or foolhardiness), for in 1909, sentenced to die, he had fled Russia with Hedy, closely pursued by his enemies. Strangely, it was not the Russian government that had tried Azef and condemned him, but his old comrades of the Socialist Revolutionary party. Even as he posed for the camera like a businessman on vacation, they hunted him, convinced beyond doubt that the chief of their Fighting Organization, the man they called their "Eagle," was actually an agent of the czar's Secret Police.

What does the man in the snapshot think about as he poses with mock formality for an unknown photographer? Once master of the chase, he is now the quarry. Did he yield uneasily to Hedy's request for a souvenir? Will he demand that the negative be destroyed? Probably not. Smiling in the surf with the sun at his back, he looks very much like a man with nothing more to lose.

ONE

Entrapment and Escape

Is this not the fast that I have chosen?
To loose the fetters of wickedness,
To undo the bands of the yoke,
And to let the oppressed go free,
And that ye break every yoke?
—ISAIAH 58:6

TO KNOW ONE'S COUNTRY of birth is a privilege of sorts. Some territories are painted a new color with every change of the political map, and some peoples are forbidden to claim any color as their own. For Yevno Azef, the matter of nationality was problematical. His birthplace was Lyskovo, a rural market town that once belonged to Poland and is now part of Belarus. In 1869, when he was born, it was formally—but only formally—Russian. For Azef was a Jew, and Lyskovo was located in the Pale of Settlement, the territory to which the Jews had been confined ever since Catherine the Great seized it from Poland in the 1790s.

For more than two centuries, Jews had been barred from entering Russia—an exclusion that Catherine wholeheartedly approved. But when Russia, Prussia, and Austria dismembered the Kingdom of Poland in the 1790s, the empress suddenly found herself possessed of more than one million Yiddish-speaking subjects: the largest concentration of Jews anywhere in the eighteenth-century world. Most of them were poor laborers; there was a mere smattering of merchants and tradesmen. Nevertheless, Catherine feared that they would spread throughout the empire like an alien plague, infecting pious Russian peasants with the diseases of commercialism and religious doubt. Therefore, she forbade them to settle or even to travel elsewhere in her domains. For more than one century, Russia's Jews were to be confined to the twenty-five formerly Polish provinces stretching from the Baltics to the Black Sea: the Pale of Settlement.

Yevno Azef's grandparents were among the first generation of Jews to be trapped in the Pale. By the time their grandson was born, Catherine the Great's unwanted million had become five million, and her ban on emigration had been supplemented by a long list of internal restrictions. The Jews were forbidden to engage in most profitable occupations, to lease land, manage inns and taverns, or employ Christian workers. They were forbidden to attend universities or enter the professions; forbidden to open rabbinical academies or operate publishing houses; forbidden to govern themselves locally or to live in rural villages. Soon they would be forbidden even to wear their traditional clothing and to defend themselves against anti-Semitic mobs.

Held in place by these restrictions, the inhabitants of the Pale were beginning to die en masse. Jobs were scarce and hunger was endemic. Crime and prostitution flourished. Disease was rampant and schooling primitive, reinforcing the image of the backward, "dirty Jew." Some Jews believed that their rabbis could fly like birds; others wore charms to protect them against the "Evil Eye" and terrors unknown. They had reason to be fearful: in the year of Azef's birth, a plague of typhus struck the region, killing thousands already weakened by starvation, mainly children and old people. That same year, the Russian government sanctioned the publication of *The Book of the Kahal,* a sensational exposé that "proved" the existence of a worldwide Jewish conspiracy directed from Paris, aimed at cheating honest Christians and overthrowing Christian governments. Shortly thereafter, Russia experienced her first modern massacre of Jews: the Odessa pogrom of 1871, which was allowed to continue for four days while the authorities stood by approvingly.

Confronted by this implacable pressure, many Jews gave up all hope of worldly advancement. Singing and dancing in their synagogues, they awaited the arrival of the Chosen One who would liberate them at last from poverty, violence, and injustice. "On that day," they chanted, "the Lord will be One and his Name will be One." But Yevno Azef's parents nurtured another kind of hope. Their inspiration was not the promised messiah but a Russian ruler: Alexander II, known by his people as the "Czar-Liberator."

Eight years before Azef was born, the czar had earned his sobriquet by emancipating Russia's serfs. He topped that generous act, so far as the Jews were concerned, by abolishing the hated system of conscription established by his predecessor, Nicholas I, an attempt to wreck the Jewish family by requiring boys as young as eight or nine years old to serve in the army for a period of twenty-five years. When Alexander equalized the conscription laws applicable to Jews and Christians, expectations rose in the Pale. When he opened the universities and professions to a limited number of Jewish students, hope surged. And when he issued decrees permitting certain classes of Jews—merchants, academicians, army veterans, and skilled artisans—to emigrate freely throughout Russia, many thought that the Day of Liberation was at hand. Wrote the poet Judah Loeb Gordon:

> Arise, my people, it's time for waking!
> The night is over; day is breaking.

The celebration, as it turned out, was premature. Alexander's Great Reform was inspired more by national pride than by liberal ideals. His nation's humiliating defeat in the Crimean War had convinced him that Russia must either modernize or become a helpless puppet of more advanced nations. By liberating certain Jews, he intended to open the Russian heartland to settlement by the "better class" of merchants and artisans, those with capital or skills essential to Russia's development. It went without saying that the useless rabble still trapped in the Pale would deserve their fate.

Those who had bothered to read the czar's decree would have noted
its ominous diction:

> All regulations at present governing the Jews are to be sub-
> jected to a revision in order to harmonize them with the
> ultimate aim of fusing this people with the native population,
> insofar as the moral condition of the Jews allows of such
> fusion.

The grateful émigrés, Alexander expected, would assimilate cultur-
ally at first, then in matters of religious belief, with the Russian
population. If they did not—if the beneficiaries of royal generosity
failed to "fuse" or proved troublesome in other ways—they would
be suitably punished.

To the Azefs, however, the czar's motives were irrelevant; what
mattered was that the doors to their prison had at last been thrown
open. Yevno's father, Fischel, was only a tailor, and not a very
successful one at that, but tailoring was a trade that qualified him
for emigration as a skilled artisan. Moreover, unlike the majority
of his compatriots, he had a source of income that would enable
him to save enough to make the thousand-mile trek with his family
to South Russia. Fischel and his wife, Sosha, knew exactly where
they would settle once they had acquired the price of the journey.
Their promised land was Rostov-on-Don, a thriving city some six
hundred miles south of Moscow, on the Don River near the Black
Sea.

Other Jews who had moved to Rostov reported that it was a
booming agricultural depot and center of new industry, a rough-
and-tumble river town where one's origins mattered less than one's
talent for trade. There an ambitious mender of clothes could become
a respected dealer in cloth: a merchant! There one could follow
Judah Loeb Gordon's advice to be "a Jew at home, but a man in
the street." In Rostov, it was said, even a mere tailor could earn
enough to put his sons through the local *gymnasium*. Yevno and his
brothers would become educated men, reading and writing in Rus-

sian and associating with Russian children of the middle class. With a little luck they would graduate, and then . . . anything was possible. They might become businessmen on a grand scale, traveling the empire in search of adventure and opportunity. Better yet, they might go on to become learned men, members of the growing but still select professional class—*intelligents*. Unless Fischel became a wealthy merchant, his daughters would not have the same opportunities; his limited funds were reserved for the education of boys. But through their husbands, they, too, would find respectable lives in Rostov. . . .

A restless soul, this little tailor, with visions far outreaching his humble abilities and station. In the spring of 1874, he and Sosha bundled their children and few belongings into a horse-drawn cart and left the Pale forever, traveling south to Odessa, on the shores of the Black Sea, and then east through Cossack territory to their final destination on the River Don. The following year, Fischel invested what was left of his savings in cheap cloth and attempted to establish himself as a draper. But he was not one of those "clever, grasping Jews" so envied and feared by Russia's anti-Semites. Expert with a needle and thread, he was baffled by the intricacies of trade. In the mid-1870s Fischel's business failed, and he was forced to return to simple tailoring. His dream of merchanthood was never to be realized; twenty years later, a Rostov police report would describe the Azefs still as "a poor family."

Even so, he and Sosha managed somehow to put their two boys through the local *gymnasium*—a significant achievement for an impoverished Jewish family. At school, their eldest son excelled at science and mathematics. Little else is known of Azef's schoolboy experiences. Decades later, after he had become notorious, tales circulated representing him as a strange, untrustworthy child with few friends—a trickster and a rebel. One story has it that he informed the school authorities of other students' misdeeds. Another alleges that he was expelled from school several years before graduation for some signal act of disobedience. But these tales seem apocryphal. So far as we know, Azef graduated from the *gymnasium* with his class in 1890. A few months later, he went to work as a correspondent for the local newspaper, the *Don Bee*. Not long after that, as his parents had done more than two decades earlier, he would dream of nothing but escape.

What Fischel and Sosha did not understand when they made their long pilgrimage into the Russian interior was that they were exchanging one sort of confinement, brutal and direct, for another, more subtle and variable. The Russia of Yevno Azef's youth was a welter of contradictions: a land of rising cities where illiterate peasants still used the traditional wooden plow; a nation modernizing, yet clinging to medieval customs and values; a place of opportunity for ambitious (or unscrupulous) entrepreneurs, but wedded still to antique notions of social gradation and privilege. Outwardly, the environment the Azefs found in Rostov was similar to that which they might have discovered had they emigrated to the American Midwest instead of South Russia. In both places, slaves or serfs had recently been liberated and new lands brought under the plow. Large populations were on the move, trade flourished, and cities of the interior blossomed overnight. But there the similarities ended.

Rostov-on-Don would not be allowed to become a Russian St. Louis or Chicago. The "Czar-Liberator's" government wanted the nation developed, but not at the price of westernizing (or, god forbid, "Judaizing") it. Economic change must not be allowed to impair the monarch's absolute power over his subjects or the landowner's authority over his peasants. Wives must remain subject to their husbands, children to their parents, and students to their teachers. Non-Russian peoples must acknowledge the supremacy of Great Russian culture, and non-Christian religions that of the Holy Orthodox Church. In practice, this meant that the Autocracy would be compelled to take back with its left hand what it gave with the right. It would be forced to suppress the political effects of the very changes that (in its capacity as modernizer) it sponsored. Every burst of reform would be followed by a longer period of reaction; every promise, raising hopes for more radical change, by bitter betrayal. And of all groups, the Jews of Russia would feel the sting of these violent alternations most keenly.

Without knowing it, Fischel Azef and his family had stepped into a devious trap. They had been liberated in order to help develop their country, but the only development permitted would be that which maintained the nation's medieval, authoritarian traditions intact. In Alexander II's ambitious plans there was no place for poor tradesmen like Fischel, who lived on the narrow margins of survival, or for ungrateful students like Yevno, who took advantage of a Russian education without accepting the three dogmas of czarist rule: Autocracy, Nationalism, Orthodoxy. Even before the Azefs reached Rostov, in fact, the czar was having second thoughts about his Great Reform. Outside their confines, his advisors informed him, the Jews were doing *too* well! The older ones worked as if possessed, buying and selling, scheming and saving—and most of them, clannish as ever, clung to their old customs and beliefs. Their children, moreover, were worse. Casting off their parents' reticence and piety, they flooded the schools and universities, devouring secular education as if it were food and drink. These young Jews *were* losing their identity as a separate people, but with whom did they fuse? The most radical student generation in Russia's history: the idealists of the 1870s, who talked of nothing but democracy, land reform, and socialism!

When one of these students—the son of an impoverished nobleman—fired a pistol at the czar as he strolled in St. Petersburg's Summer Gardens, Alexander knew that it was time to rethink his whole program of reform, starting with the "Jewish problem."

What *was* the problem? If its essential features were Jewish isolation and backwardness, the obvious solutions were emancipation and education. Let the Azefs emigrate to Rostov-on-Don. Let Fischel the tailor dream of merchanthood and work to achieve it. Let him enroll his son in a modern secular school, and let the boy believe that, with hard work and a "Jewish head," he could become what he desperately longed to be: a scientist, a professional man, and a

Russian. But if the problem was the Chosen People's refusal to assimilate, their unscrupulousness in business, and (in the case of the young) their inclination toward subversive thinking, the solution would not be liberation but "reclassification." Those outside the Pale would have to be enumerated, supervised, controlled, and, if necessary, expelled from Christian communities, while those still inside were disposed of by the simple expedient of denying them the right to make a living. In this case, Fischel the tailor must be made to understand that he was *not* safe in Rostov—that the authorities who released him from the Pale could easily return him thence for "bad behavior." And his son, too, must face facts. For him a Russian university degree was out of the question. Unless Fischel became wealthy enough to send him to college in Western Europe, Yevno Azef would never become a professional man.

The Azefs had left their little town in the Pale buoyed by the same hopes that were beginning to draw Russian Jews to America: the dreams of prosperity and freedom. The first was dashed by Fischel's commercial failure, the second by an event that shaped his son's future and that of a whole generation of Russian students: the assassination of Alexander II.

Yevno Azef was eleven years old when the blow fell. In 1881, the young militants of the People's Will organization finally caught up with the Czar-Liberator, whom they hated for betraying the earlier promises of the Great Reform. Led by a woman, Sofia Perovskaya, a squad of terrorists disabled the czar's carriage with one nitroglycerin grenade and killed him with another. Although the assassin, a boy named Ignacy Hryniewicki, was a Pole and most of his fellow-conspirators "pure" Russians of the upper and middle classes, a few were Jewish. Immediately, the government gave the anti-Semitic newspapers permission to blame the regicide on the Jews, and a wave of pogroms swept southern and western Russia. While police stood idly by or actively encouraged the rioters, 160 communities were attacked, with hundreds of lives lost and countless homes and shops destroyed. Although Rostov was spared, nearby Jewish communities in the Ukraine were devastated.

This was bad enough news for the Azefs, but worse was to follow. Alexander II was succeeded by the last Russian czar to die a natural death: the capable and vicious Alexander III. This Alexander was a fanatical reactionary whose solution to the Jewish problem, in the words of his principal advisor, was "to force one-third of them to emigrate, another third to embrace Christianity, and the remainder to die of starvation." The new czar's May Laws, passed when Azef was thirteen, restricted the movement of Jews within the Pale, curtailed their rights to own property outside it, and attempted to force those in "Russian Russia" to return to their original confines.

Now Fischel Azef and his family walked a tightrope over a yawning chasm, barely managing to escape disaster. New regulations gave guild masters the power to regulate "Jewish trades" like tailoring and provided for the expulsion of those who violated the rules. New decrees forbade unbaptized Jews to take Christian names and blocked their access to education. Three years before Azef graduated from *gymnasium,* the minister of education imposed strict quotas limiting the number of Jews allowed to attend public schools and universities. One year later, Rostov was added to the growing list of areas closed to new Jewish settlers. And the year that Azef graduated, the czar's uncle, the Grand Duke Sergei, ordered the entire Jewish population of Moscow to be expelled, with permission to remain granted only to two classes of individuals: those who submitted to baptism and registered Jewish prostitutes.

Little wonder that the Azefs remained "a poor family." Each new ordinance provided czarist bureaucrats with another method of extorting bribes from vulnerable Jews; those unable to purchase the favor of powerful officials were returned unceremoniously to the Pale. Simply to remain in Rostov and to educate their children was no small accomplishment, considering the obstacles thrown in their way by a tyrannical, capricious government. But Azef's father spent his life's energy negotiating the narrow passage between the czar's hatred of the Jews and his servants' willingness to be corrupted by them. If he had succeeded in business, his daughters might have had dowries and his sons Russian university educations despite the anti-Jewish laws. Since he did not, his children faced a world still bounded by poverty and anti-Semitism—indeed, a world more painfully limited for ambitious Jews than even Fischel's had been.

This oppression defined the environment in which Azef came to manhood. Its hallmark was dependence: not the need for parental authority that most children reject naturally (but painfully) in the course of growing up, but reliance upon forces as distant and capricious as they were omnipotent, and beside which one's own parents seemed helpless children. Almost by definition, young people subjected to this sort of official abuse bear a heavy burden of shame and rage. Many come to despise not only the public authority that degrades them, but also the parents who have failed to protect them. Perhaps most deeply, they despise that part of themselves that, like a fearful child, remains dependent upon the will of the oppressor, ever seeking his protection and approval.

It is not hard to imagine how this humiliating dependence must have galled the tailor's eldest son, whose adult life was to be dominated by a passion for personal and political independence. The czar, whom he hated, was everything that his own father was not. While Fischel schemed and struggled merely to survive, never escaping the daily dangers and humiliations visited upon Russia's Jews, the "Little Father" in St. Petersburg could allow Yevno to attend school or bar him from the classroom, grant him special privileges or subject him to public disgrace, permit him to succeed in a respectable calling or doom him to poverty and failure. One could not trust the czar's promises any more than Fischel's dreams, but in the tyrant's strength there was an . . . *effectuality* that made him a model of sorts as well as a villain.

Azef left no schoolboy diary to record his youthful hopes and fears. Nevertheless, it seems likely that he grew up hating the government for its malevolence while secretly admiring its power, just as he honored his parents' self-sacrifice while rejecting their fatal vulnerability. Long before he left Rostov-on-Don, Azef had abandoned his identity as the little tailor's son. Whatever became of him, he would not be Yevno *ben* Fischel, a hereditary victim. Never would he be another of the czar's helpless Jews.

Here is Azef, the *gymnasium* graduate, already, at the age of twenty-one, a mysterious figure, an object of rumor and speculation. His parents, it is known, are poor, and the young man himself has no regular employment. He tutors rich men's sons, peddles news stories to the Rostov paper, the *Don Bee,* sells butter and eggs on consignment for local merchants, . . . but he dresses elegantly. After work, he is often seen in the cafés and taverns frequented by well-heeled businessmen and students of the wilder sort. Some say that he is involved in illegal business activities. Others report that he borrows heavily from wealthy friends, often "forgetting" to repay his debts. Azef himself says little about his affairs (indeed, he is not one for talking much about anything), but his occasional remarks suggest a life considerably more complex and shadowy than that of his Rostov friends.

He is a fat, homely young man, with his Jewish origins stamped irrevocably on his features. With his unprepossessing appearance, his lengthy silences, his distaste for physical activity, and his air of superiority, one would expect him to be an easy target for cruel jibes and insults—but his associates learn not to take Azef lightly. Those who do soon find themselves scorched by a venomous tongue. His capacity for contemptuous rage is legendary; his detractors maintain a cautious distance between themselves and the object of their gossip. A touchy, secretive fellow, this Azef, defending his wounded pride with the bitter hauteur of an exiled prince. One would hardly suppose him to be a popular fellow, and yet within a small circle of devoted admirers, he is considered a natural leader: warm, considerate, ingenious, and daring. His unusual calmness makes him seem older than his years. He has few illusions. And he . . . *knows* things. A certain bribable inspector of food products is selling crates of slightly damaged fruits and vegetables at a fraction of their market value. A certain innkeeper has a soft spot (and a cheap bed in his

attic room) for young people in love. A certain bookseller will slip
you a dog-eared copy of Plekhanov's *Socialism and the Political Struggle* if you promise to return it after reading. . . .

What some find repellent in Azef—this peculiar combination
of outsider's alienation and insider's cunning—proves irresistible to
others. Those with unusual "deals" to make or a taste for dangerous
discussion solicit his company. Certain women of the town, as well
as schoolgirls of the more emancipated sort, seem unaccountably
drawn to him. Among the rumors that circulate about Azef is one
that he finds not displeasing: his appetite for love is said to be as
large as his capacity at table. Outwardly a cynic, he is a romantic
in his personal life, a compelling combination to those who know
him well. But there are few—very few—who know him well.

Azef's closest friends are students or ex-students like himself,
youths whose intellectual abilities and social aspirations far outrun
the opportunities available to them in Alexander III's Russia. Hopeful and desperate, these angry idealists dream of smashing the system
that holds them in thrall. Politically impotent but filled with moral
fervor, they long to play dramatic, history-making roles: Philosopher,
Liberator, Martyr. Their moral heroes are the terrorists of the People's Will, young people like themselves who sacrificed their lives
to rid their nation of a tyrant. Their political bible is Nikolai Chernyshevsky's utopian novel, *What Is to Be Done?*, which envisions a
democratic, socialist society where youths of both sexes are free to
express their individuality. But Azef and his comrades also devour
the works of Karl Marx and his leading Russian interpreter, Georgy
Plekhanov, as well as tracts illegally published by anarchist, populist,
and liberal thinkers. Endlessly, they argue the great issues of revolutionary theory: Will Russia be liberated by small groups of terrorist fighters, an uprising of the peasant masses, or a workers'
revolution? Should the nation become a liberal democracy like England or America, or should it opt for some sort of socialism? And
if socialism is the answer, should it be decentralized and agrarian,
as the populists urge, or centralized and industrial, as the Marxists
propose?

Strangely, a number of these voluble young people look for political guidance to Azef, the taciturn Jew. Or perhaps this is not so strange, since he possesses what they lack: gravity, patience, a knack for organization and planning, and knowledge of the streets. Above all, his views bear the conviction of one who lives (not just espouses) them. He does not burn with indignation for the nameless poor or concoct fanciful utopias. Not for him the "romance of suffering"—an affectation especially prevalent among those who have never known the bite of real poverty and personal humiliation. Azef's rage is the product of his own experience. His ideas are his own. And his frank intention is to liberate *himself* by destroying the czarist system.

Highly persuasive in face-to-face conversation, the young Azef was no orator. He distrusted rhetorical brilliance and had nothing but contempt for politicians who substituted words for action. In this distaste for "mere talk," he resembled the youth of the People's Will, who preferred "direct action" (that is, terrorism) to other sorts of political activity. But at this point in his life, Azef was neither a populist nor a terrorist. He did not share the former's confidence in the peasant masses or the latter's faith that acts of heroic violence would inspire the "Black People" of the villages to rebel. On the contrary, what he found most inspiring were *Western* ideas and institutions. He particularly admired German science and culture, including the "scientific socialism" of Marx and Engels. Just by looking about in Rostov-on-Don, one could see that it was the workers, not the peasants, who were beginning to challenge czarist rule. With little help from intellectuals, and at great risk to themselves, they had begun to organize their own trade unions and political associations. Activists interested in making the Revolution, as opposed to merely talking about it, should obviously address themselves to this new mass movement.

These thoughts naturally drew the young radical in the direction of the Social Democrats—the name then used by both German and

Russian Marxists. Not long after graduating from school, he joined a small circle of Social Democratic intellectuals who assigned him the task of writing tracts inciting the workers of Rostov to organize and strike. This is how Azef enters public history: as a revolutionary youth with a private library of forbidden books, a primitive mimeograph machine, and, very shortly, a police record.

His Marxism, however, was only skin deep. While the workers' rebellious temper excited his admiration, collectivism of any sort ultimately left him cold. His favorite work of German philosophy was not Marx's *Capital* but Max Stirner's *The Ego and Its Own,* a book proclaiming the individual to be the source of all value. On Azef's personal scale of values, freedom always ranked higher than equality. The Russia of his dreams was a nation in which every individual would be free to take his own chances, make his own rules, and carve out his own path in life. Had Azef's family been wealthier, and had he not been disillusioned by the government's continual betrayals, he would most likely have become a liberal— one of those reform-minded professionals working to turn czarist tyranny into constitutional democracy. But experience told him that the czar would never permit himself to be transformed peacefully into a Russian version of Queen Victoria. Violence was inevitable, even if its only purpose would be to turn Russia into a civilized nation. The problem that no political organization in Russia had solved was how to combine the ideals of urban liberalism with the methods of violent revolution.

The Rostov police, however, were not interested in these nice distinctions. Horrified by the rise of labor militancy among previously docile workers, the authorities were prepared to pay good money to obtain copies of seditious Social Democratic pamphlets and descriptions of their authors and distributors. Rostov was a small world. The police already had most of its troublemaking intellectuals under observation, and it did not take them long to discover that one source of the literary contagion was the malcontent Jew, Yevno Azef. Somehow or other—it is not clear how—the pamphleteer got wind of the fact that his role was known and that he could be arrested at any moment. At the time (in the spring of 1892), he was in possession of a shipment of butter worth eight hundred rubles, which he was to sell on consignment for a butter-and-egg merchant, one of the many businessmen profiting from the famine then ravaging the Russian countryside. Azef later told his friends that he sold the butter, pocketed the cash, and left immediately for Karlsruhe in Germany, where he enrolled in the university as an engineering student.

This may well have happened. For Azef to finance his escape from Rostov with a crime would surely be in character. He longed desperately to leave the provincial city and to become a professional man with a German university degree. Already toughened by experience, he would have found criminal acts of the more common sort easier to carry out than someone of gentler background. The restraints of what he and his comrades liked to call "conventional morality" might have prevented him from stealing earlier to finance his university education, but a strong push from the police would have been sufficient to dissolve those inhibitions. In any case, to take a little profit from a businessman enriched by famine might well have seemed more an "expropriation" than a theft.

The story of the purloined butter is quite convincing . . . but then, all of Azef's stories were convincing. When he arrived in Karlsruhe, his comrades in the Russian émigré community at the Polytechnic Institute were fascinated to learn about his narrow escape from the police, financed by a greedy speculator's ill-gotten gains. But less than one year later, when he applied to the Russian Secret Police for a job as a political informer, a report by the Rostov Gendarmerie favoring his application described him as a "clever intriguer" and a needy, "covetous" man. Moreover, when Prime Minister Stolypin described Azef's career years later in a speech to the Russian parliament, he stated that he had begun working for the police in 1892.

Did Azef enter into relations with the police *before* leaving Rostov, perhaps after discovering that they were about to arrest him? Did he, in fact, join the Social Democrats at the request of the local gendarmerie? These questions are probably unanswerable, but Azef's later activities give cause to wonder whether it was the theft of butter that purchased his freedom or whether he had some other, even more questionable, source of funds.

Newly arrived in Karlsruhe, Azef was accepted almost immediately as a valued member of the Russian student group at the Polytechnic Institute. A number of his comrades were from Rostov, many were Jews, and together they enjoyed a freedom and excitement unavailable to students at even the best Russian universities. Karlsruhe, a city of great charm and sophistication, was located in the Rhineland, for centuries Germany's "window on the West." France was within easy reach, as was Switzerland, the home of exiles and the birthplace of revolutionary conspiracies. Heidelberg's famous university was a short distance away, and some thirty miles to the north lay Darmstadt, with its advanced engineering school, where Azef would later complete his training and receive his degree in electrical engineering. At the university he studied electrodynamics, a rapidly developing field that appealed to the more philosophically minded students. But during his first few months in the Rhineland, studying was the least of his pleasures.

The German universities were considered among the best in the world. Foreign students were everywhere, living in little colonies according to their country of origin, their youthful plots and peccadilloes ignored, for the most part, by the German police. For Russian students, in particular, the experience of freedom was intoxicating. No travel restrictions! No forbidden books! One could even advocate a revolution in Russia without fear of arrest or persecution. And for Azef, what pleasure to be a European, not just a Russian Jew—to be able to move at will from country to country, to attend scientific meetings and political congresses, to sit up all night talking politics with his comrades, or to join them in joyous pursuit of more earthy pleasures. Best of all was the feeling that he was a member of the intellectual vanguard, that small group of advanced thinkers destined to transform society through the force of ideas and willpower. Science and politics: with these levers, one could move the world. For Germany, once as backward as Russia, was palpably transforming herself into a modern nation through the power of scientific learning and technology. Here, intellectuals were no moody dreamers; here, one could be both a respectable professional *and* a radical. In the year that Azef arrived in Karlsruhe, the once-banned German Social Democratic party received more than one-fourth of the total vote in parliamentary elections, prompting old Friedrich Engels himself to declare that an age of peaceful revolutions was at hand.

During the winter, Azef and his comrades organized a Social Democratic propaganda group, hoping to establish contact with revolutionary activists back in Russia. At the same time, however, he found his personal situation deteriorating. The cash that he had brought from Russia was dwindling, and the regulations applicable to foreign students in Germany made it virtually impossible to earn money locally. As the weather turned bitterly cold, he found it increasingly difficult to heat his fourth-floor walk-up at 30 Wertherstrasse, a room that he shared with another student from Rostov. Obtaining food also became a serious problem. The fat man suffered constantly from hunger and developed a chronic throat infection. Even worse, he now faced the possibility that the poverty that had dogged him from childhood might also extinguish his dreams of education and success.

This prospect now seemed intolerable. Azef survived the winter, but on April 4, 1893, his funds exhausted, he addressed two unsigned letters to Russia, one to police headquarters in St. Petersburg, the other to the Gendarmerie at Rostov. "I have the honor to inform your Highness," he began, "that two months ago a circle of revolutionaries was formed here. . . ." Shrewdly, he avoided asking for money. His letters mentioned several students' names, briefly described their activities in Germany, and noted that their intention was to link up with revolutionists in Rostov and their other cities of origin. If the authorities found this information useful, he added, they should respond by registered letter to a Karlsruhe address.

These revelations were not dramatic, but Azef judged correctly that with far more revolutionary activity taking place outside than inside Russia, the Secret Police would be thirsty for information about the networks of radical students and émigrés proliferating abroad. His letter was quickly passed to high police officials, who ordered an investigation to determine his identity. On May 16, the Police Department in St. Petersburg responded to his application, understating its interest with heavy-handed obviousness. "We know of the Karlsruhe group," the official letter said, "and we are not very interested in it. Therefore you are not of such great value to us. Nevertheless, we are prepared to pay you—on condition, however, that you reveal your name, for we have strict principles and will have no dealings with certain people." Barely concealing his enthusiasm, the would-be informer replied by return mail, demanding a payment that he termed "delightfully low"—about fifty rubles (in modern terms, about four hundred dollars) per month. He declined to state his name for fear that it might somehow be leaked to the other students, but this reticence proved useless. The Rostov police had a list of Rostov students in Karlsruhe, with handwriting samples. They identified the writer with little difficulty and passed his name to police headquarters in St. Petersburg with a short recommendation that he be hired.

> Yevno Azef is intelligent and a clever intriguer. He is in close touch with the young Jewish students living abroad, and he could thus be of real use to us as an agent. It can also be assumed that his covetousness and his present state of need will make him zealous in his duty.

This recommendation gives a tantalizing hint (but no more than that) of some previous relationship between Azef and the police. More important, it represents the first mistake—the archetype of many to follow—made by the Russian government in its dealings with him. The czar's top police officials had adopted from their French and German colleagues the technique of recruiting informers and *agents provocateurs* from the ranks of radical organizations. By the 1890s, the Russian Secret Police had become the world's leading practitioner of infiltration and provocation. Its experienced officers thought that they knew the type of needy, insincere revolutionary who would sell his comrades for money—a stereotype coinciding neatly, in Azef's case, with that of the "covetous," unprincipled Jew. The police were aware, of course, that some of their informers might attempt to play a double game. To avert this danger, they frequently employed agents to keep track of other agents. But the possibility that a man like Azef might develop an independent agenda of his own, that he might position himself *between* contending revolution- ary and reactionary forces, playing each side off against the other, was utterly beyond their imagination.

Perhaps if Azef had never met the founders of the Socialist Revolutionary party, he might not have been inspired to occupy so independent a position. During the summer of 1893, he attended an international congress of the Social Democrats and submitted reports to the Secret Police that were models of clarity and detail. But his success in spying on the Marxists inspired his police super- visors to assign him the task of keeping track of a newer group of troublemakers calling themselves Socialist Revolutionaries.

These populist agitators were deemed particularly dangerous because of their admiration for the People's Will organization and their belief (so far, purely theoretical) that terrorist acts could create the conditions for a massive popular uprising. Early in 1894, Azef traveled to Berne, Switzerland, where he met the Zhitlovskys, a married couple who had just founded an organization called the Union of Russian Socialist Revolutionaries Abroad. These SRs (as they were known) were greatly impressed by the deep-voiced, serious young man whose demeanor belied his years. One young friend of the Zhitlovskys' in particular—a petite university student named Lubov Grigorievna—was entirely captivated by the new arrival. For his part, despite disagreement with much of their doctrine, Azef found himself responding strongly to the spirit of the SR organizers. Their agrarian socialism, which held that the Russian economy could be based on traditional peasant communes, he found sentimental and unrealistic. But when they talked about terrorism, he listened raptly.

Russia's Social Democrats, the SRs argued, were little more than harmless reformers dressed in revolutionary clothing. The Marxists claimed to believe in "proletarian revolution," but in practice this required waiting until Russia had become a modern industrial nation with a working-class majority—an endless prospect in a land where more than eighty percent of the people still scratched out a bare subsistence on the land. More important, insisted the SRs, the Marxists lacked revolutionary *spirit;* they had lost faith in the power of violent deeds to challenge the czar's authority and move the masses to revolt. In Germany, perhaps, socialists could come to power through the ballot box. But what the Russian people needed were examples of heroic action; bombs, not words, would awaken them. On this point, the terrorists of the People's Will had been right, and veterans of that organization were even now joining the Socialist Revolutionary movement. The old populist prophet, Mikhailovsky, had also been right: *individual* actions, not blind historical forces, were the key to revolutionary change.

The argument was familiar. Azef had refuted it many times with quotations from Marx and Engels, but now he absorbed it with new enthusiasm. Enough intellectual hairsplitting! Enough Utopian dreaming! The point was to make the czarist bastards *pay* for their crimes against the Jews and the other inmates of Russia's "prison house of peoples." What did it matter if the Zhitlovskys and their comrades romanticized the country folk? The SRs were right: Russia was *not* Germany. Their criticism of the Social Democrats was unanswerable, and their call for violence against czarist tyranny— for heroic individuals willing to stand and be counted—struck a deep chord in him.

Before Azef came to Berne, his political activities mirrored his essential isolation. Too individualistic and impatient to be a Marxist, he was far too alienated and ambitious to remain a faithful police agent. The SRs' fascination with terrorism, which made them so interesting to the czarist police, interested him for reasons entirely his own. For the first time, the poor tailor's son imagined himself arriving in Moscow and St. Petersburg like a Jewish Monte Cristo, his diploma in hand and righteous anger in his heart. Violent action could connect him with other rebels as individualistic as himself. It promised power unavailable to mere drawing-room revolutionaries or hirelings of the police. And it held out the prospect of his continuing to live—on an even more intense level—multiple hidden lives. For reasons he did not understand, Azef found this sort of complexity and danger virtually irresistible.

It was not only their terrorist doctrine, however, that attracted Azef to the Socialist Revolutionary camp. After leaving Berne in February 1894, he thought constantly of Lubov, the young student he had met through the Zhitlovskys. A small woman with short hair and light freckles, Luba was not a great beauty, but Azef was impressed by her quick wit and fierce dedication to the SR cause and flattered by her obvious interest in him. Moreover, her revolutionary ideas and independent life had not deprived her of certain middle-class characteristics that he valued highly, perhaps because they were lacking in himself. She was transparently honest and straightforward. While not averse to comfort, she ranked duty ahead of pleasure. She deferred to his experience and confessed that one of her ambitions was to raise a happy family in the new Russia.

Azef was smitten. Politically advanced but charmingly domestic, Luba would make the perfect mate for an ambitious engineer and political activist. After returning to Karlsruhe, he wrote her constantly, declaring his determination to help overthrow the hated czarist regime. A mutual friend who read these letters described them as "full of . . . the deep sorrow of a 'popular bard,' and at the same time of the ardor of a fighter burning with the fire of idealism." Azef visited Luba often, and their friendship quickly ripened into love. Of course, she knew nothing of his relations with the Secret

Police. Before the year was out, the lovers were making plans to return to Russia as husband and wife.

Now Azef traveled at a faster pace, studying advanced engineering at Darmstadt, visiting Luba in Berne, and getting to know the expanding circle of Socialist Revolutionary thinkers and activists. At political meetings he spoke little, but his utterances carried unusual weight, impressing even experienced veterans of the anti-czarist struggle. Everywhere he was welcomed by the SRs as a young recruit of unusual promise, with a calmness, an ability to listen, a maturity of judgment, and practical skills that set him apart from other students of his generation. Soon he was discussing revolutionary strategy with the top leaders of the new organization, émigrés with names well known to the Secret Police. His reports on these meetings, written with scientific detachment and a scholar's eye for detail, were forwarded immediately to police headquarters in St. Petersburg. Since Azef was now in contact with the principal advocates of Russian terrorism, his superiors were greatly interested in his work. Long before he received his engineering diploma, he had been marked down by both the SRs and the government as a recruit well worth keeping.

Masterful as his reports were, Azef did not tell his police supervisors everything he knew about the revolutionaries. He had already discovered that it was well within his power to expose certain names while withholding others. At the same time, he managed to keep his relationship with the police secret both from Luba and from his closest colleagues at the university. In order to conceal the source of his increased income, he wrote incessant begging letters to Jewish charitable organizations, asking other students to look them over, allegedly to correct his German grammar. Even so, when several arrests in Rostov were made on the basis of information that he had supplied, a suspicious comrade openly accused him of being an informer. Azef was so greatly trusted, however, that when the accuser failed to produce evidence to substantiate his charge, he was expelled in disgrace from the group of student revolutionaries.

This surprising credibility, a capacity to inspire in his associates

something approaching absolute faith, was to prove one of his greatest assets. Azef a traitor? Impossible! There was something about
the man, some combination of skill at dissimulation, personal concern for his colleagues, and genuine hatred of czarist rule, that made
other revolutionaries discount any accusation of disloyalty brought
against him. What made him so believable? The answer may lie in
the fact that he was *not* simply a police agent pretending to be a
revolutionary or a revolutionary pretending to be an informer. His
letters to Luba were as sincere and truthful—so far as they went—
as were his reports to the Secret Police. Others might find these
dual roles incompatible. Perhaps, in the long run, they were. But
Azef's European experience had convinced him that, at least for the
time being, he could be *both* a police agent *and* an anti-czarist revolutionary.

Azef received his diploma from Darmstadt in 1899. Shortly
before graduating, he accepted a job with the Schukert engineering
firm in Nuremberg—an indication of how comfortable he had become in the free and easy West. But Luba would have none of it;
the duty of an educated professional man was to put his skills at
the disposal of the Russian people. Her views were echoed by the
SR leaders in Switzerland, who urged him to return to help organize
the new party and lay the foundations for armed revolutionary
struggle. At the same time, the Secret Police raised his salary to one
hundred rubles per month and informed him that a good job as an
electrical engineer awaited him at the General Electrical Company
in Moscow. When Azef told the SRs that he had been offered a
job in Moscow, they were delighted. As soon as he arrived, they
told him, he should get in touch with Alexei Argunov, the leader
of a secret organization called the Moscow Union of Socialist Revolutionaries.

Upon reflection, the young engineer was happy to oblige all his
sponsors. He would accept their offers and return home to an
adventure no career in Germany could match. Azef despised the
czarist system, but welcomed the opportunity to milk it for influence
and income. He had little interest in promoting the SRs' agrarian

program or in furthering their political ambitions, but he embraced the chance to strike back at the reactionaries and anti-Semites who had humiliated his family and who still held Russia in a merciless grip. Loyalty, in the conventional sense, was as meaningless a word to him as justice was to a czarist or obedience to a revolutionary. Yevno Azef would be loyal to the only authority that he recognized as legitimate: himself.

Some might say that he believed in nothing—but this would be an error. The philosophy he embraced, expressing his natural inclinations, was radical individualism. Like Max Stirner and Friedrich Nietzsche, Azef believed that the individual is superior to any collectivity; that one's own sense of justice takes precedence over conventional moral values; and that the purpose of politics is to liberate each person to fulfill his or her unique destiny. To a man espousing such views, the conservative collectivism of the czarists and the utopian collectivism of the Left were bound to prove equally abhorrent. In Azef's eyes, the enemy was not this political grouping or that, those in power or those in opposition, but the whole structure of prejudice and dogma, moralism and terror, that reduced individuals to the level of an undifferentiated mass. The point was to be *free*—to assert one's absolute independence here and now, rejecting all claims that would limit one's freedom of action. Where political affiliations were concerned, Azef could see no difference between loyalty and submission. A truly independent man, he was certain, could be far more dangerous to tyrants than any group of obedient followers.

But how, exactly, was he to make the most of his own independence? Although Azef had no clear plan of action at this point, there were already certain indications of where his future might lie. Men and women who thought as he did were to be found on both sides of the line separating the czarist regime from its enemies. The Socialist Revolutionaries were a magnet for veterans of the People's Will and for young militants who lionized the heroic terrorists of the previous generation. Some of the SRs had already begun discussing the possibility of organizing an "action wing" of the party in Russia—an idea that Azef strongly advocated, and that he refrained from reporting in any detail to the Secret Police. At the same time, he learned that his police supervisor in Moscow was to be the famous Sergei Zubatov, a brilliant innovator rumored to be a liberal thinker with ideas of his own about Russia's future. Zubatov would no doubt want to use Azef to penetrate the Moscow Union of Socialist Revolutionaries. But a free-thinking police official might also be of considerable use to him. . . .

Zubatov . . . the Moscow Union . . . an "action wing" of the party . . . the possibilities of independent action multiplied even as Azef considered them. He would have a public life as a respectable engineer, a family life with Luba, and other lives utterly his own. Financial independence also beckoned. He would begin life in Moscow with two salaries: one paid by the General Electrical Company, the other by the police; and other opportunities for gain would surely present themselves. Of course, this duplicity would entail some risks, but Azef had little doubt that he could convince Zubatov to accept him as a valuable police agent and the SRs to greet him as a dedicated revolutionary fighter. It was his gift to be convincing in multiple roles. In time, Azef understood, one side or the other might be tempted to betray him to its adversary. But he had faced this danger for six years and would deal with such problems, if necessary, when the time came.

TWO

Opening Moves

WHEN AZEF AND LUBOV returned to Russia in the autumn of 1899, they found a country much changed from the one they had left almost eight years earlier. The authorities had good reason to be concerned. A new student movement—the first in more than a decade—was sweeping the universities. Demonstrations demanding freedom and land reform erupted spontaneously and were brutally suppressed, with their leaders sent into Siberian exile. Illegal trade unions were springing up everywhere. In St. Petersburg and Moscow, the salons of prosperous intellectuals were alive with subversive discussion, and even the provinces (where a new class of educated peasants was making its presence felt) showed unmistakable signs of discontent. Revolutionary grouplets were organizing so rapidly that police officials could not keep track of them. Little wonder that Azef's services were eagerly sought by both the government and its enemies.

Alexander III had died five years earlier, leaving the throne to his inept and childish son, Nicholas II. A ghastly incident at the new czar's coronation proved a foretaste of things to come. Several hundred thousand people, workers and peasants, had gathered at the Khodynka Field just outside Moscow to participate in the traditional "people's celebration" in honor of the coronation. At dawn, free food and drink were to be distributed to the hungry crowd, the beer in special commemorative mugs that were prized as icons by the country folk.

Just before sunrise, for unknown reasons, the crowd surged wildly toward the food stalls on the far side of the field. "Suddenly," wrote the correspondent for *Le Temps* of Paris, "there was a terrible, long, drawn-out wail." People were falling into the deep trenches dug by the Imperial Corps of Engineers as part of their summer exercises in the field. Thousands more, propelled by the movement of the crowd, fell atop them and were crushed in turn by those pushed in from behind. The official figures counted 1,389 dead, but other estimates put the toll at three or four times that number. That very evening, disregarding his ministers' advice, Nicholas danced with his czarina at a lavish ball hosted by the French ambassador. And eight days later, in the finale to his coronation celebration, he reviewed a grand parade of uniformed troops . . . on the Khodynka Field! Even his most loyal supporters were appalled. Although the czar attended a funeral service for the victims and subscribed funds for their widows and orphans, the damage done to his paternal image was serious.

Still, it was not just Nicholas II's weakness that inflamed discontent throughout the country. Led by the czar's able finance minister, Sergei Witte, the government had embarked upon a program of modernization aimed at attracting foreign capital, building railroads and factories, exporting Russian foodstuffs to the world, and educating a new generation of business and professional leaders. The process of change was convulsive and uneven, enriching a few groups and impoverishing many others. Inevitably, it disrupted traditional habits and raised popular expectations that could not be fulfilled within the narrow framework of czarist autocracy.

In Moscow, Azef noted the ubiquitous signs of change: the

workers, newly arrived from farms and villages, jammed into urban slums and living military-style in huge, company-owned barracks; the new crowd of businessmen and hustlers spending wildly while the "gilded youth" entertained themselves at Moscow's new theaters and nightclubs; the increased number of university students drawn from all social classes, many of them as poor and provincial as Azef had once been, seething with aspiration and anger. . . . Clearly, the political effects of this transformation could not be contained by the old methods of intimidation and suppression. So what if a few student hotheads were shipped off to Siberia or a few labor organizers immured in Lubyanka Prison? As long as the changes continued, there would be an endless supply of malcontents to replace them.

The same thought had already occurred to Sergei Zubatov, chief of the Moscow Secret Police. This brilliant and controversial figure was to be Azef's principal police "control" until the chief's fall from power four years hence. Soon after Azef's arrival in Moscow, Zubatov summoned the young agent to a meeting at the private apartment that he used for clandestine appointments.

The two men were well matched. Zubatov was then thirty-five, six years older than Azef. While attending *gymnasium* in Moscow during the early 1880s, he had become a radical propagandist; then, like Azef, he had begun working undercover for the police. When his double role was discovered by the revolutionaries several years later, he openly joined the police department. There his knowledge of revolutionary thinking and tactics, his fascination with Western methods of "scientific" detection, his political acumen, and his capacity for innovation raised him high above the plodding bureaucratic norm. At thirty-two, a certified *wunderkind,* Zubatov had been picked to head the Moscow Secret Police. By the time Azef met him, he had already introduced modern methods of police work (fingerprinting, mug files, tactical "flying squads," and surveillance teams) to the ancient Moscow police apparatus. Now he was preparing a bold new initiative in which Azef was to play a leading role.

The slender, bearded man who sat easily in a high-backed chair drinking hot tea out of a glass looked like a typical professor of Azef's acquaintance, his clothes plain but respectable, his eyes soft behind tinted glasses. In a nation where police officials attempted to out-military the military in dress and demeanor, the Moscow chief was clearly an aberration. Zubatov sounded like an intellectual as well, outlining his ideas with the happy intensity of a senior faculty member suddenly possessed of an unusually bright graduate student. He had read Azef's reports and congratulated him on his fine work. It was his office, he revealed, that had arranged for Azef's job at the General Electrical Company. With paternal concern, Zubatov advised his new protégé to join the Intellectual Aid Society, which would put him in contact with the liberal elite of Moscow. He should also convert immediately to Christianity—Lutheranism would do—to secure both his engineering position and a permit to reside in the city. Azef must think of his wife and his children-to-be. With Grand Duke Sergei still governor of Moscow, no Jewish family was safe from expulsion.

What the old guard in St. Petersburg did not understand, Zubatov argued with astonishing frankness, was that revolutionary movements could not simply be "suppressed" by the police and the army. A relative handful of agitators or terrorists without mass support, like the People's Will, could be dealt with by the old methods. But what was developing in Russia now was something new: a *mass* movement fed by real grievances, currently centering on the urban proletariat, but with the potential, if it continued long enough, to arouse the countryside. With considerable learning and practical insight, Zubatov summarized the current state of revolutionary ideology and organization. According to a new study by "V. Ilyin" (known to be a pen name of V. I. Lenin), fundamental changes in the Russian economy were at the root of the current revival of radical politics. Capitalist development was generating a social transformation that rigid autocracy could not control. A dangerous state of affairs, when revolutionary fanatics understood the state of society better than those chosen to rule it! But Lenin was wrong in one essential respect. Warfare between contending social

classes was *not* inevitable—not if the monarchy could convert itself
into a government of all classes and peoples.

New developments required new responses. How should the
regime deal with a genuine mass movement? The answer, Zubatov
claimed, was "social monarchism." In the long run, of course, grievances must be remedied. Witte would modernize the country eventually, and national harmony would prevail over class struggle. But
considering that a growth of mass organizations was inevitable
during the transition period, two immediate steps were necessary.
First, the Secret Police must penetrate the trade unions and peasant
leagues. This process, Zubatov declared, had already begun. Second—and this is where Azef had an important role to play—it
must infiltrate the revolutionary organizations.

The important fact, according to the police official, was that all
these groupings were still at the formative stage of their development. Azef had reported that scattered groups of SRs were now
talking about uniting to create an all-national party with a central
apparatus, a newspaper, and perhaps even an "action wing." But
the same process was taking place everywhere: small groups of
revolutionary intellectuals were preparing themselves to "intersect"
(as they put it) the spontaneously developing mass movement. A
dangerous moment, to be sure, but also an opportunity to be seized,
for Zubatov was certain that his agents could beat the revolutionaries
to the punch. By intervening early enough in the organizing process,
the police could put the unions and radical parties not just under
surveillance but under effective government control.

It took Azef a moment to grasp the implications of what his
new chief was saying. The government, operating through trusted
agents, had actually *created* illegal trade unions and peasant associations! The Secret Police, operating through agents like Azef himself, would help mold the various revolutionary factions into
organized parties. Then, having played the midwife to these organizations, it would be in a position to manipulate them from birth.
Of course, Zubatov explained, different policies were called for when
dealing with workers and with intellectuals. The point was to pre-

vent the "intersection" of these two forces that revolutionary agitators were promoting. This could be done, on the one hand, by permitting the trade unions to win moderate concessions from employers, and, on the other, by driving the intellectuals to commit heinous crimes. In this way, the masses could be won to Witte's program of moderate reform while the isolated intellectuals were mopped up by the police.

"We shall provoke you to acts of terror," Zubatov told one captive intellectual, "and then we shall crush you." Azef's assignment was to win the confidence of the intellectuals. Zubatov ordered him to put himself immediately at the service of the SRs. He should ask no untoward questions, give no unsolicited advice, and refuse to push himself forward as a leader—but he was to fulfill every assignment given him and rise as high as possible in the revolutionary hierarchy.

Should he then take part in the negotiations to fuse the various SR centers into a united party?

"Certainly."

And if the subject of "direct action" (terrorism) were to arise?

"Keep us informed, but encourage it!"

Only Azef's icy composure enabled him to suppress his glee. Obviously, there were limits to Zubatov's brilliance. The police chief was proposing to further Azef's revolutionary career in the belief that his love of money and the government's power to expose him would keep him under control. But he, the "agent," would be in a position to manage the information Zubatov received, hence (information being the lifeblood of police work), to control his "principal"! He managed to mask his enthusiasm; notwithstanding Zubatov's liberal veneer, it was clear what sort of response he expected from a mercenary Jew. With a nice tremor of nervousness, Azef demanded detailed commitments to prevent accidental disclosure of his secret role. His real name would not be used or listed in any police file. He would report directly—not through intermediaries—to Zubatov, and no other agents would be planted among the SRs without his knowledge. Most important, the police were to make no arrests based on information supplied by him without warning him well in advance. If possible, he would be sent out of the country "on business" when arrests were to be made. If not, the police would provide the revolutionaries with enough information to convince them that someone other than Azef had been responsible for their capture.

Zubatov quickly agreed to all these terms. Then, citing the cost of living in Moscow, Azef demanded an increase in his salary . . . and an immediate advance!

Zubatov smiled. He had his man—a Jew after all, caring for nothing but money and his own safety. And Azef had his: an overly clever policeman who believed that he could manipulate the entire revolutionary movement from one apartment in Moscow. Of course, Zubatov was a phenomenon. He might well succeed in gaining some control over the mass organizations and the starry-eyed intellectuals. Azef himself had a low opinion of the masses' capacity for self-direction, while for the theorists' utopias he had nothing but contempt. But he was no puppet, and the delicious irony was that the would-be puppeteer was prepared to put him in a position to hold all the strings in his own hands. Azef would have the power to rid himself of ideological enemies or suspicious comrades on the revolutionary side; their plots against the state would be foiled by the police in the nick of time. But no agent could be expected to forestall *every* anti-czarist conspiracy. Azef could not be blamed, say, if certain notorious reactionaries and anti-Semites were liquidated by "unknown terrorists." Russia was a dangerous country these days. No one was safe, he thought with silent satisfaction. Not even the czar himself.

After his initial meeting with Zubatov, Azef hastened to put the police chief's plans, and his own, into effect. His first step was to take advantage of the introductions given him by the Zhitlovskys to the leaders of the Moscow Union of Socialist Revolutionaries. To begin with, he accepted an invitation to a party at the home of a leading intellectual, a woman who delighted in arranging informal debates between revolutionaries of different ideological schools. Several leaders of the Moscow Union were present. The newcomer kept his peace until a well-known Social Democrat attacked the ideas of the SRs by disparaging the ideas of the old populist philosopher, Nikolai Mikhailovsky. Then Azef joined the fray, defending Mikhailovsky's concept of "the struggle for individuality" with impressive passion and learning.

His deep voice compelling attention, Azef turned the defense into an attack. The Marxists, he declared, were simply proposing to replace the old order with a new form of despotic collectivism, and even this dark utopia would have to wait until some undefined day in the future when Russia would finally be "ripe for revolution." When, he asked scornfully, would this great moment arrive? Exactly how long were the Social Democrats planning to wait before acting? Could they not recognize "ripe" fruit even after it had fallen on the ground?

After the debate, a group of SR sympathizers clustered around the heavyset young man, congratulating him and introducing themselves. Several days later, Azef called upon Alexei Argunov, the founder and head of the Moscow Union, and then met the other leaders of the organization, who received him warmly. For the next several months, socializing in Moscow and traveling about the country (purportedly on business for the General Electrical Company), he cultivated a growing list of revolutionary acquaintances in both the Marxist and populist camps. Some names and descriptions he retained for his own future use. Most became the subjects of reports, sent directly to Zubatov, detailing their identities, plans, and activities. True to his word, the latter took no action on the basis of these communications. Zubatov's guiding principle was to protect his agents at all costs and to postpone arrests until a crushing blow could be delivered to the revolutionary organization. "Gentlemen," he told his young case officers, "you must look upon your collaborators as you would upon a woman whom you love and with whom you are conducting a secret intrigue. Watch over her as the apple of your eye. One rash step, and you have dishonored her in the eyes of the world."

For his part, Azef followed his chief's advice to the letter. He asked few questions, offered no provocative suggestions, and made himself useful to the SRs in a thousand small and practical ways. His new comrades were particularly impressed by his ability to combine revolutionary zeal with prudent practical advice. On the one hand, he warned them *not* to publish a newspaper or attempt to establish a large, mass-based party within Russia; the police, he said, were still too strong for such "mass work" to succeed. At the same time, however, without proposing any particular course of action, he became one of the most consistent advocates of terrorism within the Socialist Revolutionary movement. Open agitation among the workers or peasants would endanger the whole organization, he argued, but a small group of dedicated conspirators could create the conditions for a revolutionary upheaval. "Terror," he used to say, "is the only way."

Azef's listeners were not at all shocked by such sentiments; unlike the Marxists, the SRs had no objection in principle to terrorism. Most agreed that a terrorist campaign need not await a mass uprising in the cities or the countryside, and that the time would come to strike directly at the czarist enemy. "But why not now?" asked Azef. Of all the SR leaders, those who agreed with him most passionately were Ekaterina Breshko-Breshkovskaya and Grigory Gershuni. Breshkovskaya, known throughout the revolutionary movement as "Babushka" (Grandmother), was a former leader of the People's Will—an indomitable, gray-haired figure who had spent more than twenty years in forced labor camps and in exile. She was currently sweeping through the Volga region like a windstorm, announcing the renaissance of Russian populism and rallying discontented young people to the SR cause. Right behind her followed Gershuni, a blond, blue-eyed Jew with the intensity of an Old Testament prophet, whose task was to turn the enthusiasm whipped up by Babushka into organized commitment.

During the next three years, Gershuni would become Azef's

closest comrade on the revolutionary side. Gershuni was now engaged in uniting the strong populist group in Saratov on the Volga
with groups in southern Russia to form a "Southern Organization"
devoted to SR principles; but he lived for the commencement of
terrorism. Gershuni was one year younger than Azef. Like Azef's,
his parents had emigrated from the Pale of Settlement when he was
a child. He studied pharmacy in Kiev and bacteriology at the University of Moscow before moving to Minsk, where he established
both a chemical institute and a school for Jewish youth. It was in
Minsk that he became an active populist. In 1898, he was arrested
there and brought to Moscow, where Zubatov himself made a serious
effort to convince the young idealist that revolutionary activity was
futile and to convert him to Zubatov's own "social monarchist"
philosophy.

At the end of several long interviews with his captor, Gershuni
signed a deposition recanting his "errors." Then he was released.
In fact, he gave Zubatov no information that could be of use to the
police. Gershuni was scrupulous in protecting his associates, and no
further arrests followed his detention. Nevertheless, he had been
badly frightened and, according to his own standards, had misbe-
haved. This humiliating experience left the young populist with an
abiding determination to punish the czarists, prove his valor, and
redeem his wounded pride. A born organizer, warm, spontaneous,
cheerful, and fearless, Gershuni was later to be called "an artist in
terror" by Zubatov himself. Releasing him was to prove one of the
Secret Police chief's worst mistakes.

Azef, Zubatov, Gershuni . . . all were men who had wavered,
at one time or another, between a vision of revolution from the
bottom of society and the hope for reform from the top. All were
intellectuals with scientific backgrounds who dreamed of a Russia
brought up to Western standards in science, industry, and culture.
Each man was an individualist, and (by ordinary standards) an
immoralist, convinced that he could make history conform to his
own view of human possibility. Each was multifaceted and capable
of playing many roles. And each was an activist, impatient with

mere talk and eager to put principles immediately to the test of practice. Interestingly, despite his political differences with both Zubatov and Gershuni, Azef recognized a kinship with these fellow adventurers. In a career so filled with betrayals as to earn him, eventually, the label "the Russian Judas," there is no evidence that he ever betrayed either of them.

It was a betrayal, however, that raised Azef to the rank of a revolutionary leader. In the autumn of 1900, the SRs in Moscow decided to set up a printing press in Finland, a part of the Russian empire that nevertheless enjoyed a large measure of de facto independence from St. Petersburg. For political reasons, arrests were rarely made there by the Russian police. When Argunov, the leader of the Moscow Union, asked Azef to help him locate a "solid but not too unwieldy roller" for the press, the helpful recruit had one made—with the help of the Secret Police! It was shipped to Finland, and at the end of the year, the SRs began publication of their newspaper, *Revolutionary Russia*. Edited by the formidable émigré leader, Mikhail Gotz, the paper was well written and widely circulated. Copies were snapped up by revolutionary intellectuals of populist bent, and, with Azef's assistance, Zubatov soon had a complete list of the publication's editors, writers, distributors, and contacts in Russia.

The police director was biding his time when, in February 1901, a student named Pyotr Karpovich, who had been expelled from the University of Yuriev for participating in the student movement, shot and mortally wounded Nikolai Bogolepov, the minister of education. Six years later, after escaping from a prison in eastern Siberia, Karpovich would join the Fighting Organization of the Socialist Revolutionary party. But in 1901, not yet affiliated with any political organization, he acted on his own to avenge the expulsions, beatings, and imprisonment of his fellow students. The young man had no idea that his shot would initiate the most savage period of terrorism and repression in Russia's history. Azef, however, was jubilant, declaring that "the terror has begun," while *Revolutionary Russia* extolled Karpovich's deed in no uncertain terms. "It is personal boldness that is the real measure of revolutionary success," wrote the SRs.

> If you have boldness of heart, you will know how to hurl the precious ideas of your small group into the mass of the people, and you will know how to move them with committed speech. If you have boldness of heart, you will know how to persuade the whole world of your strength and how to make the government tremble before your decisive attitude. . . . If you have *great* boldness of heart, go with courage straight up to the enemy and strike him with your sharpened dagger. . . .

For Zubatov, that was enough. He decided to suppress the paper before it could incite further violence. But first he wanted the press and all its supporters on Russian soil, where they could be arrested without offending the Finns. His solution—a technique that became part of the Secret Police's stock-in-trade—was open surveillance, a practice known in Russian intelligence circles as "frightening." Zubatov had all known revolutionaries traveling to or from Finland followed and watched in an obvious manner by persons who could be none other than detectives. Convinced that a raid on their Finnish headquarters was imminent, the SR leaders decided to disassemble their press and move it to Tomsk, a remote Siberian city whose emigration center was staffed by SR sympathizers. The emigration center was deep in the forest outside the city—a perfect location for a secret printing operation. The transfer of the machinery in small pieces, with each courier taking a different route to Siberia, took several months. But Azef, supplier of the "solid but not too unwieldy roller," was now sufficiently trusted to be given the new location, which he immediately conveyed to Zubatov.

The spymaster moved quickly. In September 1901, after learning that a new issue of the paper was already on press, Zubatov ordered the Tomsk police to raid the emigration center without delay. The police promptly descended upon the center, made multiple arrests without encountering any resistance, and confiscated the printing press. Correspondence, notes, and lists of contacts were seized; the entire "Northern Organization" centered on the Moscow Union was now in danger of being rolled up. Zubatov then detailed one of the top officers in the Moscow Gendarme Corps—Aleksandr Spiridovich, who was later to become a czarist general, and after that a historian of note—to conduct the inquiry. Arriving on the heels of the police, he casually let drop the "fact" that suspicious local residents had noticed the increased activity at the emigration center and reported it to the police. Azef was entirely in the clear.

Not only was Azef's role in the affair unsuspected, but precisely at this juncture, Alexei Argunov came to the conclusion that the young engineer was the logical choice to become the leader of the Moscow Union! In the wake of the Tomsk disaster, Azef had hastened to the SR leaders' favorite meeting place, a public bathhouse in Moscow. There, in an atmosphere thick with steam and anxiety, he expressed his great sorrow over the arrests and offered his services to the SRs as a full-time organizer and activist. Argunov and his comrades had every reason to accept the offer. To begin with, they trusted the man, who, as Argunov later said, "wholeheartedly shared our sorrow. It might have been his own grief." Furthermore, they were convinced that, after Tomsk, it was only a matter of time until the Secret Police identified and arrested *them*—but Azef, the new man, was not implicated. He was not mentioned by name or by pseudonym in any documents that the police might have seized; in fact, so far as the SRs knew, he was not known to the police at all. And they had no doubt of his ability to manage the most important task now confronting the Socialist Revolutionary movement: the fusion of its various branches into one united party.

Prompted by Sergei Zubatov, Azef had already informed Argunov that he was planning a European trip. The General Electrical Company, he alleged, had asked him to go abroad on business. This suited the SRs perfectly, since the negotiations to unite the Moscow

Union with Gershuni's "Southern Organization" and other groups were to take place in Berlin, Berne, and Paris. With suitable solemnity, Azef agreed to represent the Moscow comrades in this important negotiation. But as a relative newcomer, he pointed out, it would be advisable for him to be accompanied by a senior member of the Moscow Union . . . perhaps Argunov himself? The SR leader considered this suggestion, which would have put him at least temporarily out of reach of the police, but decided finally that his place in the hour of danger was with his comrades. He would stay in Moscow and take his chances. Maria Seliuk, a three-year veteran of the union, was to join Azef abroad to assist him in the negotiations and to vouch for his authority.

At the end of November 1901, Azef and his wife left Moscow for Berlin. Luba carried with her their year-old son. Azef bore a heavier burden: virtually all of the secrets of the Moscow Union had been entrusted to him. "Like dying men on their deathbeds," Argunov later recalled, "we confided everything to Azef. We revealed all our passwords, all our connections (literary and organizational) without exception, all our people, their names and addresses, and we recommended him by correspondence to our friends. He was to appear abroad with full power to represent the Union, on the same footing as 'Q.' " ("Q," of course, was Seliuk.) Two weeks later, after Azef was safely out of the country, Zubatov had Argunov arrested. The SR leader would spend the next four years in a Siberian prison, never once suspecting that the young engineer he had picked to head the Moscow Union was responsible for his arrest. Upon his escape from prison, Argunov would immediately put himself at the disposal of "Comrade Valentine Kuzmich," the name Azef had chosen as his party pseudonym.

Meanwhile, with the support of both the police and the revolutionaries, Yevno Azef, alias Comrade Valentine, became one of the founders of the Socialist Revolutionary party.

THREE

A Message for the Minister

SHORTLY BEFORE 11:00 A.M. on April 15, 1902, the morning train from Vyborg pulled into St. Petersburg's Finland Station. The train was crowded, but not unpleasantly so. Through windows opened to admit the mild air, calls rang out, arms waved, and heads projected, faces searching the platform for signs of welcome. Although it was only Tuesday, the waiting crowd was in a holiday mood, buoyed up by the end of the long winter and by the arrival of friends and loved ones. Disembarked passengers were embraced and whirled away through clouds of steam and tobacco smoke by chattering, gesturing well-wishers.

From a car near the rear of the train, a young man wearing the uniform of an army aide-de-camp descended to the platform without benefit of a welcoming committee. Quickly he made his way toward the station's main exit, where a line of horse-drawn cabs stood in readiness. Ignoring the competitive shouts and waves of drivers further down the line, he climbed into the nearest cab and snapped a brief instruction to the driver.

Stepan Balmashev leaned back in his seat and closed his eyes, and feeling the rhythm of the cab as the horse settled into a well-paced walk, he willed himself to relax. The young nobleman had had a difficult morning. Two hours earlier, as his train sped through the Finnish marshes toward the Russian capital, Balmashev happened to glance down and notice, with a shock that made his ears ring, that his uniform was incomplete. He had left his sword in the hotel! There was no way that he could present himself at the Maryinski Palace improperly attired. The cabinet meeting was scheduled for one o'clock that afternoon, and it was essential that he meet Sipyagin, the minister of internal affairs, at least fifteen minutes beforehand, preferably in the small anteroom that permitted guests to converse privately before joining the throng in the grand salon. If the train arrived on time, he calculated, he would have slightly less than two hours to find a military outfitter, buy a replacement sword, drive to the palace, and present himself to the minister.

Theoretically, that was time enough, but Balmashev had spent the rest of the trip wound up like a spring. To avoid conversation with other passengers he had pretended to read a military journal, but what ran repeatedly through his mind was a poem for children: for want of a nail, the shoe was lost; for want of a shoe, the horse was lost. . . . For want of a sword, the mission might be lost, and with it the career he longed for. He could imagine what they would say at headquarters if a ridiculous fit of absentmindedness were to prevent him from delivering the all-important message to Sipyagin. All his military training would be for nought; he would be written off as a scatterbrained, untrustworthy dilettante.

As the cab turned sharply left into moderately heavy bridge traffic, Balmashev opened his eyes and sat upright, looking down at the rain-swollen Neva. His breathing slowed; he unclenched his hands. All was well. The train had arrived precisely on schedule, the traffic was moving slowly but steadily, and at this hour the military supply house just off the Ismailovsky Prospect would certainly be open for business. He would restore his uniform and meet the minister as planned.

Balmashev had never met Dmitry Sipyagin, but he knew that the Russian Empire's top police official was no ordinary politician. Now in his late forties, Sipyagin had held important government positions ever since taking his law degree. In 1899, when the revival of student protest rocked Russia, he was the internal affairs ministry's chief administrator, just one step (but that a long one) from the top job. Ironically, it was the student movement that raised Sipyagin's status from that of dutiful bureaucrat to royal intimate. Outmaneuvering more "enlightened" and timorous officials, he mobilized support for a draconian response to the disorders: Close the universities for the entire year. Arrest the student leaders, try them as adults, and set them to hard labor in Siberia. Expel all the lesser activists permanently, and subject them to immediate military service. The tenderhearted liberals were appalled, but Sipyagin's decisive recommendations won the enthusiastic approval of the czar's chief spiritual and political advisor, Konstantin Pobedonostsev. His subsequent appointment to head the ministry—a position giving him control over all the police forces of the empire, including the Secret Police—therefore came as no surprise to knowledgeable insiders.

The czar's ministers, advisors, and their aides were now alighting from their carriages at the main entrance to the Maryinski Palace. Balmashev stood aside for one moment, watching the parade of dignitaries; then he removed the sealed letter from his pocket and strode briskly up to an elaborately uniformed police guard.

"Urgent message for Minister Sipyagin from His Highness, the Grand Duke Sergei Alexandrovich."

The guard stiffened briefly at the mention of the name. Grand Duke Sergei was not only the czar's uncle, he was the military commandant and virtual dictator of Moscow. "The minister will arrive shortly," he replied, motioning the officer toward a marbled anteroom adjoining the entrance. Balmashev entered the room and stood rigidly at attention, his back to the window, the hilt of his ceremonial sword glinting in the early afternoon sun. A few minutes later, Sipyagin entered through the open door opposite, squinting against the glare.

"You have a message for me?"

The young officer stepped forward, holding something in his hand. Not an envelope, but a pistol. It spoke twice. For a moment after the echoes faded, there was absolute silence; then two palace guards rushed into the room with absurdly drawn swords. Balmashev threw down his weapon and allowed one guard to pin his hands behind his back. The other dropped to the floor where Sipyagin lay openmouthed in a spreading crimson pool. He lay his head on the minister's chest, listening for a heartbeat, then squatted by the body, his cheek smeared with blood, shaking his head. The minister would be dead within the hour.

Soldiers and officials jammed the room, yammering in disbelief. They stared at Balmashev with curiosity and loathing. Someone cursed him; someone else searched him roughly, tearing the sealed envelope from his tunic pocket. Necks craned for a better view as the envelope was opened. The letter was very brief. It read, "You are condemned to death. Organization."

The assassination of Sipyagin created an international sensation, especially when the meaning of the cryptic signature, "Organization," was revealed. The next day, hundreds of leaflets appeared in St. Petersburg under the heading, "The Fighting Organization of the Socialist Revolutionary Party." Immediately beneath this title was a slogan: "You will be repaid according to your work!" The text announced "the dawn of a great struggle," declaring that the assassination was the work of an "awakened minority" that abhorred violence, but found itself powerless to combat the government's crimes in a peaceful manner. There was no need, the authors stated, to justify the killing of Sipyagin, a man whose death would be celebrated by the Russian people. "The whistle of bullets, that's the only possible reply to our ministers so long as they refuse to understand human language and to listen to the voice of the nation. . . ."

The pamphlet, like the assassination itself, was the brainchild of Grigory Gershuni. It was he who had arranged for Balmashev's trip to the Finland Station and his appearance at the Maryinski Palace in military uniform. The killing of Sipyagin was to have been only one of several blows directed at the czarist leadership. At the minister's funeral, Gershuni planned to have the czar's chief advisor, Pobedonostsev, assassinated by a cavalry officer whom he had recruited to the SR cause, while the officer's lover, dressed like a college student, was to shoot the governor-general of St. Petersburg, General Kleigels. But Pobedonostsev stayed away from the funeral, and the lovers may have changed their minds about killing Kleigels. (They later on gave testimony to the government that proved quite dangerous to Azef.) In any event, these attempts did not take place, and Gershuni quickly left St. Petersburg for Kiev. There, by chance, he met an SR comrade at the railway station. Smiling grimly, he announced, "It is only the beginning. The Gordian knot has been cut; the terror has justified itself. It has begun! All discussion is now superfluous."

Stepan Balmashev was tried by court-martial—the method that would now be used to convict accused terrorists without making public the evidence against them—and convicted. He refused to cooperate with his captors and was hanged at Schlüsselburg Fortress on May 16, 1902. Gershuni, still in Kiev, replied to the execution with a hastily mimeographed poem by the revolutionary poet Lenzevich. It was soon being quoted by intellectuals all over Russia.

> A comrade has gone to his death,
> And given his life in the night.
> His corpse freshly strewn with the earth
> Lies buried in ominous night.
>
> Remember and find a true friend,
> Then sharpen the keen dagger bright.
> It's time not to cry, but avenge,
> —Avenge the lives lost in the night.

Did Azef help plan this assassination? In one sense, Grigory Gershuni's terrorist activities were "unplannable"; Gershuni was an inspired improviser with a gift for the rapid fabrication and alteration of plots. But Viktor Chernov, the brilliant young writer who was already the Socialist Revolutionaries' leading theoretician, stated later that Azef and Gershuni plotted together to kill Sipyagin, and circumstances suggest that he was right.

Azef had arrived in Berlin at the end of November 1901. Early in December, he was joined by Maria Seliuk, who would help him represent the Northern Organization in the fusion negotiations, and by Gershuni, who represented the SR activists centered in Kiev (the so-called "Southern Organization") and St. Petersburg (the "Northwest Organization"). The two survivors of the Pale were together constantly during the winter, meeting with other leaders and conducting the talks that, by the end of January, would result in the creation of a united party. Their easy partnership soon ripened into intimate friendship. Such was Gershuni's faith in Azef that the veteran organizer asked the Moscow leader to work with him decoding the party's secret correspondence from Russia. On most matters of principle the two men agreed, but one issue, in particular, united them passionately: the need to begin the terrorist struggle.

Now, with famine stalking the countryside, the universities still in disorder, and signs of awakening appearing everywhere—*now* was the time to strike a series of dramatic blows against the czarist dictatorship. Terrorism would announce their organization's existence. Terrorism, aimed not at Nicholas II directly but at his most brutal servants, would demoralize the government and embolden the masses to overthrow it. To implement this policy, the two comrades dreamed up a bizarre contest: the first group of SRs to assassinate a leading czarist official would be entitled to call itself the party's "Fighting Organization" and to take the lead in organizing further attacks. According to Chernov, Gershuni made it perfectly clear to the inner circle of SR leaders that he intended to capture this honor himself. He even named the target—Minister

Sipyagin—and announced that before leaving Russia he would recruit volunteers for the operation.

Interestingly, the party chiefs made no objection to this scheme,
even though it threatened in time to split their organization. The
SRs, who viewed themselves as the spiritual heirs of the People's
Will movement, clearly had a penchant for political violence. At the
same time, under Chernov's influence, they had adopted a relatively
moderate program calling for representative government, legaliza-
tion of trade unions, respect for the rights of nationalities, and
distribution of land to peasant communes. The "land question" was
the SRs' particular obsession; their concern for the "organizational
question" was marginal at best. Unlike Lenin's Bolsheviks, who had
just split the Social Democratic movement in order to create a highly
selective and centralized "vanguard party of the proletariat," Chernov's party was a loosely organized coalition based on autonomous
trade unions and peasant associations. Virtually anyone could join
it who wished, and its policies were subject to unending debate and
revision.

But now, side by side with this open-ended mass organization,
Chernov and his comrades proposed to create a tightly organized
conspiratorial group specializing in terrorism. Typically for the SRs,
the contradictory relationship between the democratic party and the
elite Fighting Organization remained essentially unresolved until
the Organization was finally dissolved in 1909. Once chartered, the
terrorists demanded and received a large degree of independence
from the party; "autonomy" was their constant refrain. But the SR
leadership was never content to grant in theory what the Organization largely achieved in practice: the right to manage its own
affairs. Close coordination between the Organization and the Central
Committee was a matter of great importance to Chernov. SR terrorism, he insisted, would be part of the mass struggle, done "with
the people" rather than behind their backs or against their wishes.
The Central Committee would therefore appoint the Organization's
leader, and the Organization as a whole would be responsible to the
party leadership. But by its very nature, secretive terrorist work

defied party control. Wittingly or not, Chernov was playing the role of Dr. Frankenstein, and the Organization that of his monster.

To Azef, however, the "problem" that agitated Chernov was meaningless; his heart belonged to the terrorist struggle, not to any party. And so, while reporting to the Secret Police in great detail on the negotiations to form the Socialist Revolutionary party, he carefully covered up the leadership's extracurricular plans to inaugurate a terrorist campaign. His letters to Zubatov were a treasure trove of information. They described the persons present at each meeting, the positions taken by the various SR factions, the agreements they reached, and their plans for the immediate future. Grigory Gershuni appears in these reports as a mastermind of the political fusion; yet of the "contest" to establish a Fighting Organization and the plot against Minister Sipyagin there is no word. When Gershuni left for Russia at the end of January in order to organize the Sipyagin operation, Azef informed his superiors both of his departure date and of his travel plans. He hastened to add, however, that since Gershuni had become such a valuable source of information, he "must not be arrested yet under any circumstances."

Azef was certain that Zubatov would comply with this request. Why arrest Gershuni when, merely by trailing him, the police could penetrate virtually the entire SR underground in Russia? Moreover, Azef's very existence inspired his superiors with confidence. As one official wrote to Zubatov, "Gershuni will not escape us now. Since he is in such close contact with our agent, his immediate arrest would leave us in the dark as to his plans and furthermore might compromise the agent." Either way, the man his comrades called "The Fat One" was now in a position to play an independent game with a minimum of risk to himself. If the police somehow discovered the plot to kill Sipyagin, Azef could take at least partial credit for foiling the assassination. But if (as was likely) the wily Gershuni succeeded in shaking off his surveillants, the powerful internal affairs minister, nemesis of the student and labor movements, a bureaucrat hated for his oppression of Finns, Jews, and other national minorities, would die a richly deserved death.

When Sipyagin met his end, Azef celebrated the assassination with the other SR leaders in Switzerland, but he had his own reasons for enthusiasm. Gershuni, his closest comrade, was now chief of the new Fighting Organization—a position that gave Azef increased leverage over both the government and the SRs. This victory would be dangerous to him, however, unless he could justify his failure to forewarn the Secret Police. Immediately following the assassination, he wrote Zubatov, professing astonishment. The conspiracy, he declared, had apparently been organized by an unknown group of militants far from the party center. Gershuni, so far as he knew, had had nothing to do with it. Zubatov accepted this explanation, but as summer approached, rumors that the charismatic SR organizer had been involved in the plot began to spread among the lower-level comrades. When Azef learned at the end of May that Gershuni had left Russia and was expected in Switzerland, he decided to prepare the authorities to learn at least part of the truth, lest they discover all of it.

Gershuni may have been "an artist in terror," as Zubatov later remarked, but Azef was now to prove himself an artist in deception. It was necessary to reveal Gershuni's involvement in the assassination, but to do so in a manner that would allow his friend to continue to lead the Fighting Organization. Azef therefore wrote a series of letters that both accused Gershuni and protected him: a bravura performance that was soon to cost several top czarist officials their lives.

First, he described a mythical conversation with the remarkable editor of *Revolutionary Russia,* Mikhail Gotz, whose record was well known to the Secret Police. In the mid-1880s, this millionaire's son had been arrested for revolutionary activity and deported to Siberia. While a prisoner at the Yakutsk camp, he had been beaten savagely on the spine with a rifle butt as punishment for leading a protest of political prisoners against the camp administration. Although in constant pain, Gotz cheerfully directed the political work of the SRs from his base in Geneva until 1904, when it was discovered that he had a spinal tumor; he would die during an operation to remove it two years later. But in 1902, still full of energy and hope, he was the SRs' chief political strategist as well as editor of their journal— a man convinced that terrorism in the People's Will tradition could be combined with "mass work" among the workers and peasants. Shortly after the Sipyagin killing, he had visited the Azefs at their house in Berlin to report in detail on the assassination. Azef had never reported this conversation to the police. Now, however, he informed Zubatov that he had offered Gotz five hundred rubles to support the activities of the Fighting Organization. Gotz had refused to accept the donation, he wrote, but had advised him to give the money to Gershuni, who would be arriving shortly in Berne.

Azef had now raised the possibility that Gershuni was connected in some undefined way to the Fighting Organization. Early in June, the triumphant terrorist did reach Switzerland, excited by his success and planning a series of daring new exploits. Gershuni's list of targets included the new internal affairs minister, the despotic Vyacheslav von Plehve; the Secret Police chief, Sergei Zubatov; and—above all—Prince Obolensky, the Governor of Kharkov Province, who had just smashed a peasant uprising by flogging scores of rebels to death. Azef wrote Zubatov again, reporting that he had interviewed Gershuni and discovered that he was, indeed, "connected" to the Fighting Organization. But Gershuni was not its operational head, he insisted—he served merely as a party liaison and fund-raiser. As he had previously suspected, the Organization's terrorist activities were directed by unknown persons based somewhere in Russia, very likely in the Odessa region.

Azef could no longer plead that his comrade be spared arrest, but he could, and did, throw sand in Zubatov's face in order to keep the terrorist chief alive. In subsequent letters, he reported that he had heard rumors of plans to assassinate both Zubatov and von Plehve, as well as to establish a dynamite factory in Switzerland. But he misled the police about the location of the Swiss laboratory, and, more important, he said nothing about the plot against Obolensky, although he knew that the "butcher of Kharkov" was Gershuni's primary target. To be sure, protecting Gershuni was risky, but Azef was determined not to dissolve his partnership with the founder of the Fighting Organization. The terror had begun, and whether or not Azef already saw himself as Gershuni's potential successor, he was beginning to act as the Organization's leading advisor.

After conferring with Azef about the upcoming campaign, Gershuni again departed for Russia. The terrorist originally selected to carry out the killing of Prince Obolensky was Alexei Pokotilov, a high-strung young man who had earlier volunteered to shoot Minister Sipyagin. But when Gershuni arrived in Kharkov, he learned that a young worker of the province whom he had recruited to the Organization several months earlier was eager to strike the blow himself. He interviewed this fellow—Foma Kachura by name— and decided on the spot to accept his offer. Far better that the killing be carried out by a local man and a worker than by an outsider and an intellectual, even if the would-be assassin's soldierly qualities were untested.

The operation that followed illustrated the limitations of Gershuni's improvisatory style. As usual, his plan of attack was concocted at the last minute. As usual, a lone assassin was to carry it out, using only his wits and a Browning revolver. On an evening when Prince Obolensky was scheduled to attend the summer theater in Kharkov's Tivoli Garden, Kachura would position himself outside the theater. During the intermission, when the theatergoers stepped outside to take the air, the assassin would kill him with two shots from his revolver. Assuming that he were not killed himself, Kachura would then surrender to the police. The arresting officer would find Obolensky's "death sentence" in his pocket.

On the night of August 11, Gershuni put the scheme into effect. With his usual disdain for danger, he personally accompanied his inexperienced recruit to the Tivoli Garden. Kachura was armed with a revolver on which he had scratched the words, "For the blood spilled by the peasants. Fighting Organization. Death to the czarist executioners." During the first intermission, Obolensky remained in the theater, but he came out during the second entr'acte and stood near the main entrance, chatting with friends. Kachura approached him, raised his weapon, and fired twice, missing the prince with both bullets. Seized by nearby onlookers, he fired once more, this time hitting the local chief of police. Since he had laced his bullets with strychnine, the wound might have proved mortal, but the police officer somehow survived.

In Kachura's pocket the police found a document entitled, "Judgment rendered against the Governor of Kharkov, Prince Obolensky," which listed Obolensky's "crimes against the people" and condemned him to death in the name of the Fighting Organization. But it was the terrorist who suffered trial and condemnation. Kachura's behavior under interrogation revealed the weakness of Gershuni's spontaneous methods of recruitment; after several months of threats and cajolery by the police, he named Gershuni as the man who had recruited him to the Organization and "persuaded" him to become a terrorist. (By contrast, when Azef became chief of the Organization, none of his recruits, when captured, ever revealed his name.)

The elusive Gershuni, of course, had disappeared from the Tivoli Garden before the first shot was fired and was again at large. Although he had not yet been identified as the chief of the Fighting Organization, the police now began to search for him in earnest. The situation was dangerous for Azef as well, but he had already taken steps to protect himself. Late in June 1902, while his friend was planning the attempt against Obolensky, he wrote Sergei Zubatov requesting that he be returned to Russia for "a personal conversation about my further work." Clearly, with Gershuni preparing to wreak havoc in Russia, Azef could not remain cut off from his sources of information in the movement and from his police contacts. He had to return to the center of action. "My position has become somewhat dangerous," he stated truthfully enough. "I am now playing a very active part among the revolutionaries. It would be unprofitable to retreat now, but any action calls for the greatest care."

Zubatov quickly agreed to a meeting and recalled Azef to Russia. In July, the latter returned with his family to Moscow, where he reestablished his household after an absence of almost eight months. At the end of the month, he arrived in St. Petersburg and plunged immediately into talks with the Secret Police officer, whose star was rising fast. Zubatov told him the whole story at his mistress's apartment, which he used for clandestine meetings with his secret agents. A few months earlier, on the anniversary of the liberation of the serfs by Alexander II, he had enjoyed a tremendous success. His agents in the Moscow labor movement had organized a massive march of workers to the monument of the Czar-Liberator—fifty thousand factory hands peacefully demonstrating their loyalty to the monarchy. When the great crowd cheered as the band played "God Save the Czar," even Grand Duke Sergei, Russia's leading reactionary, was impressed. Shortly afterward, with the Grand Duke's support, Zubatov was promoted to the position of chief investigator—the director of Secret Police operations on a nationwide basis.

In effect, Azef was "promoted" with him. Strangely parallel circumstances had suddenly increased his influence both on the Left and on the Right, for at the same time that his closest comrade among the SRs, Gershuni, was taking command of the Fighting Organization, his principal supervisor on the government side was given effective control over the Secret Police. Emboldened by this good fortune, Azef now made a proposal that startled even the unflappable Zubatov. The Secret Police, he said, should authorize him to join the SRs' highest policy-making body—the Central Committee—and, from that lofty position, to establish relations with the members of the Fighting Organization.

Now, as Zubatov well knew, Azef's proposal contravened a cardinal rule of Secret Police practice: no agent must accept a policy-making position in any revolutionary organization. The department expected its employees planted in the revolutionary movement to function primarily as informants, supplying their superiors with data about the personnel and plans of radical groups. On occasion, with prior consent of his supervisor, an agent might also be authorized to play the role of *provocateur*—to suggest or help plan a criminal act that could be used to expose wrongdoers and to crush their organization. But officially, at least, secret agents were not to be entrusted with wide discretionary powers. What would ensure that an operative directing the affairs of a revolutionary group would serve the government rather than its opposition? Double agents could be troublesome enough even at the foot-soldier level. At higher policy-making levels, they might do incalculable damage.

Thus the rule forbidding the Secret Police to accept proposals like Azef's. But the logic of what was now called "Zubatovism"—the use of secret agents to create and manipulate illegal organizations—pointed in the other direction. If an agent could help *found* a revolutionary party, as Azef had already done, why not take the next step and have him help *direct* it? If he or she were trustworthy, how better to achieve control over the organization? And if a terrorist campaign were afoot, how better to expose and defeat it than to have one's own agent in direct contact with the terrorists? Zubatov was not unaware of the risks of this strategy, but in this case, he was sure of "his man." So far as he knew, Azef had been representing the government's interests faithfully for almost ten years, and for the most comforting of reasons—for money! The new chief inspector therefore began the process of securing his superiors' consent to Azef's unusual request.

Zubatov obtained the first of these approvals without difficulty, for Police Director Alexei Lopukhin, technically his commander, was also his longtime protégé. When Zubatov first met him, Lopukhin was a young prosecutor with a reputation for handling difficult political cases effectively. In 1890, he had been given the job of supervising the Moscow branch of the Secret Police, whose relationship with other police department agencies was highly competitive and friction-laden. This task brought him into contact with Zubatov, who soon won the young prosecutor over to his way of thinking by initiating him into the fascinating world of secret agents, coded reports, clandestine meetings, and provocation. Lopukhin, who had been influenced by liberal professors at Moscow University,

embraced Zubatov's "social monarchist" philosophy along with his
police techniques.

In 1902, as public prosecutor of Kharkov, Lopukhin came to
the attention of the new internal affairs minister, Vyacheslav von
Plehve, who knew how to use a talented young bureaucrat with
liberal pretensions. Disarmingly, the minister asked him for a "completely candid" report on the causes of the recent peasant uprising
in Kharkov Province. Lopukhin responded with a carefully researched document that attributed the riots not only to the ill will
of the peasants but the indifference and inefficiency of the government. Claiming to agree wholeheartedly with this report, von Plehve
promised to bring Lopukhin's views directly to the attention of the
czar himself. But in the meantime . . . what was to be done about
the revolutionary scum that were taking advantage of this quite
understandable discontent? The Socialist Revolutionaries, in particular, were said to be making tremendous gains in the "Black Earth"
region stretching across South Russia from the Ukraine to the Cas-
pian Sea. Eventually, all grievances would be remedied. But what
would the prosecutor recommend in the short run?

His "studies" with Zubatov had prepared Lopukhin to answer
this question in detail. The revolutionaries could be smashed only
if their organizations were thoroughly penetrated and brought under
invisible government control. Therefore, competition between the
"political branch" and other branches of the police department must
cease. The Secret Police must be strengthened and expanded in
order to infiltrate opposition groups with an army of spies and
provocateurs. It should operate as autonomously as possible, unre-
stricted by bureaucratic red tape, and its leadership should report
directly to the minister of internal affairs. Of course, this was exactly
what von Plehve wanted to hear. Lopukhin's reward was the di-
rectorship of the department. When Zubatov requested that he approve Azef's proposal, the young ex-prosecutor had been in office
for only two months. He quickly consented and agreed to bring the
matter directly to the attention of Minister von Plehve.

Von Plehve's approval, Zubatov understood, was not a foregone conclusion. Notwithstanding his fondness for daring intrigue, no one knew the internal affairs minister's mind or could predict with any certainty what strategy might win his favor. Von Plehve was perhaps the most unpopular official in Russia, an ambitious figure almost as feared and distrusted by his government colleagues as by the common people. Despite his fanatical devotion to the monarchy and his well-known anti-Semitism, many conservatives at court believed him to be tainted by liberalism, while to the liberals, he was Reaction personified. A self-made man, he had been orphaned at an early age and adopted by a Polish landowner (thus the "von" preceding his surname). It was commonly believed that he had denounced his adopted father as a Polish patriot to General Muraviev, the gravedigger of the Polish rebellion. In any case, when the boy was seventeen, Muraviev had hanged the elder von Plehve and confiscated his estates. Although impoverished, the young man put himself through university, adopted the Russian Orthodox faith, and began to climb the bureaucratic ladder. His ruthless suppression of dissidents and those of "inferior" nationality won the praise of Grand Duke Sergei, and when Sipyagin was assassinated, von Plehve achieved the position he had long craved.

Von Plehve took Lopukhin's recommendation under advisement, but it did not take him long to decide the matter. The key to the minister's power was the Secret Police, a large but cumbersome apparatus that he was in the process of modernizing and expanding. Both von Plehve and his enemies recognized that the master of this internal army might well claim to be de facto the master of Russia. But to continue to build the power of the Secret Police, he needed victories; even his friends at court were insisting that the terrorists be mopped up before more officials met their deaths. The minister had to admit that Azef's proposal was unexpected—but that was also its strength. What revolutionary would suspect that a member of the SR Central Committee and a leading advocate of terrorism might also be a government spy? Whether von Plehve would have sanctioned such an innovation if he had not been assured that the agent in question was an unprincipled Jew is not certain, but he clearly shared his subordinates' confidence in Azef's greedy reliability.

The plan was therefore approved. With the knowledge of the Secret Police, Azef accepted appointment to the SR Central Committee and immediately took command of the St. Petersburg party apparatus. He was soon engaged in a full range of political activities, from organizing student and factory committees to supervising the importation of illegal party literature from Finland and establishing a hidden cache of weapons for use on the Day of Reckoning. Several weeks later, Foma Kachura fired his pistol at Prince Obolensky. Azef had by now learned that those closest to Gershuni in the Fighting Organization were two members of the party's committee in Saratov, Mikhail Melnikov (Gershuni's principal "lieutenant" during the Sipyagin operation) and Pavel Kraft. This presented a dual opportunity: he could get rid of those who stood between him and Gershuni in the Organization while demonstrating the value of his new role to the Secret Police. Azef therefore informed Zubatov that, according to his sources, the real leaders of the Organization were Melnikov and Kraft. Grigory Gershuni, he insisted, was only their party liaison.

Zubatov ordered an immediate search for the two "chiefs." Once again, as Azef expected, the hunt for Gershuni was relegated to less urgent status. When the search for Kraft and Melnikov proved fruitless, the newly empowered agent came to the aid of the Secret Police. He sent word to Gershuni through party channels that he had important news to communicate on behalf of the Central Committee. A meeting with the leading Organization activists would be necessary. In a few days, Gershuni replied, convening a meeting in Kiev at the beginning of October. Azef relayed this information to Zubatov, and when he traveled to Kiev for the meeting, he was followed at a discreet distance by a team of Secret Police detectives. What "news" Azef delivered at the meeting is unknown. What is certain is that he met in Kiev with Gershuni, Melnikov, and Kraft, and then returned with his police "escort" to St. Petersburg, where his superiors were anxiously awaiting his report.

Zubatov began by assuring Azef that no one present at the Kiev meeting would be arrested until sufficient time had passed to eliminate any suspicion of his involvement. Satisfied by this solemn promise, the agent reported that the main topic of discussion had been a plot against the life of his master, Minister von Plehve. Azef warned his superiors to keep a careful watch on two St. Petersburg cavalry officers, Grigoriev and Nadarov by name, who were planning to attack von Plehve's carriage on one of his frequent trips between the Ministry of Internal Affairs and the czar's Winter Palace. The police followed this advice, using the technique of "frightening" developed by Zubatov, and the cavalry officers hastily abandoned the plot. Azef also supplied his chiefs with accurate information about the whereabouts and movements of the two Organization "leaders," Melnikov and Kraft, who were to be kept under observation until the appropriate time arrived for their arrest. About Gershuni's plans, on the other hand, he claimed to be uncertain, and the police lost track of him immediately after the meeting.

So successful was this trip from Zubatov's point of view that the chief inspector asked Azef to visit other towns where the party was gaining influence and members. Azef did so at frequent intervals during the winter of 1902–1903, traveling as a representative of the Central Committee, but functioning as lead dog for the team of detectives that followed inexorably in his tracks. Lopukhin and von Plehve were more than pleased with the results. In November, the police arrested sixty-six SR activists in the current center of party activity, Saratov, along with copying machines, false passports, party literature, and a large library of illegal books. In December, they struck again in Saratov, forcing the removal of the regional party headquarters to Ekaterinoslav. And in January 1903, Zubatov's blows fell like rain; mass arrests swept up whole groups of activists in Ekaterinoslav, Odessa, Koslov, Penza, Kursk, Moscow, and Kiev. Four working printing presses were confiscated; lists of party members, addresses, and safe houses were captured; and the communications links between local SR branches and the Central Committee in Switzerland were severed. Most important, from Azef's point of view, Mikhail Melnikov, Gershuni's chief lieutenant in the Fighting Organization, was swept up with his non-terrorist comrades in the Kiev raid.

Although von Plehve took credit for dealing the Socialist Revolutionaries a major defeat, the blow was not as devastating as the government had hoped. True, the party's apparatus was damaged and many dedicated workers were lost, but disaffection with the government had spread so far that new members quickly took their places. By the following year, the party had regained its former strength. Furthermore, the temporary disorientation of the SRs' mass organizing work gave new importance to the activities of the Fighting Organization, and with the capture of Melnikov, Azef was now in a position to become that group's second-in-command. The police agent and would-be terrorist understood far better than did other party leaders the *inverse* relationship between mass organizing and terrorism. While Chernov lectured on the need to "join the terror to the mass struggle," Azef recognized that the fortunes of the Fighting Organization would rise as those of the party's socialist organizers fell, and vice versa. During the great mass upheavals of 1905, he was not surprised to find the Central Committee abandoning terrorist work altogether.

With the events of 1902–1903, another pattern, more personal to Azef, emerges: Each of his terrorist acts spawns a more serious betrayal of revolutionaries, while each betrayal presages a more dramatic attack on the government. Thus, the affair of the Tomsk printing press and the betrayal of Argunov positioned Azef to help found the Fighting Organization, protect Gershuni, and launch the SRs' campaign of assassination. The assassination of Sipyagin necessitated larger-scale betrayals, including the sacrifice of Kraft and Melnikov. Those betrayals, while bolstering Azef's credibility as a police agent, also brought him closer to control of the Fighting Organization. . . . Clearly, if the war between the terrorists and the state escalated, these oscillations would tend to become progressively more violent, increasing Azef's vulnerability along with his power. He became painfully conscious of this dilemma at the beginning of

1903 when threats of exposure began to emanate both from party sources and from the police.

The first threat was unrelated to the mass arrests. As party leader in St. Petersburg, Azef had recruited a student named Kristianinov to do propaganda work among the factory workers. A romantic, somewhat neurotic young man, Kristianinov was repelled by Azef's appearance but fascinated by his power to command. "From this ponderous figure," he later recalled, "sitting heavily on a chair, with its dark and, as it seemed to me, immobile face, radiated strength and willpower. . . ." What the student did not know was that his mysterious and impressive leader had sent him to propagandize a group of workers composed almost entirely of Zubatov's agents. He discovered the deception when one of the agents—an ordinary worker with a bad conscience—confessed that the group was a police front and asked Kristianinov to help him become a true revolutionary. "The Secret Police know all about your party, comrade," the penitent worker informed him. "It must be one of your leaders who is giving them information."

Kristianinov was bowled over by the extent of the worker's knowledge. "Your people think that everything is aboveboard," declared the informant, "but there is somebody laughing up his sleeve. For example, I heard today that your party has a secret arsenal called 'Energy' in an electrical appliance shop, and that your arms and literature are hidden there. The Secret Police won't raid it because they have an agent there already, so neither your arms nor your literature can run away."

Kristianinov verified the existence of "Energy," which was one of the party's largest arsenals; Azef had set it up several months earlier with the help of two of his old university comrades. This information proved too much for the young man to handle. His mental balance gave way, and he raved incoherently about traitors high in the party leadership.

Finally, he accused Azef of being an *agent provocateur*. Ever scrupulous about investigating such matters, the party promptly appointed a local commission of inquiry, but the outcome was never in doubt. Kristianinov's testimony was rambling and confused. The worker's story proved the existence of a "leak" somewhere in the SR ranks, but no more; and Azef's brief statement to the commission made short shrift of the charges. Obviously, he pointed out, Zubatov had riddled the labor movement with his agents. Obviously, he, Azef, had no knowledge of such spies, nor was there one shred of evidence to suggest that he did. "This young man may be forgiven for making a mistake," he told the investigators, "but you, men of experience . . ." Azef shook his head sadly. The commission recommended a finding of innocence to the Central Committee, which immediately issued a report stating that their accused comrade stood "above suspicion."

This faith in Azef was not so unquestioning, however, on the police side. In February 1903, on a day that the czar was scheduled to review his cavalry troops in St. Petersburg, the police seized officers Grigoriev and Nadarov, who would otherwise have been within easy pistol range of His Majesty. Grigoriev's lover, Zoe Yurkovskaya, was arrested at the same time. These young people, recruited as a result of Gershuni's charm, were not hardened activists. After the Sipyagin assassination, Gershuni had had to persuade them to remain in the Organization, and recently they had been further rattled by Zubatov's technique of "frightening." Their Secret Police interrogators therefore found them easy game. The three made full confessions, implicating by name all the SRs with whom they had been working, and making it clear that, contrary to Azef's reports, Grigory Gershuni was the real leader of the Fighting Organization.

Zubatov was furious. Ignoring Azef's anguished protests, he ordered the arrests of all those named by the captured SRs. Obviously, even if the agent had not appreciated Gershuni's true role in the Organization, he had concealed a great deal of information from the police. Moreover, his failure to name Gershuni as the Organization's mastermind greatly embarrassed not only Zubatov but Lopukhin and von Plehve. Nicholas II took a personal interest in the matter; the czar criticized his internal affairs minister and offered a huge reward, said to be 15,000 rubles (the equivalent, in modern terms, of about $130,000) for Gershuni's head. Von Plehve informed Zubatov that he would keep the "terrorist murderer's" index card on his desk until he was captured and ordered the chief investigator to organize a top-priority, nationwide manhunt for him. Zubatov took his rankling suspicion of Azef to Police Director Lopukhin, who ordered the agent brought before him without delay.

At this meeting Azef immediately took the offensive. Of course he did not know about Gershuni's leadership of the Organization! There was a great deal he did not know, since Zubatov's raids had severed his contact with party headquarters in Switzerland. But what he did know was this: the Secret Police had not made good use of the plentiful information that he *had* given them. Moreover, by ignoring his recommendations and arresting virtually the entire St. Petersburg SR committee without touching its leader, the police had endangered his position in the party—perhaps even his life. How dare Lopukhin question his good faith! Had not his information saved the czar from possible assassination? The performance was vintage Azef. The suggestion that he could help the police locate Gershuni he dismissed with a wave of the hand. Scornfully, he suggested that if, despite his paltry stipend from the department, Lopukhin needed his assistance so badly, he had better send him back to Switzerland to confer with the SR Central Committee.

The nonplussed official could do little but agree. Without Azef and his contacts on the Central Committee, he and Zubatov would be operating entirely in the dark. Furthermore, although it was clear that the agent had not disclosed everything he knew about the SRs' activities in St. Petersburg, a certain self-protective concealment was to be expected of such spies. No one really expected him to endanger his life by turning in all his comrades. While Azef's services to the government were undeniable, there was no real evidence of disloyalty on his part. Lopukhin ended the interview on a softer note,

promising to consider carefully the matter of another foreign assignment. For the moment, he counseled, it would be advisable for
Azef to lie low.

This, of course, was precisely what he did not do. In March,
without a word to the police, Azef arranged to meet Gershuni in
Moscow at the house of a Darmstadt classmate who was then serving
as assistant director of the Moscow Electrical Station. For three days,
taking little time out to sleep, the two friends discussed the future
of Russia, the problems of the party, and the need for new initiatives
by the Fighting Organization. A target was designated: Governor
Bogdanovich of Ufa Province, who had recently called out the troops
to suppress a long, disorderly strike organized by Social Democrats
and SRs at a factory in Zlatoust, deep in the Ural Mountains. The
soldiers had fired on the strikers, killing 69 of them and wounding
about 250. The workers' funerals became a mass demonstration at
which scores more were arrested. Clearly, millions who were neither
SRs nor Marxists would applaud this bureaucrat's "execution." In
recent months, the wave of peasant uprisings that began striking
South Russia in 1902–1903 had been succeeded by an even more
serious and widespread series of industrial strikes. Factory workers
were proving easier to organize and more hostile to the regime than
peasants ever had been. Terrorism by the Organization against one
of their notorious oppressors (a tactic strongly disapproved of by the
Social Democrats) would help align the working class with the SRs.

Gershuni was now treating Comrade Valentine as his chief
associate in the Organization. Azef's immediate task, he suggested,
was to get back to Switzerland, interview the young comrades who
had volunteered for terrorist work, and send a team of assassins to
Ufa. Then Gershuni went on to say what Azef had hoped to hear.
During his last trip to Switzerland in January, he revealed, he had
advised Mikhail Gotz and Viktor Chernov that in case he were
arrested on his return to Russia, Azef should be appointed chief of
the Fighting Organization. He had given Gotz documents containing all the information his friend would need to direct the Organization's affairs: membership lists, suppliers and other contacts, safe

houses, passwords, and the rest. The two SR leaders had enthusi-
astically agreed. Azef, the methodical engineer burning with a deep,
controlled hatred of the whole established order, Azef, with his
commanding presence, his talent for organizing, his apparent bourgeois respectability and obvious passion for terrorism, was clearly
the man for the job.

Solemnly, Gershuni embraced his new second-in-command. He
understood that virtually every policeman and informer in Russia
was now looking for him. "If I am captured," he told Azef with
great emotion, "you will continue the work."

This meeting took place at the end of March 1903. In April, as
Azef was preparing his family to return to Berlin (again, to serve
as ostensible representative of the General Electrical Company), an
even more fateful event occurred: the Kishinev pogrom.

Kishinev, a city in the Pale of Settlement about equally divided
between Christians and Jews, had been in an uproar ever since
February when the body of a Christian boy was found in a nearby
village. Later investigation revealed that the boy had been murdered
by his uncle, but his grandfather claimed that he had been the victim
of a ritual killing—his body tortured and drained of blood by Jews
who required the blood of living Christian children to make their
Passover *matzoh* (unleavened bread). This ancient lie was part of
Russian folk culture. Gradually, the popular belief in Jewish malevolence was dying out, but it was given new life in Kishinev by
The Bessarabian, a newspaper published with financial support from
the Ministry of Internal Affairs by one Pavolachi Krushevan—
perhaps the most vociferous anti-Semitic propagandist in Russia.
With many Jews playing an active role in the revolutionary movement, von Plehve sought to inflame traditional anti-Semitism both
to "teach the Jews a lesson" and to turn the people against radical
organizers.

Early in April, a Christian servant girl died in Kishinev's Jewish
hospital, allegedly a victim of another ritual murder. Although
it was later proved that she had poisoned herself and that her
Jewish doctors had tried desperately to save her, the local Christian

population was outraged anew. Leaflets, appearing throughout the city on Easter Sunday, April 6, announced that the czar had granted his faithful subjects permission to visit "bloody punishment" upon the Jews. About fifteen hundred rioters, organized into some thirty gangs, attacked the Jewish community at noon. They killed forty-five people, injured more than six hundred, and looted or destroyed more than thirteen hundred homes and shops. Women were raped and men castrated; one Jew was blinded by a sharpened stake driven into his eyes while onlookers told him, "Never again will you look at a Christian child!" The Bishop of Kishinev blessed a mob carrying out "the czar's punishment" as he passed them in the street, and von Plehve did not order troops in to stop the killing until late in the afternoon. In response to worldwide protests against the massacre, he deplored the violence—and then blamed the Jews for starting it by attacking helpless Christians! According to another high official, the Jewish community had brought the disaster upon itself by "propagating disobedience and opposition to the Government among uncivilized people."

On the following day, Azef visited Zubatov and raged against von Plehve, whom he accused of instigating the massacre. According to Zubatov, he "shook with fury and hate" during this tirade, declaring that he did not see how he could continue to work for such a monster. Zubatov sympathized, but defended his minister against the charge of directly ordering a pogrom. In fact, the matter was considerably more complex than Azef realized. Chief Investigator Zubatov and his immediate superior, Director Lopukhin, were probably as anti-Semitic as von Plehve, although considerably more discreet. Zubatov threw the support of the Secret Police behind the government's anti-Jewish campaign, and Lopukhin defended the Jew-baiting journalist, Krushevan, against his opponents in the Writers' Union, stating that he was one of the few Russian writers not "bought by the Jews." Both men were quite happy to whip up popular anti-Semitism as a method of turning the masses against the opposition, and Zubatov, not to mention von Plehve, may well have had advance notice of the Kishinev massacre. On the other hand, no evidence has been found to prove that either of them gave the order to carry it out.

In any case, Zubatov did not defend his minister very strongly. In fact, the chief investigator had become involved in a political intrigue against von Plehve that was shortly to cost him his career. Alexei Lopukhin later alleged that Finance Minister Witte, who despised von Plehve, and who believed Nicholas II incapable of steering Russia through her present crisis, had approached him with a desperate scheme: using its agents in the revolutionary movement, the Secret Police should "allow" the czar to be assassinated! Then, Nicholas's brother, Prince Michael, would come to the throne, von Plehve would fall, and the Secret Police chiefs would be suitably rewarded. Not only would the assassination alienate the masses, turning them away from revolution, but Russia would gain a czar strongly influenced by Witte and capable of preserving the empire.

Neither Lopukhin nor Zubatov ever attempted to put this plan into effect, but they agreed that von Plehve had become an embarrassment to their cause as well as an obstacle to their further advancement. While refusing to participate in the plot against the czar (if, indeed, Witte had made this suggestion), they were not averse to conspiring with von Plehve's enemies to get their minister dismissed. But von Plehve, having gotten wind of the Zubatov-Witte alliance, waited for a suitable opportunity to destroy his disloyal subordinate. In July, a strike conducted in Odessa by one of Zubatov's "pet" unions got out of control, and troops had to be summoned to put it down. Von Plehve used this failure to turn the czar against the chief inspector. He summoned Zubatov to his summer home on Aptekarsky Island in St. Petersburg, accused him of betraying state secrets to "the Jews," and fired him, giving him twenty-four hours to leave the capital.

It was the end of a brilliant if eccentric career. Zubatov's efforts to manipulate the labor movement were already failing; as word of this campaign (dubbed the *Zubatovschina*) leaked out, the infiltrated unions tended either to collapse or to take on a life of their own. By contrast, the extent to which his agents had succeeded in penetrating the organizations of revolutionary intellectuals remained secret, and "provocation" remained the policy of the Secret Police under his successors. Exulting in the defeat of his political enemies, the minister of internal affairs had no idea of the personal danger to which this policy exposed him. For by this time, Grigory Gershuni's career had also been brought at least temporarily to a close, and the Fighting Organization had acquired a new chief who blamed him personally for the Kishinev Massacre. Comrade Valentine, von Plehve's "mercenary Jew," was now the most dangerous terrorist in Russia.

In April 1903, at Gershuni's suggestion, Azef returned to Switzerland to recruit terrorists for the campaign against Governor Bogdanovich. Gershuni had meanwhile arrived in Ufa, site of the recent massacre of workers, and discovered that the local SRs were already contemplating an assassination. Two party members eagerly volunteered to perform it: a railroad worker (formerly a student expelled from the University of Moscow for radical activity) named Igor Dulebov, and an intellectual known only as "the Apostle." The two volunteers had been keeping track of the governor's daily movements and were able to inform Gershuni that Bogdanovich was in the habit of strolling alone in the cathedral garden every day at noon. This insouciance was made to order for an improviser like Gershuni. He armed Dulebov and the Apostle with Browning revolvers, scribbled a condemnation of the governor on a piece of paper, and hurled them into action. On May 19, the two terrorists joined Bogdanovich on his midday stroll. In an isolated corner of the garden they emptied their revolvers into him and shoved the death sentence into his hands. Then they jumped the garden fence and disappeared into the woods, easily escaping their astonished pursuers.

Gershuni, however, had worse luck. He left Ufa undetected, stopping on the way to Saratov to write an account of the assassination for the party press and an Organization manifesto for public distribution. He then made his way by train to Kiev, hoping to travel from that city out of the country. Azef, who might have betrayed him, did not; Gershuni betrayed himself, or rather, his daring individualistic style, hinting both at a sense of invulnerability and willing martyrdom, betrayed him. The terrorist leader made several mistakes in the course of this journey that might seem, for an experienced conspirator, to be incomprehensible, but at this stage in the development of the war between Russian terrorists and the government, neither side was yet fully aware of the other's reach or of its own vulnerability. Just as Bogdanovich had continued walking daily in his garden, Gershuni continued to rely on the good faith of all comrades and the stupidity of all policemen.

En route to Kiev, the fugitive terrorist sent an unsigned telegram asking one of the SRs in that city to meet his train at Darniza, a suburban railway station. A student named Rosenberg, one of Zubatov's low-level spies, saw the telegram and passed it on to Secret Police officials in Kiev. Suspecting that the sender might be Gershuni, these officers quickly stationed plainclothesmen both at Darniza and at the Kiev railway terminal.

Gershuni left the train briefly at the suburban stop and looked for his party contact, but the latter was nowhere to be seen. Either he had not received the telegram, or someone had scared him off. The hunted man returned to his compartment, exiting at last when the train arrived at the Kiev station. He must have understood that he was in serious danger, for he emerged wearing an engineer's cap, and, carrying only a briefcase, walked along the track with his head down, pretending to examine the train wheels. The detectives (who had been given a good description of him) were not fooled. "That's our man," their chief said. "He's got slanting eyes."

The policemen allowed Gershuni to leave the station. In the street, he bent down to tie his shoelace, peering around to see if he was being watched. What he saw was not reassuring. He walked to a nearby lemonade stand and ordered a glass, but his hand trembled so much that he spilled part of his drink. It was almost a relief when the police finally closed in.

Gershuni was put in chains. When arraigned in Kiev in open court, he bent down and kissed them, demonstrating his proud willingness to sacrifice everything for the people. The gesture created a great sensation. He was transferred immediately to St. Petersburg where, after a period of imprisonment in the Peter and Paul Fortress, he was tried by court-martial together with Foma Kachura, officers Grigoriev and Nadarov, Zoe Yurkovskaya, and other party members in what came to be known as "the affair of the Fighting Organization of the Socialist Revolutionary party." Gershuni was condemned to death by hanging, but on appeal his sentence was commuted to life imprisonment at hard labor (for most prisoners, a slow death sentence). He was sent to Akatui Prison in Eastern Siberia, from which he escaped in 1906 in finest Gershuni style—hidden in a barrel of sauerkraut! The terrorist leader made his way via China to America, where he raised a considerable amount of money for the revolutionary cause before rejoining the Organization one year later.

And what of Azef? Throughout the spring of 1903, he divided his time between representing the General Electrical Company in Berlin and interviewing terrorists on behalf of the Fighting Organization in Berne and Geneva. He also reported regularly by telegraph to the Secret Police, conveying a good deal of information of general interest, but establishing his ignorance of the Organization's current activities and his lack of connection with Grigory Gershuni. The assassination of Governor Bogdanovich, he reported, had taken the Central Committee completely by surprise. When Gershuni's arrest was made public at the end of the month, Azef traveled immediately to Geneva where the party's leaders acclaimed him as the new chief of the Fighting Organization. The celebration over, Mikhail Gotz asked him privately if he had chosen the group's next target. Azef's brief answer was as much a hiss as a name.

"Von Plehve!"

FOUR

Valentine Takes Command

MORE THAN ANY OTHER member of the Organization, Boris Savinkov fit the popular image of the romantic revolutionary. When he met Azef, Savinkov was twenty-four—ten years younger than his future chief—a slender, aristocratic Russian from the Kharkov region with dark hair, dark slanting eyes, and a hint of cruelty about the mouth. He was already a poet and novelist and would go on to write one of the classics of terrorist literature: *Pale Horse,* a novel published in 1909 under the pen name "V. Ropshin." His wife, Vera, was the daughter of the well-known writer, Gleb Uspensky. Savinkov's political views were similar, in general, to Azef's. An individualist to the core, he cared little for socialism, yearning for a society where freedom of thought and action would prevail over restrictive rules. But he was governed by a moody, artistic temperament and a hunger for new sensations. More enamored than Azef of the military virtues, and even more inclined than he to pursue violent action as an end in itself, he was to be Comrade Valentine's second-in-command for five stormy years.

Savinkov fled Russia in June 1903, one step ahead of the Secret Police. He had been sentenced to spend five years in Siberia for anti-czarist activity but escaped to Norway with the help of Babushka—the veteran SR leader, Ekaterina Breshkovskaya. In July he reached Geneva, eager to begin a terrorist career. He applied first to Mikhail Gotz for membership in the Organization, but Gotz put him off, asking him to remain in the city while the matter was considered further. One month later, he received a visit at his apartment from "a man about thirty years old, very stout, with a broad, calm face which seemed to have been hewn from stone, and big, gray eyes." The visitor did not introduce himself, but immediately asked in an everyday conversational tone, "I have been told you wish to take part in terror. Why precisely in terror?"

Savinkov replied as calmly as he could that he believed in the necessity for terrorism, and that—to speak frankly—fighting was the only political activity that really interested him. When Azef did not reply, he added that he considered the assassination of von Plehve the most important task of the moment, but that he would carry out whatever duties the party assigned him. Azef's only response was a further question: "Have you any comrades?" Savinkov named three, giving their biographies. The visitor listened carefully. Then he rose, said good-bye, and left the apartment without uttering another word.

From what we know of Azef's recruiting technique, it is clear that Savinkov must have impressed him immediately as good terrorist material. Unlike his old comrade, Gershuni, Azef was as systematic about recruitment as he was about every other aspect of a terrorist campaign. Ordinarily, he argued at length with eager volunteers, emphasizing the importance of the party's mass activities and stressing the boring, "unheroic" side of Organization work: the long periods of inaction, the fear and isolation, the need for meticulous planning, and the likelihood that one's duties would consist entirely of technical support work. Frequently, he devised tests designed to weed out impulsive romantics, rebels incapable of discipline, and mere psychopaths. One volunteer panting for combat would be assigned to transport propaganda into the provinces; another would be left waiting for "orders" that never arrived while Azef watched to see what he would do next. Virtually all the recruits who passed through his hands were impressed (indeed, sometimes overwhelmed) by Azef's impassive tone, his calm authority . . . and his silences.

Savinkov, however, was not subjected to extensive testing. Totally committed to violence and unafraid of death, yet coldly detached from "sentimental causes," he seemed a natural soldier. Capable of acting boldly, but always awaiting some trusted superior's orders, his destined rank—lieutenant—was equally clear. Azef visited him several times in Geneva, talking little and listening much. Then, late in September, he announced, "It is time to go to Russia." He dispatched Savinkov and his friend, Josep Matzeyevsky, to Freiburg in southern Germany with orders to make sure that they had not been shadowed and to wait there for further instructions. Two weeks later, Azef joined them. In a Freiburg café he unveiled both the Organization's next target and its new *modus operandi*.

The target was a foregone conclusion; the despicable von Plehve must die. The method by which Azef proposed to eliminate him, however, was novel. The days of daring improvisation were over, declared the Organization's new chief. No longer could the lone terrorist with his Browning catch senior officials unprotected and unawares. Following the assassination of Bogdanovich, von Plehve had ordered all important bureaucrats to be surrounded night and day by well-trained security officers. The internal affairs minister, who was no fool, had gone so far as to move his own household into the police department compound on St. Petersburg's Fontanka Quay. This made his assassination difficult but all the more desirable, since killing von Plehve would prove that no one was invulnerable to Organization attack. Gershuni's terrorist technique—a throwback, really, to the "bandit-hero" traditions of an earlier day—was admirable but obsolete. The new situation required more modern virtues: scientific planning, precise coordination, and military discipline.

The goal, Azef explained, was to attack von Plehve where his defenses were weakest, that is, *outside* the police department compound. It was known that the minister drove several times per week in a fast horse-drawn carriage to report to the czar either at the Winter Palace or at suburban Tsarskoye Selo, depending upon where Nicholas was residing. Clearly, it was during these trips that he was most vulnerable—not, of course, to individual assassins carrying revolvers, but to a trained Organization team armed with heavy bombs. Von Plehve's staff had attempted to minimize this danger by varying the timing and routes of their master's journeys. Neither the day, the hour, nor the destination was ever announced in advance. Therefore, said Azef, the Organization's first task was to map these official visits for a time long enough to ascertain the regularities in his travel patterns and to establish the best time and place for the attack.

This would be the job of a team of observers supervised by Savinkov. Terrorists disguised as cabdrivers, peddlers, and beggars, well rehearsed in their roles, would infiltrate the St. Petersburg streets, watching and waiting. By the time they had mastered von Plehve's schedule, they would have become part of the environment, invisible to the police. It would take weeks, perhaps months, to get a fix on their target's movements and to establish the best point of attack. During this period, other units located outside the city would collect dynamite, oxyhydrogen blowpipes, and other necessary materials, establish a chemical laboratory, and prepare the bombs needed to destroy both the ministerial carriage and its passenger. At the appropriate time, Azef—the only link between these units—would act. It was he who would select the assassination team and give the terrorists their final instructions. The plan required great patience, but, Azef asserted, its outcome was inevitable. "If no one betrays us," he told Savinkov, "Plehve will be killed."

At the beginning of November 1903, Savinkov arrived in St. Petersburg as instructed and registered at the Northern Hotel under a false name. He still did not know the identities of the other members of the observation team but had been told to look for Josep Matzeyevsky among the crowd of street vendors peddling their wares in Sadoyava Street, not far from the police department building. Savinkov walked the street for hours without meeting his friend. Then he heard a familiar voice: "Your Honor, buy a pack of 'Doves.' Ten for five kopecks." Turning, Savinkov discovered Matzeyevsky disguised as a cigarette peddler—so well disguised, in fact, that he hardly recognized this thin, pale, unshaven man as his old Geneva comrade. At a shabby café nearby, Matzeyevsky revealed that his brother Ignatz, now driving a hansom cab in the vicinity of the Fontanka, was the third member of the observation squad. The brothers had easily identified von Plehve's entourage—black horses, a coachman with medals on his chest, a liveried lackey on the coach box, and two secret service men following behind the carriage— and had traced a few of the routes he customarily traveled on his way to and from the Winter Palace. But they were having great difficulty carrying out Azef's orders in the face of police harassment, hostile competitors, and the need to earn their daily bread.

Savinkov's own attempts to decipher the patterns of von Plehve's travel were equally unsatisfactory; occasional glimpses of the black carriage were not enough. Clearly, it would be necessary to talk to Comrade Valentine about fielding a larger, more capable observation team. The terrorist chief had promised to appear in St. Petersburg early in December, but day followed day without any sign or word of him. Azef seemed to have vanished from the face of the earth. In mid-December, feeling isolated and increasingly insecure, Savinkov traveled to Vilna to seek out news of his leader, but without success; Azef's whereabouts were still unknown. He returned to St. Petersburg in a gloomy frame of mind and immediately developed the conviction that he was under police observation. In some panic, he ordered the Matzeyevsky brothers to flee the capital and took the next train for Kiev. There, in an SR safe house, he met Igor Dulebov, Governor Bogdanovich's assassin, who was planning to escape from Russia with a group of Jewish emigrants. Early in

January 1904, the accomplished terrorist and the novice escaped with several Jewish families across the German frontier, arriving in Geneva a few days later.

At Viktor Chernov's suggestion, Savinkov then traveled to Nice, where Mikhail Gotz, now in agonizing pain, was vainly attempting to recuperate. Savinkov complained bitterly about Azef's unexplained absence. The campaign against von Plehve, he said, was a failure; the observers were far too few and the St. Petersburg police too many. As an alternative, he proposed returning to Kiev to organize the assassination of its governor, General Kleigels.

Gotz received this suggestion coldly. The organization of the von Plehve operation, he said, was much more complex than Savinkov realized. The SR leader explained that Maximilian Schweitzer, a brilliant and personable engineer well known in the party, was in charge of preparing the weapons. He was now awaiting Azef in Latvia, while in Moscow, Alexei Pokotilov and several of his comrades were collecting supplies of dynamite. Meanwhile, a third comrade recently escaped from Siberia—an ex-student of Moscow University named Igor Sazonov—was already in St. Petersburg learning the cabdriver's trade. "You must leave immediately, this very day, for Russia," Gotz commanded Savinkov. "Go to Moscow and wait there for Comrade Valentine."

Savinkov agreed, but ventured one further question. Even with the addition of Sazonov, the observation team would still be too small to carry out its work. Why not send Savinkov back with his oldest and dearest comrade, Ivan Kaliayev? Kaliayev, known in the party as "the Poet," was a passionate revolutionary with a tender heart, some literary talent, and a mystical faith in sacrificial violence. According to him, it was one's duty to take the lives of tyrants, but only if lives were given in return. To right the moral balance of the universe, assassination must be balanced by martyrdom. Azef had met the Poet the previous summer in Geneva and had deferred his admission to the Organization, pronouncing him "quite strange." Kaliayev had had the same opinion of Azef. But Gotz, who considered Kaliayev entirely reliable ("a good hand," as he put it), agreed to Savinkov's request. The two friends left together for Moscow. One week later, they met their chief in an out-of-the-way restaurant.

Savinkov had never seen Azef so angry. "How dare you leave St. Petersburg?" he demanded. Savinkov answered in an injured tone, accusing his chief of abandoning the observation squad in the capital.

"But *you* abandoned *us* in St. Petersburg," was the stern reply. "It was your duty to wait for me and to keep an eye on von Plehve. Did you do that?"

Savinkov gave a brief report of his team's activities.

"That isn't much. You will be kind enough to return to St. Petersburg!"

Much chastened, Savinkov meekly consented. Azef, no doubt recognizing that he had left his young "soldiers" too much on their own, ordered all the comrades involved in the von Plehve operation to meet him in St. Petersburg at a masked ball to be given at the Merchants Club. This was a typical security measure; Organization members met rarely and always in public places (cheap restaurants, bathhouses, public theaters), with lookouts posted and signals agreed upon if it proved necessary to disperse. They were forbidden to correspond with or visit their friends or families and were required to act and dress in an inconspicuous fashion. "Very bold in his plans," Savinkov was later to write of Azef, "he was extremely careful in their execution."

The group that met at the Merchants Club in February represented, in a way, the cream of Russian youth. With the exception of Azef, all were men in their early to mid-twenties, well educated, with deep devotion to the revolutionary cause and considerable experience working for the party in factories or at other working-class jobs. Virtually all were "alumni" of the student movement of 1898–1901—students expelled from their universities for revolutionary activities. Many had been exiled or imprisoned in Siberia and had escaped to join the Socialist Revolutionary movement. In the initial group there were no women, but Azef had had no hesitation in recruiting female terrorists to the Organization. Those meeting at the Merchants Club would be joined a short time later by Dora Brilliant, the alienated daughter of a wealthy Jewish merchant, and Praskovya Ivanovskaya, an elderly veteran of the People's Will organization. Together, under Comrade Valentine's leadership, these unlikely soldiers would shake Russian society to its core during the next two years.

The outstanding personality among them was the chemist, "Marc" Schweitzer, a businessman's son from Smolensk in western Russia. With his clean-shaven face and Germanic features, Schweitzer looked younger than his twenty-five years. A well-informed and convinced socialist, he struck all the comrades as unusually calm, happy, and well balanced. His expertise in chemical engineering earned him the most dangerous of all Organization jobs short of bomb throwing: preparation of the highly volatile weapons in makeshift labs . . . or kitchen sinks. A former czarist official later described him as "a man gifted with a great mind, an energetic character and an iron will"—an evaluation shared by Yevno Azef.

Igor Sazonov, another happy warrior, was prized for his folksy good humor and common sense. Sazonov's father was a peasant of the Ufa region who had become a lumber merchant; naturally, the old man was passionately loyal to the czar. His cheerful but rebellious son attended the University of Moscow and was expelled in 1901 for participating in student demonstrations. He returned to Ufa, where he spent the next year working in a factory as an agent of the allied SRs and Social Democrats. Arrested and deported to Siberia, he escaped and fled abroad, returning after a brief period to join the SRs in Geneva. Like Josep Matzeyevsky, he was now acting the part of a cabdriver, and, having cultivated the rough humor and shabby elegance of the St. Petersburg cabbies, he was already an accepted member of that fraternity.

The remaining members of the initial group, assigned to work as peddlers, were Ivan Kaliayev, Alexei Pokotilov, and two comrades then en route to St. Petersburg: Bogdanovich's assassin, Igor Dulebov, and Abram Borishansky, a Jewish worker from Byelostock. Kaliayev, the Poet, was a police officer's son and high-school chum of Savinkov's from Warsaw. Strongly inclined toward terrorism, he had been arrested several times and finally deported to Siberia before escaping to join the Organization under Savinkov's auspices. Pokotilov, a blond, pale-faced young man, was a jittery fellow inclined to eczema and other nervous afflictions; Gershuni had twice denied him the privilege of assassinating czarist officials, and he was determined to be the killer of von Plehve. Of the ten members of the group, only two—Kaliayev and Pokotilov—fit the popular image of the wild-eyed terrorist, but both men, although political zealots, were also quite sane. The most disturbed personality among them was Dora Brilliant, who suffered long bouts of agonizing depression. Her illness did not interfere with her work, however, and she was cherished as a younger sister by the other comrades.

Although thoroughly committed to terrorism, few of these young people shared Savinkov's devil-may-care attitude toward personal violence. Students without a university, they continually debated the morality of taking life and the relationship of their activities to the mass movement. All had been SR activists, but their activities would soon mold them into a self-conscious elite corps jealously guarding its independence and its "honor." Carefully selected and briefed by Azef, there is no doubt that they understood the risks they were taking, but the price they paid was nevertheless appalling. Not very long after their meeting at the Merchants Club, one would be executed and two would die in explosions. Two more would die by their own hands, one would go mad in jail, and the rest would be imprisoned at hard labor.

But now, emboldened by their meeting and by Azef's presence, the group assembled in St. Petersburg threw themselves with new spirit into the painstaking work of observation. Savinkov's previous nervousness vanished; his terrorist "cabmen," "tobacco peddlers," and "panhandlers" *were* invisible to the policemen who swarmed about the Fontanka Quay. By mid-March, the observation squad had established the probable times and days of von Plehve's visits to the czar, although they were still uncertain about which route his carriage might take after leaving the police department building or the czar's residence. To Azef, this meant that the work of the squad was unfinished. Urging his eager followers to be patient, he proposed to reposition the observers and to continue the search for the best point of attack away from the waterfront and police headquarters. But Savinkov insisted that the young comrades had waited long enough. They could spot von Plehve's carriage leaving for the Winter Palace and estimate its time of return to the police department. Why not attack it right on the Fontanka Quay, as the beast drove confidently back to his lair?

Azef was unconvinced, but he agreed to meet Savinkov, Sazonov, and Matzeyevsky in a field outside the city to discuss the idea further. Dressed, for once, in the rough jacket and baggy trousers of a peasant, he planted himself on the still-frozen soil and attempted to demolish Savinkov's plan. In the first place, he argued, there were too many policemen outside the department building. Even if the comrades were now "invisible," some suspicious detective might well notice a nervous gesture or a bulky object hidden beneath a tattered jacket and blow his police whistle. Second, the squad's ignorance of von Plehve's exact route would overcomplicate the plan of attack. What if his carriage returned along the Liteiny Prospect, which would enable him to enter the police department compound through another gate? The point was to *concentrate* attackers, not to spread them out with each one looking in a different direction! Finally, he warned, a failed attempt now would set the Organization's plans back months and might even put von Plehve permanently out of reach. Better to wait and do the job right.

Azef might have saved his breath. The comrades, Savinkov replied, were unable to wait any longer. Moreover, they had developed a plan that accounted for all possible contingencies. Three armed men would await von Plehve's return from the Winter Palace. Pokotilov, in his role as peddler, would stand with two bombs in the pockets of his greatcoat near the Stiglitz office building on the Fontanka Quay. Borishansky, also carrying two bombs, would take up a position on the same thoroughfare, but closer to the river Neva. Sazonov was to position his cab on one side of the entrance to the police department, his seven-pound bomb within easy reach, while the unarmed Matzeyevsky, also in a cab, occupied the other side. If von Plehve's carriage somehow got by the first two terrorists, Matzeyevsky would raise his hat, signaling Sazonov to prepare to throw his bomb. Meanwhile, Kaliayev would stand alone on the Tzepnoy Bridge with the job of signaling if the carriage returned to headquarters by an alternative route.

Azef stood silently, considering the matter. The plan was clever, but far too complex; he strongly doubted that it would succeed. On the other hand, however, it *might* work—and vetoing it now could demoralize his young followers to the point that the entire plot would have to be abandoned. As always, Josep Matzeyevsky agreed with everything his friend Savinkov suggested, but Azef had a high regard for Igor Sazonov's judgment. He asked Sazonov, who had been listening quietly to the argument, to state his views. The young man replied that his only reservation sprang from the fact that he had never seen von Plehve's carriage and might not recognize it; but since Matzeyevsky knew it well and could give the signal as planned, he believed that the plan was worth trying. Like Savinkov, he did not feel that the group could tolerate a long delay. Their nerves were steady; now, if necessary, they were ready to die. Later on, they might not have the same determination.

Azef was quiet for a long moment. Then he spoke with finality. "Very well. If that's the way you want it, let's try our luck."

The terrorist chief had reason to be concerned; there were risks involved in killing one's own employer! Particularly after the Kishinev Massacre, he would have no hesitation in ridding the world of von Plehve, but he was still working for the Secret Police as well as for the Organization and wished to continue playing a double game. Assassinating czarist monsters was a vital part of the play, but so was remaining in the good graces of the government. For it was in the uncharted space *between* the forces of revolution and reaction that freedom was to be found: free choice, the power to control events, and the thrill of matching his wits against all of them, revolutionaries and reactionaries alike.

Police Director Lopukhin and Minister von Plehve knew, of course, that Azef was "close" to the Fighting Organization. They had permitted him to join the SR Central Committee for this very reason. But they had no idea that he had become the Organization's new chief! To be exposed as the instigator of von Plehve's assassination would not only terminate his dual career, it would very likely end his life. Thanks to him, scores of comrades, including several beloved party leaders, were now being worked to death in the Siberian wilderness. If Azef was exposed as von Plehve's killer, the Secret Police would not even have to arrest him; Lopukhin could simply let the SRs know that he was a police agent. Since the penalty for such treason was death, the chief of the Fighting Organization could easily become its next target.

The goal, then, was to kill von Plehve, but to convince the police that he had done his best to foil the plot—that it was not he but they who had bungled the minister's defense. In this game Azef had one great advantage: the Secret Police official recently designated as his "control," a man named Leonid Ratayev, had fallen entirely under his influence and was now, without knowing it, part of the conspiracy. Ratayev had become Azef's supervisor in the latter part of 1903, after Zubatov was dismissed. This high-ranking officer understood police work well enough, but much preferred the pleasures of Paris to the mundane challenges of his job. His appointment as head of the Secret Police's foreign affairs division was a product of the petty intrigues and factional warfare that continually wracked the bureaucracy. Von Plehve, who considered him a "blot" on the department, had originally removed him as chief investigator to make way for the vastly more talented Zubatov; but then, to settle an old score, he named him head of foreign operations in place of Pyotr Rachkovsky, a brilliant and ruthless spymaster whom von Plehve loathed. Unceremoniously fired after twenty years of service to the Crown, Rachkovsky remained in his Paris mansion, awaiting his revenge.

Azef, meanwhile, had moved quickly to bring his new "master" to heel. He visited Ratayev in Paris, establishing himself as a fellow *bon vivant,* a man well worth knowing to one ceaselessly in search of new pleasures. Along with news of the most interesting new cafés and artistes, he conveyed tantalizing bits of information about the SRs and their plans, while the talkative Ratayev revealed exactly what the police knew—and did not know—about the Organization. Azef's reports carefully mingled bits of truth with false leads; for example, he gave accurate descriptions of several "important terrorists" whom he claimed to have met briefly, but coupled them with false names, roles, and itineraries. Ratayev's revelations, on the other hand, were entirely candid. In November, he told Azef that a friend of Igor Sazonov, who was then believed to be in Western Europe, had reported to the police that Sazonov had sworn to kill von Plehve. "I do not know Igor Sazonov," Azef replied coolly, "but I have met his brother, Izot. I can question him further if you like."

In fact, Azef had sent Igor Sazonov to St. Petersburg just a few days earlier, and was anxious to return to the capital, as planned, to meet with Savinkov and the observation squad. But a new piece of information proved most unsettling. From the SR leaders in Geneva he learned that a controversy over the Fighting Organization had broken out in the Central Committee. With Gershuni in jail and the Organization temporarily quiescent, impatient party leaders in South Russia had decided to challenge Azef's monopoly on violence by fielding a terrorist group of their own. Its leader was one of Gershuni's old comrades, a woman named Serafima Klichoglu. This was bad enough; worse was the news that the group was assembling in St. Petersburg with the intention of killing Vyacheslav von Plehve.

It flashed upon Azef, as he considered this news, that it actually presented the solution to his problem. Obviously, for his own plan to be realized, the Klichoglu group would have to be eliminated. Betraying these competitors to Ratayev would enhance the latter's standing in St. Petersburg, which was to his advantage. More

important, since von Plehve was fated to die, Azef's exposure of a
serious plot against him would go far toward clearing him of suspicion when the blow finally fell. It might even make killing him
less complicated, since the minister, believing himself "protected"
by his agent on the Central Committee, might feel secure enough
to become careless. Yes . . . he would expose the Klichoglu conspiracy
to Ratayev. Better yet, why not convince the foolish fellow to return
with him to St. Petersburg to make his report in person? It would
be convenient to travel back to Russia under the protection of the
Secret Police.

During December, then, while his terrorist squad awaited him
anxiously in St. Petersburg, Azef proceeded to document the case
against the Klichoglu group. The information had to be gathered
discreetly, but by the turn of the year he had the essentials—the
leading terrorists' names, their addresses in the capital—all that was
necessary to guarantee the group's destruction. Once in possession
of these facts, Ratayev agreed immediately to Azef's plan; they
would travel together to Russia. Thus in January 1904, while a
desperate Boris Savinkov sought news of him in Geneva and Nice,
Azef returned to St. Petersburg with his "control" to report the
existence of a conspiracy against Minister von Plehve. The trip back
by train was convivial, but Azef had an additional reason to smile
as the countryside rolled past his window. Taking advantage of
Ratayev's immunity to border inspections, he had loaded a suitcase
with dynamite for use in his own conspiracy!

A day or two later, however, Azef was feeling considerably less
comfortable. Lopukhin congratulated him on his report, but instead
of proceeding to arrest Serafima Klichoglu and her comrades, the
police director insisted that his information was incomplete. Who
were the unnamed conspirators? What were their sources of supply?
What moves did they plan to make after von Plehve's assassination?
Who were their contacts in Kiev and Rostov-on-Don? Azef would
have to visit Klichoglu personally to fill in the missing details. The
agent objected bitterly; meeting the terrorists now was unnecessary,
he argued, and could be fatal to him if they were arrested soon after

his visit. The SRs trusted him, but they weren't complete fools! Lopukhin allowed him to vent his spleen and then spoke calmingly. The visit must take place, he said, but Klichoglu and the others would not be arrested until a decent period of time had elapsed after the visit. Azef could go abroad again if he liked before the police struck.

Although the evidence on this point is not clear, it appears that some figure or figures high in the government—perhaps Count Witte, who was now conspiring with the old Secret Police chief, Rachkovsky—were determined to deny Leonid Ratayev his triumph and to embarrass his agent, Azef. In any case, Azef *did* meet Klichoglu and her comrades in January at an SR safe house in St. Petersburg. His offer to assist the conspiracy was gratefully accepted, and the information he was able to gather as a result of this pretense was enough to implicate an entire network of terrorists and their suppliers extending from St. Petersburg and Moscow to the major party centers in South Russia. A few days later, however, without warning either Ratayev or Azef, the police seized Klichoglu and her entire group in the capital. Early in February, the trap closed on their supporters in Moscow, Kiev, Kharkov, Rostov-on-Don, and Odessa. Fifty-eight activists were arrested, and materials discovered in their hideouts permitted the Secret Police to smash an independent plot against the minister of justice, as well as to seize six printing presses, documents inculpating other party supporters, and a mass of propaganda material.

With Ratayev's help, Azef managed—barely—to avoid disaster. The story "leaked" by police agents and accepted by the SRs was that the Secret Police had planted an agent directly inside the Klichoglu group. Nevertheless, Azef raged against this "betrayal," warning Ratayev that he was considering severing his relations with the government. Before returning to his Paris headquarters, Ratayev brought Azef's complaint to Lopukhin's attention and extracted the police director's promise to take over direct supervision of Azef's work himself. In mid-February, Azef met with the members of his assassination squad at the Merchants Club. Some five weeks later, after giving his followers permission to attack von Plehve's carriage on the Fontanka Quay, he demanded an interview with his new "control," Alexei Lopukhin. He had urgent news, he said, to impart.

The two men met near the end of March in a private apartment. Azef's manner was solemn. Gravely, he informed the astonished police director that, according to his informants, the Organization's next target was . . . Lopukhin himself! Yes, he was sure of it; his sources were entirely reliable. Yes, he could supply additional details: the attempt would be made on the Fontanka Quay, near the police department building, and the weapons used would be bombs, not revolvers. No, he could not supply the names or descriptions of the terrorists or indicate precisely where or when the attack would take place. But it would probably be soon, and the director should take particular care to protect himself in the vicinity of the department compound. Lopukhin expressed his gratitude. Azef would henceforth be treated with the care and respect such a valuable agent merited. But a salary increase now? No, no, that was out of the question. The Department's budget for such payments had recently been reduced. A little later, perhaps . . . he would see what he could do.

Azef left the apartment with no salary increase, but in high spirits nevertheless. No matter what happened on March 31, the day set for the bombing, his relationship with the Secret Police was secure. If suspicious security men arrested any of the comrades on the Fontanka Quay (an unlikely prospect, since he had not revealed their disguises), he would be credited with foiling the assassination. If, on the other hand, his "soldiers" succeeded in killing von Plehve, he could argue that he had given the police both the exact place and method of attack, and that their failure to make proper use of this information had cost the minister his life. Obviously, he would have had no way of knowing if the terrorists decided to switch targets, or if von Plehve had been chosen at the last moment as a target of opportunity. After all, he was not the chief of the Organization!

This would settle matters with the police; as for the party, Gotz and Chernov must be told that an attempt on von Plehve's life was imminent, but that he believed that the effort was premature and had tried to discourage it. With his usual caution Azef had arranged to be out of the country when the assassination took place; he told the comrades to meet him after the event in the Latvian city of Dvinsk. But on March 27 he went instead to Geneva to convey his information to the party leaders and then left immediately for Paris to report to Ratayev on the fictitious "plot" against Director Lopukhin. All eventualities were now covered. Whatever the outcome of the conspiracy, Azef would receive the credit for it, or at least avoid the blame. Safe in Paris, he awaited news of the expected attack.

Marc Schweitzer worked through the night of March 30 preparing the bombs. The mechanical part, the soldering and sawing, was easy. What was tricky was assembling the volatile elements that, when thrown or dropped, would leave nothing of *Barin* von Plehve's carriage but a few pieces of charred wood and metal. He mixed the potassium chloride and sugar quickly in his sink, trying to avoid breathing the noxious fumes, and then poured the mixture into glass test tubes. To each tube he attached a small lead weight with a thin piece of wire, before slipping it into a cylinder filled with fulminate of mercury. The cylinders fitted neatly into their dynamite-filled containers, which he placed carefully on the floor, cushioned above and beneath by heavy blankets. Schweitzer was a precise and careful workman. He knew that any blow to the container would cause the lead weight to shatter the glass tube, igniting the mercuric fulminate and detonating the bomb. By dawn, his work was finished and he managed to catch a few hours' sleep before Igor Sazonov's cab drew up to his apartment.

The cabdriver helped his passenger load five blanket-wrapped packages into the passenger's seat. He then drove along the Vassily Ostrov Tramway line to a previously established stopping point. Alexei Pokotilov entered, and Schweitzer eased two four-pound bombs into the pockets of his overcoat. The cab proceeded to the Tuchkov Bridge, where Pokotilov exited, ambling off in the direction of the Fontanka Quay. Abram Borishansky took his place and received his two bombs, and when the cab stopped for a third time near the Fontanka Quay, Schweitzer and Borishansky descended together, leaving Sazonov in possession of the last bomb—a large seven-pounder that lay in his lap, fastened under his leather cab cover. Meanwhile Boris Savinkov, the field commander, walked with his old friend Kaliayev to the Tzepnoy Bridge, listening to the Poet complain about his relatively safe role as lookout.

"There is no bomb for me. Why for Borishansky and not for me? . . . I do not want to take fewer chances than the others." Savinkov assured Kaliayev that he was in sufficient danger standing alone on the bridge and that, if arrests were made, he would suffer the same punishment as his comrades. Then, in accordance with the plan, he went down into the Summer Garden just off the Fontanka Quay and sat down on a bench to wait for the surviving assassins.

Shortly before noon, Sazonov returned to the quay with his cab and took up a position among several other drivers standing adjacent to the main gate of the police department. He gave a friendly wave to a cabman waiting patiently at the other side of the entrance, a driver wearing a hat: Josep Matzeyevsky. Almost immediately, there was trouble. In order to keep his eyes on Matzeyevsky and to get a good view of the quay sweeping down to the Neva, Sazonov sat in his cab facing the river; but the other cabbies, as was their custom, faced in the opposite direction, toward the business district. A few catcalls rang out: "Hey, brother—you're going the wrong way!" "Dimwit, your behind is in my face!" When Sazonov waved away the few fares that attempted to engage his cab, the ridicule mounted. "Hey, you! What are you waiting for . . . the Second Coming?" Heads were beginning to turn in his direction. Sazonov had no choice but to turn his cab away from the river like the other drivers, even though this meant losing sight of Matzeyevsky.

About thirty minutes later, a sudden scurrying among the uni-

formed police and plainclothesmen on the quay announced the approach of a dignitary. Sazonov heard the clatter of horses' hooves
as the ornate black carriage with its liveried lackey on the coach
box came dashing up the Fontanka Quay from the river. He leaned
down to unpin his cab cover and free the bomb for throwing, but
too late: von Plehve's carriage turned sharply into the main gate of
the police compound without slowing down. As he sat catching his
breath, Sazonov heard a familiar voice.

"Cabman!"

It was Pokotilov, attempting to engage his cab. Sazonov shook
his head and waved the "fare" away. One minute later, Boris Savinkov approached him with the same entreaty.

"Cabman!"

"I'm busy."

Savinkov drew closer to Sazonov, who was deathly pale, and
whispered, "Get away, quick!" But the cabman only shook his head,
as did Matzeyevsky when similarly warned. The two men stood at
their posts for one hour on the forlorn chance that von Plehve would
leave the police department again; then they drove slowly back to
the agreed-upon meeting place—a restaurant called the North
Pole—where the whole story of their failure was told.

Coming up from the direction of the river, von Plehve's carriage
should have passed close by the first two bombers, Borishansky and
Pokotilov. But before any sign of it appeared, Borishansky had left
the Fontanka Quay in a great hurry and disappeared into a side
street. Pokotilov, astonished by this behavior, had gone immediately
to the Summer Garden to report it to Boris Savinkov, and the two
men were on the quay, walking back toward the river, when the
carriage drawn by two black horses swept by at top speed. Pokotilov
did not have the time even to get a bomb out of his pocket. Abram
Borishansky explained his strange behavior; he had run away, he
said, because he was absolutely certain that he was being watched
by two policemen and would have been arrested before getting the
chance to throw his bomb. "I am not a coward," he said stolidly.
"Anyone else in my place would have done the same." The comrades

accepted this explanation; there were no recriminations. And from what we know of Azef's prior warning to Lopukhin, Borishansky's impression that he was under surveillance was very likely justified. Igor Sazonov, grief-stricken, took full responsibility for the failure himself, but Savinkov put the blame where it was due: on the plan of attack itself, which, as Azef had said, contained too many opportunities for mischance and error.

Savinkov's self-confidence was shattered; now, more than ever, the lieutenant needed his leader. He ordered his men to scatter, sending Pokotilov to Dvinsk to wait for Azef as agreed. When Azef did not appear, Savinkov sent word to the comrades to assemble in Kiev. In his despair, he assumed that his chief had been arrested, but he did not feel up to commanding the group himself. Therefore, he put a proposition to them. What would they say to remaining in Kiev in order to assassinate Governor Kleigels?

Predictably, the group split. Kaliayev and Schweitzer agreed to remain in Kiev with Savinkov, while the other comrades insisted upon returning to St. Petersburg to redeem their failure by killing von Plehve. Their plan this time was, if anything, more unrealistic than the first. With fewer men, and without knowing which route their target might take, they proposed to position bomb throwers at various places that von Plehve might pass on his way from the Winter Palace to the police department. On April 6, Pokotilov prepared two bombs. The following morning, he and Borishansky attempted to intercept the minister's carriage in the neighborhood of the Winter Palace, but never even caught sight of it. Disheartened, Pokotilov left for Dvinsk to seek news of Azef. He learned nothing, but met his chief unexpectedly on the train back to St. Petersburg.

Azef listened to Pokotilov's report with growing dismay. The failure of the first attempt had been foreseen, but to split the group now was unpardonable. Kleigels was of minor concern; killing him would have no impact whatsoever. Plehve, Plehve, and only Plehve was the target—and he *could* be eliminated if the Organization concentrated all its forces in St. Petersburg under Azef's direct supervision. Using all his persuasive power, the terrorist leader urged

Pokotilov to abandon his brave but utterly unrealistic plan. Von Plehve would not be killed by a few terrorists roaming the streets in search of him with bombs in their pockets! But Pokotilov was beyond persuasion. Twice he had been denied the opportunity to assassinate a tyrant, and the third time his comrades let him down. Now, whatever the Organization decided, he would do the deed himself.

At the railway station in St. Petersburg Azef said good-bye to Pokotilov, sadness and resignation in his voice. He boarded the next train to Kiev in order to call off the plot against Kleigels. A few days later, while assembling bombs in his room at the Northern Hotel, Alexei Pokotilov blew himself to pieces. In the war against czarism, Azef's Organization had suffered its first casualty.

FIVE

"That's for Kishinev!"

W HEN A ZEF ARRIVED IN K IEV, he found his followers utterly demoralized. At every turn their plans seemed mocked by powerful, malevolent forces beyond their control. Pokotilov's death had struck them not only as a personal tragedy but as a defeat, ending all hope of killing the apparently invulnerable von Plehve. Moreover, in Azef's absence, Boris Savinkov had developed the morbid conviction that his chief had been arrested and would never again be seen alive. Feeling isolated and frightened, but determined to assert his authority, Savinkov returned to an old fixation: the assassination of Governor-General Kleigels. Although there remained only enough dynamite for one bomb, he and Kaliayev agreed to hunt Kleigels down in Kiev, while Marc Schweitzer went to St. Petersburg to disband the group there.

Schweitzer left for the capital only two days before a grim-faced Azef confronted his disobedient lieutenant. "What's all this about?" Azef growled. "Why this idea of assassinating Kleigels? And why are you not in St. Petersburg?" Now his voice rose to a roar. "What right have you on your own initiative to alter the decisions of the Central Committee?"

Savinkov's delight in seeing his leader alive and free gave way to acute embarrassment. Shamefacedly, he offered explanations. With the arrest of Gershuni, he said, the government believed that the Organization was finished. Since it was clear that the group did not have sufficient forces to kill von Plehve in St. Petersburg, a local victory was better than none at all. One bomb would be enough to finish Kleigels, who was not very well protected. . . . Azef listened attentively, his face impassive. Then he spoke at greater length than usual, quietly, but with an absolute authority that etched every word in Savinkov's memory.

"What are you trying to tell me? What do you mean we have no forces for the assassination of von Plehve? Pokotilov's death? But you must be prepared for *any* kind of misfortune. You must be ready for the death of the entire organization, to the last man.

"Why are you disturbed? If we do not have the men, we must find them. If we do not have dynamite, we must make it. But we must *never* abandon any task. Von Plehve will be killed, no matter what happens. If we don't kill him, no one will."

With Azef's return to leadership, the Organization regained its will to live. As Savinkov later noted, "Azef's firm insistence upon action, his calmness and self-assurance, buttressed our spirits, so much so that I could not understand how I ever ventured to liquidate the von Plehve enterprise and embark upon the provincial, politically unimportant undertaking to assassinate Kleigels." Azef instructed his lieutenant to make contact with the two women recently recruited to the Organization and bring them to a meeting place near Kharkov. Then he sent Ivan Kaliayev to gather up the St. Petersburg comrades, while he traveled with the remaining terrorists to their assigned destination. In a matter of days, the entire group had gathered at a chemical laboratory owned by the Kharkov provincial assembly. Their task there, as Azef wryly put it, was to learn "a trade": the manufacture of dynamite for use in the operation against von Plehve.

The atmosphere at the laboratory resembled that of a family reunion. The frustrations of the past month were forgotten as the comrades worked quietly together under Marc Schweitzer's cheerful tutelage. Soon there would be laughter and poetry, political discussions, and renewed enthusiasm for the terrorist campaign. This understanding of his "soldiers' " needs was, perhaps, Azef's greatest strength as a leader. It was necessary to keep his followers active, but they also needed time together to recuperate, to reestablish personal relationships, to restore their energies, and to regain their taste for action. How better to revive morale than to bring them closer to Schweitzer, whose spirit was inextinguishable? And what Schweitzer would teach them—how to handle dangerous chemicals—would be just the thing to strengthen their ability to work cooperatively, their self-confidence, and their nerve.

The scheme worked exactly as Azef had hoped, although Schweitzer, who remained in the lab to complete the work after the group departed, had a narrow escape. Late one night, while stirring the mixture of chemicals that, once congealed, would become dynamite, the young chemist recognized the unmistakable signs of an impending explosion. Immediately he poured water from a nearby pitcher into the volatile gelatin, which scattered, some of it exploding on his body. Schweitzer was quite badly burned. Still, he finished manufacturing the dynamite and brought it to St. Petersburg in time for the renewal of the campaign against von Plehve.

At the end of April 1904, Azef gathered his followers in the University Gardens at Kharkov and gave them their orders. At first, the plan seemed familiar, although richer in detail than previous efforts. Four men, two disguised as tobacco peddlers and two as cab-drivers, would follow the movements of von Plehve's carriage in the streets, searching for the best place to attack it. But this time, they would live with other tradesmen and cabbies in St. Petersburg, getting to know their ways, gaining their trust, and using them as additional sources of information. This time, no horse's head would be pointed the wrong way!

Then Azef announced an innovation: the remaining terrorists, posing as the members of a wealthy household, were to rent a luxury apartment in the very center of the city. Information unobtainable by mere peddlers and cabmen would be within the reach of a rich Englishman (Boris Savinkov) and his fashionable mistress (Dora Brilliant). Once established as residents of 31 Zhukovsky Street, they and their "servants" could go where they wished without being harassed by the police or being forced to serve customers. Moreover (here Azef, who loved technology, positively glittered with enthusiasm), they could buy an *automobile*—a machine that might prove useful both for observation and for attack.

Savinkov had his doubts about the automobile—in fact, it was never purchased—but he threw himself eagerly into the role of Arthur Muir McCullough, the successful English representative of a West European bicycle company come to St. Petersburg to trade with the Russians. Now he understood why Azef had assigned him to travel to Kharkov with Dora Brilliant and Praskovya Ivanovskaya. He had already gotten to know both of them well. The black-haired, black-eyed Brilliant was a novice terrorist but one fanatically dedicated to the cause; she had been Pokotilov's lover and was determined to complete his interrupted mission. Savinkov found in her a strange combination of softness and monomania, aversion to violence and desire to throw the bomb herself, but there was no doubt of her determination and loyalty. The ancient fighter Ivanovskaya (whom Savinkov first mistook for an ordinary servant) had been a member of the conspiracy that, more than twenty years earlier, ended the life of Alexander II. According to Savinkov, the role she played, quietly and undemonstratively, was that of the group's mother. "She spoke no words of kindness, she tried not to console, nor to encourage, she did not conjecture of success or failure, but all of those close to her felt the inexhaustible light of her great, tender love."

The terrorists were entirely convincing in their assigned roles. Like many of the comrades, Savinkov had studied English in *gymnasium,* and although his accent was not perfect, the novelist had spent enough time in London to convince the Russians with whom he came in contact that he was, indeed, a wealthy English gentleman.

Dora Brilliant made good use of her fine voice and moodiness; so persuasively did she act the part of Savinkov's lover, a former light opera singer, that their landlady urged her to leave the penurious "McCullough" for a more generous man who could buy her fine jewelry and more elegant dresses! Igor Sazonov played the part of the illiterate manservant with his usual cheerful boldness (in fact, he was considered a "catch" by the marriageable servant girls of the quarter), and Ivanovskaya had no difficulty gaining acceptance as the family's faithful cook. Azef, who frequently stayed at 31 Zhukovsky Street, coached his little company carefully, and they were soon integrated into the life of the apartment house and the neighborhood.

Savinkov's memoirs make it clear that this was an extraordinarily happy time for the group, although he seems unaware of Azef's complex motives for establishing this ménage. Of course, there were tactical advantages to be gained. Through the network of servants and their gossip, Sazonov and Ivanovskaya learned more about von Plehve's habits in days than they would have discovered in weeks on the street. But street observations as well proved easier to manage and coordinate. During the day, Savinkov left the house "on business" and Dora Brilliant took Sazonov on shopping trips, while in the evening, Savinkov and Brilliant went out together, leaving their "servants" free to wander the city. These excursions provided the terrorists with ample opportunities to shadow von Plehve and to meet with the other comrades, who were also (by dint of specialization) enjoying greater success. Kaliayev, in particular, proved a mine of information. The Poet learned to recognize the faces of von Plehve's plainclothes spies and could tell by their movements whether the minister's carriage was expected or whether it had just passed a certain street. He was also the first to pick up changes in von Plehve's schedule, and by June he was able to intersect the path of the black carriage almost at will.

Yet tactical advantage was only one of Azef's goals. The other was to mold his terrorist squad into a team animated by confidence, comradeship, and a spirit of willing sacrifice. Whether through instinct or calculation, he recognized the importance of women to the process of cementing the group. By incorporating Ivanovskaya and Brilliant in the operational center, he turned the mock family into a "real" family, with the elders, himself and Ivanovskaya, as father and mother, and the younger comrades as brothers and sister. Boris Savinkov (the "eldest son") recognized this effect without understanding its cause. "Both the old and new members of the organization felt this strong bond of union," he stated later, "and the line of division between the older and the younger among us, between the workers and intellectuals, had become obliterated. We were one fraternity, living by one idea, by one aim." Sazonov was of the same mind. "The word 'brother,'" he wrote, "expressed but inadequately the reality of our relations."

Indeed, there is reason to believe that Azef himself was caught up in the network of strong emotions that he had created. ("When I kissed Sazonov," he said years later, referring to an embrace given prior to the attempt on von Plehve's life, "it was *not* the kiss of a Judas.") As always, he had been careful to maintain his relations with the police, but this time he told them nothing that could possibly compromise the conspiracy against von Plehve. In May, after taking his ailing mother to a spa in the North Caucasus, he visited Ufa and Samara at Ratayev's suggestion. His purported mission: to help the Secret Police locate Igor Sazonov and to discover the identity of the "mysterious terrorist" who had blown himself up in St. Petersburg! He could not locate Sazonov, he reported; his brother Izot had not heard from him in months. As to the identity of the dead terrorist, he was almost certainly Alexei Pokotilov, a member of the Fighting Organization who had been involved in a plot of some sort against Minister von Plehve. But his death had apparently crushed the Organization's spirit, Azef suggested, for the SRs had decided to postpone the attempt on von Plehve's life indefinitely.

With this bold lie, Azef committed himself entirely, if temporarily, to his role as the Organization's paterfamilias. Returning to St. Petersburg in mid-June, he spent ten days at the Zhukovsky Street apartment, reviewing the situation and taking time to lecture

Savinkov on the need to observe minor but important rules of conspiratorial behavior. By now, the squad's observation work had been completed; the comrades understood von Plehve's movements as well as did the detectives that followed his carriage through the streets. Azef spoke at length with each member of the group, calming, encouraging, answering questions, and preparing each one for the great day of battle. This essential work completed, he left for Moscow. Savinkov, Sazonov, Kaliayev, and Schweitzer were instructed to join him there in the first week of July.

The five conspirators met in a quiet corner of Moscow's Sokolnichy Park to draw up their final plans. The time and place of the attack were easily agreed upon. Lulled by his apparently invulnerable security system (including the reports from "his man" on the Central Committee), the minister had allowed his schedule to become somewhat routine. He had moved his family back to his villa on Aptekarsky Island and left the house every Thursday morning for the Tsarskoye Selo Station, where he took the train to Nicholas's summer residence. His route was invariable; always the black coach came storming down the Ismailovsky Prospect with police detectives bringing up the rear in a cab of their own. Clearly, the point of attack must be on the broad Ismailovsky, preferably in the few blocks separating the Obvodny Canal from the First Regiment Armory. As to personnel, Azef decided on four bomb throwers. One would allow the carriage to pass and then step into the street behind it, blocking von Plehve's way back to his villa. The second—the key figure in this scenario—would throw his bomb at the passing vehicle. The third terrorist, some forty paces further down the street, would strike if von Plehve escaped the second, and the fourth was to attack only if the minister succeeded in running the whole gauntlet. Large weapons were decided upon: six-pound bombs for comrades one, three, and four, and a twelve-pound bomb for the second man. If von Plehve survived this time, it would not be for want of men or dynamite.

Additional meetings were needed to deal with technical issues, in particular, the problem of hitting a carriage moving at high speed with heavy bombs. To Kaliayev, the solution was obvious: a suicide attack. "Imagine the carriage coming along," he said. "I throw myself with my bomb under the horses. The bomb will either go off, and then the carriage must stop, or it will not explode, the horses will become frightened—again the carriage must come to a halt. It will then be up to the second man to finish the job."

"But you will be killed," Azef replied.

"Of course."

Azef refused to sanction the plan. However foolproof it might seem, suicide missions were not part of the Organization's repertoire. A few comrades, the Poet among them, were committed to the principle of moral compensation: a life for a life. Most, however, although quite willing to die to fulfill the mission, preferred to leave the question of their own survival to circumstances or fate. In short, they considered themselves soldiers on a highly dangerous mission, not suicides. Furthermore, Kaliayev's plan ensured that von Plehve's carriage would be halted, but even if the bomb exploded under the horses' hooves, a second or third terrorist might well be forced to finish the job. If it could be done by one man, so much the better. Azef wanted to keep as many comrades as possible out of the hands of the police; von Plehve was not the last tyrant that he planned to remove from the earth. "The plan is a good one," he announced, "but I don't think it's necessary. It is possible to reach the carriage so that one can hurl the bomb under the carriage or through the window. In that case, one man can do the trick."

This question answered, Azef called a last meeting to select his assassination squad. To block von Plehve's retreat he chose Borishansky, and to hurl the first bomb, Sazonov. The Poet was appointed secondary bomber (a choice that naturally displeased him), and Leiba Sikorsky, a friend of Borishansky's recently arrived from Byelostock, was to be the last man between the black carriage and the railroad station. All contingencies seemed to be accounted for— but the male terrorists had failed to consider one possibility: that a female comrade might want to be directly involved in the assassination. When they returned to St. Petersburg, their beloved and melancholy "sister," Dora Brilliant, detonated an explosion of a different sort by demanding to be chosen as one of the bomb throwers.

"I want it," Brilliant told Savinkov in a mood both exalted and depressed. "I have to die."

At a special meeting called to consider the matter, the high-minded Schweitzer came to her support. Dora had the strength to throw a bomb, he insisted, and she had as much right as any man to participate in the attack. Sazonov, although agreeing with this in principle, was so overcome by concern for her that he could hardly speak, while Savinkov, her protector offstage as well as on, was adamantly opposed. Women should never be sacrificed, he argued, unless there were insufficient men to launch an attack. Azef disagreed with his lieutenant and said so: "In my opinion, there is no reason for refusing Dora." But either because he doubted her mental stability or because he did not want the attack group's composure disturbed by special concern for her, he allowed Savinkov's view to prevail. Dora Brilliant's request was denied.

The "family" vacated the apartment at Zhukovsky Street. Only Savinkov remained in the city with the bomb maker Schweitzer and the two cabmen, Matzeyevsky and Dulebov. Azef traveled with Praskovya Ivanovskaya to Vilna, not far from his birthplace in the Pale, to await word of the attack. The assassination squad would meet again in St. Petersburg on the morning of July 21. Before leaving, Savinkov had taken a long walk around the city with the primary bomb thrower, Igor Sazonov. "You will probably not return from your task," he had offered, thinking to draw Sazonov into a conversation that might help him conquer hidden fears. But Sazonov merely gazed at him with calm, youthful eyes.

"Tell me," Boris persisted. "What do you think we will feel after the assassination?"

"Pride and joy."

"Is that all?"

"Of course! Only that."

Azef waited in a state of great agitation for the telegram that would signal von Plehve's end. He knew that the train to Tsarskoye Selo left promptly at ten o'clock each morning, and that the minister never failed to arrive at the station on time. The comrades should have intercepted his carriage at about 9:45, in which case Savinkov's telegram would have been delivered by early afternoon at the latest. But the sun was setting over Vilna, and he had not heard a word. Pacing the small apartment that a local comrade had made available to Ivanovskaya and himself, he swore softly and muttered, "This means a complete failure—or a betrayal." Auntie Ivanovskaya, knitting in an armchair, looked up placidly without replying. Azef left the room and went into the street. When he returned, he was carrying a newspaper and seemed more relaxed. There was no news of an assassination attempt *or* of any arrests; the operation must have been called off.

Azef heard the whole story the next day, when the members of the squad arrived in Vilna. The four bomb throwers had taken up their prearranged positions on various streets near the Ismailovsky Prospect. Schweitzer had appeared exactly as planned in Dulebov's cab, with a bagful of bombs to distribute to the terrorists. But Igor Sazonov, who was to be the first recipient of a bomb, failed to meet the cab, the result, apparently, of heavy traffic on the street and a mix-up about the corner at which the rendezvous was to take place. Since the bomb delivery schedule was timed to the minute, this contretemps blew the carefully arranged plan to pieces. Schweitzer managed to hand a bomb to the Poet before returning to look for Sazonov, but the delay forced the two other terrorists to abandon their positions, as they had been instructed to do in such a case. Ivan Kaliayev was thus the only man to receive a weapon. Von Plehve's carriage came into view precisely at 9:45 A.M., moving at top speed down the Ismailovsky Prospect, and Kaliayev watched it pass, bomb in hand. All the comrades had strict orders not to attack the carriage until Sazonov had thrown his bomb, for to fail in "single combat" would delay the assassination indefinitely.

Naturally, Azef's soldiers were downcast. They were exhausted as well by the strain of preparing themselves for heroic action, only to have their expectations dashed again. For the first time, there were recriminations: Kaliayev blamed Abram Borishansky for leaving his position, Borishansky blamed Schweitzer for being late . . . and Sazonov, as usual, blamed himself exclusively. Indeed, he seemed more crushed by this failure than by the comic opera foul-up four months earlier on the Fontanka Quay. If only he had been at the right place to receive his bomb, he told Azef miserably, the Organization would now be celebrating von Plehve's death. The responsibility for failure was entirely his. Sazonov hung his head, waiting for one of Azef's patented tirades.

Instead, his chief offered gentle reassurance. The problem had been foreseeable. It was the plan—Azef's plan—that was defective, not its brave executors. Like a historian researching some ancient battle, Azef questioned his men quietly, objectively, and in great detail, probing for flaws in the strategy. He made several suggestions concerning placement of the comrades and delivery of the bombs; then his tone became richly, almost gaily, confident. Hadn't von Plehve's carriage appeared precisely at the time and place expected? Wouldn't the monster have been destroyed if all fighters had been properly positioned and armed? Certainly! Minor mix-ups like yesterday's were to be expected when delivering weapons to four men in four different places. Simplifying the delivery system would not be difficult. But what was more important, the group had had a "dress rehearsal" for the assassination—a practice run that, with one minor exception, had been flawless. The real performance would take place one week hence . . . and this time they would surely succeed.

The terrorist band spent the remainder of the week with Azef and Ivanovskaya in Vilna. They walked the city streets together, talking, strengthening their resolve, and making adjustments to the plan. The night before they were to leave for St. Petersburg, the four bombers sat all night in a tavern with their fictive parents, Comrade Valentine and Auntie. "In a small, dimly lit room," Ivanovskaya remembered, "sat thoughtful men, whose fate was already settled, exchanging trivialities. Azef alone seemed calm, attentive, and unusually kind." At dawn, with obvious emotion, he kissed each man farewell. He would go to Warsaw with Ivanovskaya, he told them, to await news of their victory.

Early in the morning of July 28, the comrades reassembled in St. Petersburg. Sazonov, dressed as a railway employee, and Kaliayev, wearing a porter's cap, arrived at the Warsaw Station at eight o'clock, followed by Borishansky and Leiba Sikorsky, who had taken the next train. Savinkov met them at the station and escorted them to a quiet street corner near the Maryinski Theater. Minutes later, Dulebov's cab drew up and his passenger, Marc Schweitzer, quickly handed packages to all four terrorists. Azef had been right; there were no police in this neighborhood, and distributing the weapons to everyone at once eliminated the possibility of mischance. Sazonov's bomb was a twelve-pound cylinder wrapped in a newspaper and tied with a string. Kaliayev's six-pounder was wrapped in a scarf. Both could be carried openly, while Borishansky and Sikorsky were given theirs in small boxes, which they hid under their capacious sailors' coats.

The four men walked to a small church on Sadovaya Street, five minutes by foot from the Ismailovsky Prospect. In the little garden they sat down to wait for Savinkov, Borishansky on one bench by himself, Sazonov and Sikorsky on another, and Kaliayev on a third. Sazonov was concerned about Sikorsky, the new arrival who did not know the city well. Speaking quickly and gesturing for emphasis, he instructed him for the third or fourth time how to dispose of his bomb in case the mission failed. Sikorsky was to hire a boat in Petrovsky Park—Borishansky had taken him there earlier to make sure he was familiar with it—row out to the juncture of the Neva with the sea, and lower his package gently into the stream. Sikorsky listened, nodding. Suddenly, the impetuous Ivan Kaliayev rose from his bench and walked over to the church gate, where an icon was displayed. He removed his hat and crossed himself, murmuring an inaudible prayer. Just at this moment, Boris Savinkov arrived at the church. He made a signal, and the comrades walked off toward the Ismailovsky Prospect at an easy pace, Borishansky in the lead, each man following the next by a distance of about twenty yards. Kaliayev stopped to embrace Savinkov, then hastened to take his place in the unnoticed procession.

Minutes later, the terrorists were on the Ismailovsky Prospect, walking in the direction of von Plehve's villa. Sazonov carried his heavy package on his shoulder, like a workman. Fifteen yards or so behind him, Kaliayev strolled as if at leisure, humming a song aloud. Suddenly, the air was alive with tension; Kaliayev saw several plainclothesmen that he recognized taking assigned positions, their eyes searching the oncoming traffic. Sazonov began to move forward at a half-trot and Kaliayev, momentarily losing sight of him, stepped up on the Obvodny Canal Bridge for a better view.

The black carriage appeared, drawn by two horses. It kept to the middle of the street, moving fast. A red-bearded coachman drove alone on the coach box, and a detective bicycled furiously at the left wheel. Two other detectives followed in a cab. Just as Sazonov stepped into the street, the carriage reduced its speed, impeded by a slowly moving cart. Sazonov ran directly toward the window of the carriage and hurled his heavy burden through the glass.

The explosion was enormous. Savinkov later described it as "a strange, heavy, ponderous thud . . . as if someone had struck an iron plate with a heavy hammer." Windows were smashed for blocks around, and a huge column of smoke rose from the ground, obscuring the scene. Standing on the footbridge over the canal, Kaliayev strained for a clearer look; should he run ahead to throw his bomb or leave the area and sink it? Suddenly, out of the smoke dashed two black horses, spattered with blood, dragging fragments of carriage wheels behind them. Crowds of people followed, running in every direction. Kaliayev understood that the attack had succeeded. He walked toward the Warsaw Station, sank his bomb in the pond nearby, and left the city by train, according to plan.

Savinkov felt the explosion internally, as a psychological blow. He felt dazed. Without thinking, he found himself running through the fleeing crowd toward the pall of black smoke. All he could see when he came to the wreckage of the carriage was Sazonov, his face deathly pale, lying on the paving stones with his left arm flung out and his head cocked to the right. The young terrorist's cap had been blown off; there was blood on his face and stomach, and his eyes were half-closed. Savinkov bent over him. The body seemed lifeless. Then a police captain who knew him as "McCullough" approached him, waving his hands.

"Go away, sir, please go away."

As he withdrew, Savinkov heard someone remark, "They say the minister escaped." With the same pessimistic conviction that had led him earlier to assume Azef's death, he "knew" then that the conspiracy had failed—that Sazonov was dead and von Plehve still alive. He found Dulebov's cab, told him the sad news, and went immediately to the Yusupov Garden, where members of the group were to meet in the event of failure. Finding no one there, but still assuming the worst, Savinkov rented a room in a bathhouse and remained there for two hours, until the time fixed for a meeting to prepare for a second assassination attempt. He emerged at about three o'clock and bought a newspaper from a vendor on the Nevsky Prospect. Von Plehve's portrait stared at him from the front page, draped in black. "Von Plehve Killed!" The paper revealed that the minister's unknown assailant, seriously wounded but conscious, had been taken to a hospital where an operation was performed on him in the presence of Muraviev, the minister of justice. The captured terrorist had refused to give his name or to reveal any other information.

Sazonov was, indeed, alive. In a letter smuggled out of prison, he described his condition at the time of his arrest.

When I was arrested my whole face was bathed in blood; the eyes were out of their sockets; in my right side there was a gaping hole; two toes were torn from my left foot;

the sole was crushed. I was well-nigh mortally wounded. The police agents, masquerading as doctors, kept waking me, and would not let me rest. They repeated again and again the horrors of the explosion, and told me lies about "the little Jew," Sikorsky. It was torture!

The enemy is contemptible without limit. It is dangerous to surrender oneself to them alive. Please let this be known. Farewell, dear comrades! I salute the rising sun of liberty!

In order to break Sazonov, the police told him that Sikorsky had betrayed the cause and that he was working with them to identify other members of the conspiracy. In fact, little Leiba *was* in jail, having been arrested less than two hours after the assassination. As Sazonov had feared, he had panicked and disregarded his instructions. Instead of going to Petrovsky Park and rowing out to sea to dispose of his bomb, he had hired a skiff at the nearby Engineering Institute and had thrown his package into the water halfway across the river, near a battleship that was under construction. When the boatman noticed this and asked him what he was doing, Sikorsky compounded his problem by offering the man a ten-ruble bribe. The boatman took him immediately to the police station, where he was arrested. Once in custody, however, he regained his poise and told his captors nothing.

Similarly, despite his helpless condition and the efforts of the police doctors to break his spirit, Sazonov revealed little to the agents hovering over his bed. In his delirium, he muttered words that might have proved dangerous to others if they had been understood, among them "Auntie" and "Valentine." But in the end, the only information wrung from the assassin was his own name, a declaration that he was a member of the Fighting Organization, and a militant statement of his belief in the terrorist cause.

It was not until the fall that a fisherman brought up Sikorsky's bomb in one of his nets, providing the evidence needed to tie "the fourth man" into the assassination. On December 13, 1904, he and

Sazonov were tried together before a jury in the St. Petersburg High Court. Both expected to hang, but the government, which was in one of its "moderate" phases, decided to show mercy. Sazonov was sentenced to life imprisonment at hard labor and Sikorsky to twenty years in jail. Both men were incarcerated in the Schlüsselberg Fortress, from which Sazonov wrote, "I did not at all expect that I would not be killed, and I do not rejoice at the verdict: what joy is there to be the captive of the Russian government? I hope it will not be for long."

It was not to be for long. In 1906, Sazonov was transferred to the notorious Akatui prison camp in Eastern Siberia, the same camp from which Gershuni had escaped several months earlier. Shortly thereafter, in protest against the mistreatment of prisoners by authorities, he soaked himself in kerosene and set himself afire, injuring himself mortally. This self-immolation may also have served another purpose. In a letter to Savinkov describing his feelings about the assassination, Sazonov had written, "The consciousness of guilt never left me."

As for Azef, he had been galvanized by the explosion on the Ismailovsky Prospect. On the morning of the assassination, he and Ivanovskaya were walking down one of Warsaw's main streets when newsboys came running toward them shouting, "Bomb thrown at Plehve! Bomb thrown!" There was no other news. "Can it have failed?" Azef asked his companion. Then another newsboy rushed up with a later edition of the paper, and he read the headline aloud: "Plehve Assassinated!" According to Ivanovskaya, he suddenly complained of feeling faint and went limp, letting his arms drop loosely by his sides. But the scent of danger revived him more quickly than any stimulant, for Azef could easily imagine the reaction at police headquarters when it was discovered that the killing was the Organization's work. The last thing he needed now was to be seen in any part of the Russian Empire in the company of Auntie or—god forbid!—Boris Savinkov. He and Ivanovskaya had arranged to meet Savinkov the next day at the Café de Paris restaurant in Warsaw, but without warning her, Azef took the next express train to Vienna. From Vienna he immediately telegraphed Leonid Ratayev: "Deeply shocked by what has just happened. . . ."

Azef's instincts served him well. According to Police Director Lopukhin, the Secret Police at first refused to believe that the Organization could have been involved in the assassination. "Their man" on the inside would surely have warned them in time to prevent it! All doubt was removed, however, by Sazonov's statement in the hospital and by the appearance of a special edition of *Revolutionary Russia,* which proudly proclaimed, "Plehve is assassinated. . . . All Russia has not ceased repeating these three words since July [28]. . . ."

> Who ruined the country, who submerged it in torrents of blood? Who carried us back to the Middle Ages with his ghetto, with the slaughter of Kishinev and the decomposed corpse of St. Seraphim? Who strangled the Finns for the sole reason that they were Finns, the Jews for the sole reason that they were Jews, the Armenians because of Armenia, the Poles because of Poland? Who fired on us, starving and unarmed, who violated our women and dispossessed us of our remaining goods? . . . Who? Always he, the unlimited master of Russia, the old man in the gold-bedecked uniform, blessed by the czar and cursed by the people. . . .
>
> Plehve's death is only one step forward on the way to popular liberation. The road is long and hard, but we have begun and the way is clear. Karpovich and Balmashev, Gershuni and Pokotilov, unknowns at Ufa and unknowns near the Warsaw Station have shown us this way. The day of judgment of the autocracy is at hand!

Azef hastened to Paris, where he found Ratayev packing. His supervisor had been recalled to Russia to explain his failure to protect von Plehve from Organization attack. Azef briefed the nervous official carefully, reminding him that they had warned Lopukhin specifically against Organization bomb throwers, that they had provided descriptions of the leading terrorists, and had even indicated that von Plehve would be most vulnerable to attack during his trips by carriage to visit the czar. But rather than use this information intelligently, the Secret Police had flooded the streets with inept plainclothesmen, arresting minor figures, putting the terrorists on their guard, and cutting off Azef's sources of information. They had not even had the sense to vary von Plehve's timetable or to guard his carriage from the front as well as from behind! Ratayev should not bother to defend himself or his agent; he should attack the obvious incompetence of the St. Petersburg police.

In fact, Azef was not as confident as he sounded. If the authorities conducted an exhaustive investigation, he might well be implicated despite his telegram from Vienna. The Secret Police now knew, for example, that Leiba Sikorsky had been in Vilna prior to July 28, and that Azef had telegraphed Ratayev from that city during the same period. Lopukhin also knew that Azef's party name (uttered in hospital by the delirious Sazonov) was Valentine. What else did the police know? What else might Sazonov or Sikorsky have revealed? But Azef's anxiety was soon relieved; his supervisor's explanations were accepted by Lopukhin without question. In fact, the department conducted only the most desultory sort of inquiry, going through the motions of an official investigation without any real energy or enthusiasm.

Years later, this lassitude would lead some suspicious souls to conclude that the assassination was an "inside job." According to them, Azef was really working for Count Witte, or for Ratayev's predecessor as foreign affairs chief, the vengeful Pyotr Rachkovsky, or for some one or another of the internal affairs minister's innumerable enemies. It is far more likely, however, that the police had no heart for a real investigation. Von Plehve had offended virtually everyone—those outside the government by his dictatorial measures and bloodthirsty repression, and those inside by his ceaseless

intriguing, insatiate ambition, and use of police spies against bureaucratic competitors. As one contemporary noted, "Hated during
his lifetime, Plehve went to his grave deserted by all."

The joy was greatest, of course, in the Socialist Revolutionary
camp. On the evening of July 28, a congress of SRs living abroad
was being held at Hermance, a little village not far from Geneva.
According to one of the participants, Stepan Sletov, a member of
the Central Committee burst in in the midst of a discussion, waving
a telegram and shouting the news of the assassination. "For several
minutes, pandemonium reigned. Several men and women became
hysterical. Most of those present embraced each other. On every side
there were shouts of joy. I can still see N——. He was standing a
little apart; he dashed a glass of water on the floor and, gnashing
his teeth, shouted, 'That's for Kishinev!' " Indeed, the celebration
went on at such volume and length that neighbors called the village
police, thus ending both the evening and the party conference.

Party leaders were somewhat more restrained, but no less joyful,
when Azef arrived in Geneva a few days later for a joint meeting
of the Central Committee and the members of the Fighting Organization. When he entered the room in which the Central Committee had assembled, all heads turned toward him and conversation
ceased. Before any demonstration could erupt, Ekaterina Breshkovskaya, the revolutionary veteran, rose to greet him. Without a word,
she prostrated herself at his feet in the ancient Russian style, touching
her head to the floor. This act of submission was all the more
significant because Babushka had not been one of Azef's supporters;
she had previously told several friends that she disliked him and
distrusted his cold nature. But now, as the cheers rang out, all was
changed. From a terrorist organizer of unproved talent whose leadership had provoked rebellious challenges within his own party,
Azef had become the Organization's "Eagle"—the very embodi-
ment of its revolutionary will. "Formerly we were led by a romantic,"
declared Mikhail Gotz. "Now we have a realist. He is not a talker,
but he will carry out his plans with a ruthless energy which nothing
can withstand."

   As he stood acknowledging these tributes with his customary half smile, Azef was inclined to agree. Already he was contemplating a new operation: a triple assassination that would decapitate the czarist bureaucracy. The ineffectual czar he would leave alive—for the time being. But Nicholas's uncles, the leaders of the reactionary, anti-Semitic party at court, were now within his reach.

The Eagle at His Zenith

THE ASSASSINATION OF Vyacheslav von Plehve must rank among the most popular political killings of the century. Russians of all classes and nationalities (including more than a few government officials) celebrated the death of the ruthless upstart. Praise rang out around the world for his young assassins, embodiments of selfless courage and desperation. Editorials in Western journals deplored terrorist violence in the abstract, but took obvious satisfaction in the "lessons" it was hoped this particular deed would teach the reactionaries in St. Petersburg. Telegrams of support and financial contributions, the latter amounting in a short time to tens of thousands of rubles, poured into Socialist Revolutionary party headquarters in Geneva. Although hard-line socialists like Lenin and Trotsky warned that terrorist heroics would never incite a mass revolution, the von Plehve operation put the SRs on the political map, accelerating a process that would eventually make them the leading opposition party in the countryside and a major participant in revolutionary events to come.

In this heady atmosphere, the SR Central Committee and its Fighting Organization met to define their future relationship. The major subject for discussion was the "organizational question." Should the party bring the Organization more firmly under its control, as several members of the Central Committee contended, or should the armed fighters be declared independent of all "civilian" leaders, as Boris Savinkov and Ivan Kaliayev wished? A narrow, rather bureaucratic issue—but behind it lay others of more general importance. Was armed struggle to remain an adjunct of the SRs' mass organizing work, or should it become their principal business? Suppose the killing of von Plehve were followed by more numerous and devastating attacks. Could terrorist activity expand to become the Revolution itself, and, if so, what sort of revolution would that be? Assorted liberals were now clamoring for an alliance with the SRs. Should the party join with them to overthrow the autocracy, postponing the question of socialism to a later date? Or should it form a common front with the more radical—but anti-terrorist—Social Democrats?

Barely one week after the assassination, the taciturn figure chiefly responsible for this triumph found himself at the center of this debate. Typically, Azef focused on the immediate practical issues, occupying a middle position that gave him the freedom to maneuver between opposing forces. Before the Central Committee, he argued that *political* control over the Organization was paramount. This could be secured if the party were given the exclusive right to decide both the type of target to be attacked (for example, the czar and his family, cabinet officials, army officers, or lower-level bureaucrats) and the duration of terrorist campaigns. At the same time, he easily persuaded his comrades in the Organization that *operational* independence was all that mattered. Let the Central Committee decide issues of general policy, so long as the matters he liked to call "technical" were left to the fighters themselves. The Organization alone would recruit new members, choose specific targets, and control its own burgeoning treasury. Coordination between the party and its military wing could be guaranteed by appointing an executive committee of the Organization whose director would be the sole intermediary between the two groups, responsible to both. Obviously, this could be none other than Azef himself.

The negotiators accepted Azef's "compromise." Reduced to writing, these principles became the "Statutes of the Fighting Organization." In order to shorten the debate, it was provided that they would go into effect on the approval of Mikhail Gotz without the necessity for confirmation by the full Central Committee. Gotz approved immediately; Azef, Savinkov, and Schweitzer were named to the executive committee, and Azef was elected director.

On the surface, this agreement did little more than ratify the status quo. The Fighting Organization retained its practical independence under Azef's leadership, with ultimate authority residing (distantly) in the Central Committee. But the agreement's real effects were more far-reaching. The wing of the party favoring mass organizing over terrorism was dealt a serious defeat. Azef, whose indifference to socialism was well known, emerged as a powerful force on the Central Committee. And the party moved rapidly into a loose alliance with the Union for Liberation, an organization of liberal intellectuals led by a history professor named Pavel Miliukov. Several months later, the SRs played a leading role in the 1904 Conference of Revolutionary and Opposition Organizations of the Russian Empire, which agreed to fight for a democratic—not necessarily socialist—republic.

The agreement also placed Azef in a uniquely influential position: he alone could control the flow of information between the Central Committee and the terrorists. Moreover, it gave him both the prestige and the resources needed to deliver a telling blow to his enemies in the government. The leaders of the reactionary party at court, dyed-in-the-wool autocrats and anti-Semites opposed to all reform, were the czar's uncles, Sergei and Vladimir Alexandrovich. The Grand Duke Sergei, who exercised dictatorial power in Moscow as military commandant of that city, was particularly loathed by the democratic opposition. A religious fanatic wielding great influence over the weak-willed Nicholas II, he was considered "obstinate, arrogant, and disagreeable" even by members of his own family. Sergei was widely considered responsible for the disaster at Khodynka Field during the czar's coronation. It was he who had expelled the Jews from Moscow in the 1890s, he who had supported Zubatov's spy system and Plehve's atrocities, and he who publicly declared his hatred of all "inferior peoples."

At a meeting in Paris, Azef persuaded the Central Committee that attacks should now be directed against the royal family, although not yet against the czar himself. He then set to work organizing three more or less simultaneous assassinations. One Organization squad was to kill Sergei in Moscow; another would liquidate Vladimir in St. Petersburg; and a third would dispatch General Kleigels in Kiev.

The terrorist chief's first problem, however, was to reestablish his credibility in the eyes of the Secret Police. True, Director Lopukhin had accepted his and Ratayev's explanations for their failure to stop the von Plehve assassination, but a successful attack on the royal family would be another matter altogether. The deaths of two grand dukes would convulse the government; this time there would be a *real* investigation of the Internal Affairs Ministry and its spy system. Azef's only protection when this happened would be his distance from the crime and a record of continuous, significant service to the government. His instinct told him that security lay in keeping his roles as a terrorist and counter-terrorist symmetrical; that is, he must make himself almost as valuable to the police as to the Organization. Fortunately for him, events in Russia were now moving in a direction that made it possible to furnish important information to the government without compromising either his terrorist mission or his liberal goals. Revolutionary breezes were freshening into a gale, providing abundant opportunities for revenge and betrayal.

The new factor provoking mass discontent was war. Several months before his death, von Plehve had declared: "In order to suppress revolution, we need a small victorious war." In January 1904, the Japanese furnished the war by attacking the czar's fleet at

Port Arthur, Manchuria, but no Russian could have described the sequel as either small or victorious. By the time von Plehve met his fate, Port Arthur was under siege (it would fall in December), and Russia's massive Far Eastern army, composed almost entirely of peasant conscripts, had taken its first lumbering steps on the road to destruction.

By the late summer and fall, as defeat followed defeat, the country burned with dissent. Popular anger had not yet reached the point of open rebellion, but all opposition groups made significant gains, with the SRs forming new party committees, labor unions, and student groups throughout the country. In the autumn of 1904, while their leaders attended conferences of liberals and socialists in the West, red-shirted SRs demonstrated openly in the streets of St. Petersburg and Moscow. At the same time, terrorism boiled up spontaneously, inspired by the Organization's success, but entirely out of its control. In September, a worker in Odessa fired a pistol at the governor of that city. He missed, but when the local party member who had incited the attempt was arrested a few days later, he managed to stab the arresting officer to death. In October, two SRs bombed the police station in Byelostock, wounding several policemen and killing one of the bomb throwers. And in December, SR militants made unauthorized assassination attempts against the chiefs of police of Kharkov and Moscow. Meanwhile, without the party's assistance or foreknowledge, peasants in the "Black Earth" region were launching a series of violent, unorganized, and apparently unpremeditated attacks on landowners and their property. Among the SRs, a group calling itself the "Agrarians" was formed with the intention of persuading the Central Committee to support this growing tendency toward "terror from below."

Azef could hardly have wished for a better opportunity to demonstrate his usefulness to the police. Prime Minister Stolypin later declared that "Immediately following this assassination [the von Plehve killing], Azef sent in extremely important and valuable reports that led to the discovery of a whole series of criminal plots." But what Stolypin failed to understand was that the only criminal plots exposed by Azef were those of his political enemies—and that, in some cases, they were the products of his own fertile imagination. As usual, Azef distorted the truth just enough to lead the Secret Police away from the most dangerous conspirators, while providing himself with future defenses to the charge of complicity in terrorism. He reported in great detail on conferences of revolutionaries abroad, giving accurate information about the Social Democrats, the Finnish and Polish revolutionaries, the liberal parties, and (up to a point) the Socialist Revolutionaries. He called attention to the formation of the Agrarian group, and then—a self-protective masterstroke— reported that SR terrorists were planning to attack the royal family. But rather than indicate their real targets, he suggested that the Organization's intended victim was Nicholas II himself!

Electrified, Police Director Lopukhin demanded more information. "The Center of the Fighting Organization's activity," Azef replied, "is in Odessa"—a blatant lie, but one impossible to disprove, since there was a large and active party organization in that city. He named several members of the alleged "Center" who were, in fact, nothing more than SR propagandists, Agrarians, and labor organizers. But the most dangerous terrorists by far, he declared, were Stepan Sletov and Maria Seliuk, both members of the Central Committee. It was they who had been sent into Russia to organize the czar's assassination.

This was not only a lie, it was a complete inversion of the truth. If the czar's assassination *had* been on the SR agenda (of course, it was not), Sletov and Seliuk would have been the last members of the party to undertake such a mission. In reality, they were Azef's most determined critics—the core of the small group on the Central Committee opposed to his policy of "autonomous terrorism." While admiring the tactical brilliance of his campaign against von Plehve, these convinced socialists considered violence by Azef's elite corps a diversion from the party's main task, which was to prepare the ground for the "mass terror" of a popular revolution. *That* is why they were returning to Russia—not to kill officials, royal or otherwise, but to organize workers and peasants for the coming upheaval. In short, they were exactly the sort of opponents whom Azef, who loathed doctrinaire Reds as much as he did freelance terrorists, had little hesitation in turning over to the police.

Thanks to these disclosures, Sletov was arrested at the frontier and Seliuk in the capital. Both were imprisoned in the Peter and Paul Fortress, but released one year later (as luck would have it) when the czar declared an amnesty for political prisoners. Other groups of "dangerous terrorists"—that is, mass organizers—were captured on Azef's say-so in Odessa, Nikolayev, Saratov, Kiev, and Byelostock, and information that he provided led to the confiscation of the party's new printing press at Nijni-Novgorod.

The authorities had good reason to value such information. What they could not know was that Azef was continuing to conduct a war on two fronts: against the advocates of "mass terror" within his own party and against the practitioners of state terror within the government. The Organization was now, in effect, his private army—a situation that gave him unprecedented freedom to mislead both the Central Committee and the Ministry of Internal Affairs. Both these bodies considered him a somewhat unorthodox but highly useful tool. But while the party basked in its newfound eminence and the Secret Police congratulated themselves on foiling a plot against the czar, it was the "tool" who had the most reason to celebrate. In a few short months he had killed von Plehve, redeemed his reputation as the government's top spy, rid himself of powerful enemies on the Central Committee, and disrupted the SRs' mass organizing activities—all while protecting his terrorist comrades from party control and police exposure.

Now he was ready to move against the grand dukes.

In August 1904, Azef established his base in Paris. Luba had given birth to a second child, a daughter, and for his family's sake as well as his own, he wanted the security of a permanent home outside Russia. The General Electrical Company assigned him to represent its interests in Western Europe, and he installed his wife and children in a comfortable apartment on the Boulevard Raspail. This would be the family's principal residence for the next five years. In Paris, Luba had the company of other Russian émigrés and played an important role among the local SRs. The children enjoyed educational opportunities unavailable to Russian Jews; according to one acquaintance of the family, they soon became more French than Russian and were known by their French nicknames. And Azef could now travel on lengthy "business trips" without worrying about his family's safety.

His first task, however, was to expand the Fighting Organization so that it could carry out simultaneous operations in three Russian cities. As usual, he selected virtually all the new members himself. Among the dozen or so new recruits was his own younger brother, Vladimir, a chemist educated (as he had been) in Germany, who was admitted with the understanding that he would confine himself to bomb making under Marc Schweitzer's supervision. Abram Borishansky's younger brother, Jacob, was also accepted, as was Tatiana Leontyeva, a young aristocrat with excellent connections among the St. Petersburg elite. She might soon be presented at court—a prospect that Azef found most intriguing—but for the time being, her assignment would be to supply the Organization with information about the habits and movements of government officials in the capital. Boris Moiseyenko, an old friend of Savinkov's, was admitted at the same time without conditions. Azef recognized him immediately as an ideal operative: worldly, self-contained, quietly committed to the cause, and utterly fearless.

In September, Azef instructed Savinkov and Schweitzer to establish a dynamite laboratory in Paris for use in the upcoming campaign. Posing as a Greek merchant, Schweitzer rented an apartment in the Rue Gramm and transformed it into a bomb factory with the help of his "roommates," Dora Brilliant and Vladimir Azef. They were joined shortly by the other members of the squad, including Igor Dulebov and the redoubtable Poet, Ivan Kaliayev. The purposes of this enterprise, reminiscent of Schweitzer's "dynamite school" in Kharkov, were to produce explosives and teach the new comrades the bomb maker's trade, but also to integrate the new members into the terrorist clan. Schweitzer's "students" soon produced enough dynamite to make several dozen bombs of various sizes. At Azef's suggestion, the soft-spoken engineer also engaged in a series of electrochemical experiments aimed at developing a remote-controlled bomb. The results were inconclusive, but Azef remained convinced that with new technology, a small group like the Organization could mount an effective war against the czarist regime. One new invention—the flying machine—particularly fascinated him, but there was no time in Paris to pursue this interest.

When Auntie Ivanovskaya arrived in Paris in October, Azef called a series of meetings to outline the three-part assassination campaign. Marc Schweitzer, he announced, would lead the largest squad into action in St. Petersburg. Its task was to prepare the assassination of Grand Duke Vladimir and to scout out the possibilities of doing away with several other high officials, including General Dmitri Trepov, a leading reactionary who had recently been named military commandant of the city. Because this group of fifteen would include many untested comrades, Azef asked Ivanovskaya and Dulebov to assist Schweitzer in training and supervising them. A smaller group led by Jacob Borishansky was directed to kill Governor-General Kleigels in Kiev; although Kleigels was not a target of great importance, Azef thought that a triple killing would have enormous impact on the nation at large. Finally, the smallest but most experienced squad was entrusted with the assassination of Grand Duke Sergei in Moscow. Directed by Savinkov, it was composed of Kaliayev, Brilliant, and Moiseyenko, with a fifth member scheduled to join the group in Russia.

All three squads were instructed to employ the tactics that had proven effective against von Plehve. Once again, Organization cabmen and peddlers would infiltrate the streets to track their prey, while other comrades prepared dynamite bombs and laid out detailed plans of attack. But this time, Azef warned, the group leaders must be prepared to operate independently without relying on his direct assistance. He could not be in three places at once! They should also avoid unnecessary contact with local party groups that might be under police observation. Each leader would have the right to augment his forces by adding new members on the spot from a list approved by Azef. And each would decide for his group the time, place, and method of attack, as well as establishing contingency plans and escape routes. Azef would try to meet each of them in Russia before they went into action, but if this proved impossible, they must act on their own.

Vague promises aside, it seems clear that Azef had no intention of returning to Russia before the attacks were made. If he were to be implicated in the grand dukes' assassinations, the game would be over; even Paris might not be a safe haven for him. In mid-November 1904, he met his soldiers for the last time, gave them their final instructions, and embraced each comrade warmly. He advised Schweitzer and Savinkov to obtain passports from English party sympathizers then residing in Paris, and they did so without difficulty. (Several years later, the British comrades who aided them were tried in London and fined one hundred pounds each for furnishing false papers to Russian revolutionaries; their fines were paid by the Organization.) Meanwhile, Schweitzer's chemical team had divided the dynamite into small portions, wrapping each portion in a well-cushioned box. During the next several days, the terrorists left Paris in groups of two or three, each taking a different route home to Russia. The small boxes went with them, hidden neatly in their clothing.

It seemed at first that the hunt for Grand Duke Sergei would go quickly. The members of Savinkov's squad needed little further training or bonding; they were already intimate friends sharing a common passion for terrorism, contempt for politicians, and distrust of all centralized authority (not excluding that of the SR Central Committee). Dora Brilliant, now playing the relatively passive role of bomb maker, was another "Anarchist" (as the militants playfully called themselves) and a familiar member of the family. With the

exception of Moiseyenko, who proved a quick study, all were experienced at the game of tracking down well-guarded officials. While
Brilliant shuttled between Moscow and Nijni-Novgorod, where the
group's dynamite lay hidden, Kaliayev and Moiseyenko fell easily
into their cabmen's roles, meeting frequently in their carriages or
in secure public places with a free-spending Englishman known in
the city as James Halley.

Halley/Savinkov was gratified by the speed with which his cabmen zeroed in on their famous target. Within one month, the group's
observation work was substantially completed. Sergei, who possessed
three palaces in Moscow, was currently residing at the Tverskaya
Palace, from which he drove regularly two or three times a week
in his dazzling carriage, which had a white harness and bright green
lights, to an office in the Kremlin. His carriage was not as well-
guarded as von Plehve's had been; intercepting it in the vicinity of
the Kremlin would not be difficult once an additional terrorist had
been recruited to work the street with Kaliayev and Moiseyenko.
Early in December, Savinkov notified Dora Brilliant that the operation was moving into its action phase. As planned, he traveled
to Baku, the Azerbaijani capital, to meet the worker whom Azef
had recommended to be the team's "third man." But there he discovered that this comrade had lost interest in terrorist work and
had left the city. The Baku party committee recommended in his
stead a local party member: an intellectual named Pyotr Kulikovsky.
Savinkov interviewed Kulikovsky and quickly selected him for the
squad.

On his return to Moscow, Savinkov received shocking news:
the local committee of the Socialist Revolutionary party in Moscow
had publicly threatened the grand duke's life. Responding to the
harsh repression of a political demonstration in St. Petersburg, it
had issued the following proclamation:

The Moscow committee of the Socialist Revolutionary Party
considers it necessary to declare that if the political demonstration called for December [18] and [19] is marked by

the same brutality on the part of the authorities and the police as was the case in St. Petersburg a few days ago, we shall hold Governor-General Sergei and Police Chief Trepov responsible. The committee will not stop short of executing them.

Technically, of course, this was a serious breach of party discipline. The SR Central Committee had not given the Moscow branch permission to execute anyone, much less the czar's uncle. But Viktor Chernov was no Lenin, and the SR local committees tended to act on their own impulses. Moreover, since Savinkov had deliberately avoided making contact with the local committee, Vladimir Zenzinov, the dynamic leader of the Moscow group, had had no idea that an Organization assassination team was in the area or that it was hunting the grand duke. Nevertheless, the proclamation infuriated Savinkov. How like a group of amateurs to announce an assassination rather than performing it! Naturally, Grand Duke Sergei immediately moved out of the Tverskaya Palace and altered the days and hours of his visits to the Kremlin. Uniformed guards and plainclothes police agents now appeared where none had been seen before. The observation work would have to begin now—after the Moscow SRs had been warned off.

In late December, Nikolai Tiuchev, a longtime member of the Central Committee, visited Moscow and gave Savinkov clearance to meet with the Moscow leader, Zenzinov. The two men met at a safe house used by the local comrades. The first question Savinkov asked was whether the Moscow committee was actually planning to assassinate the grand duke.

"Yes, it is," replied Zenzinov.

"Has the committee any information concerning his mode of life and has it been watching him?"

Yes, Zenzinov reported, it was watching Sergei and had information to impart. The grand duke had moved to the Neskuchny Palace and drove to the Kremlin several times each week, usually on Wednesday and Friday afternoons between two and five o'clock.

But his schedule and routes varied, making it difficult to predict his movements on any particular day. This confirmed Savinkov's own data, procured by the Organization's street operatives. After interrogating Zenzinov further, Savinkov ordered him, in the name of the Organization, to discontinue the Moscow committee's efforts, which could only interfere with the principal plot against Sergei. The Moscow leader agreed without complaint, and Savinkov left the meeting satisfied. Unknown to either man, however, the Secret Police had already put Zenzinov under observation. They arrested him the following morning, tried him two months later, and convicted him for complicity in an independent plot against General Trepov.

Savinkov spent the weeks following the arrest in a fever of worry. Obviously, Vladimir Zenzinov was in a position to expose the Organization's conspiracy in exchange for his freedom. How would he stand up under police interrogation? But Zenzinov's reputation for courage was well earned; he maintained absolute silence and was sentenced to five years imprisonment in eastern Siberia. En route, he escaped and fled the country, rejoining the party some months later and, finally, enlisting in the Fighting Organization. Azef had great respect for this plainspoken, vigorous merchant's son who had protected the Organization when it was most vulnerable. But, clearly, his own concerns about contacting the Moscow committee had been justified. "Had the police spies been cleverer," Savinkov later remarked, "they could have come upon my track and, through me, upon the track of our entire small group."

In January 1905, the hunt for Sergei began again in earnest, complicated by frequent changes in the grand duke's travel schedule. Savinkov was wrestling with the problems caused by these variations when an event occurred that was of much greater consequence than any assassination, real or imagined. Savinkov heard about it from an eyewitness: Pyotr Rutenberg, a party sympathizer who had just arrived in Moscow after fleeing the czar's capital with the police on his heels. Breathless with excitement, Rutenberg declared, "There is an uprising in St. Petersburg!"

Throughout January, the capital had been in turmoil. Shortly after the New Year, several workers at the giant Putilov steel factory, where Rutenberg worked as an engineer, were fired for insubordination. Twelve thousand men and women—the entire workforce—had then gone on strike, demanding an eight-hour day, higher wages for unskilled workers, better medical facilities, and other improvements. Workers from other factories spontaneously joined the strike, and by mid-January more than twenty-five thousand men and women had laid down their tools. At this time, the principal labor organization in the city was the St. Petersburg Assembly of Russian Factory and Mill Workers—another creation of Sergei Zubatov, Azef's former supervisor, who had put at its head the charismatic priest and police agent, Father Georgy Gapon. Rutenberg knew Gapon and (having no inkling of his relations with the police) admired his dedication to the workers' cause. The wave of strikes caught both men by surprise, but when Gapon proposed a massive, nonviolent march on the Winter Palace to demand justice of the czar, Rutenberg agreed to help him lead it.

The march took place on Sunday, January 22. With Rutenberg at his side, Gapon led a crowd of thirty thousand in a peaceful procession to the Winter Palace, where he planned to present a petition to the czar's representatives. "We, the workers of St. Petersburg," it began, "our wives, children, and helpless old folk, have come to you to seek justice and protection." Both Gapon and Rutenberg anticipated trouble, but vowed that they would do nothing to provoke it. The workers and their families, all in their best dress, were unarmed. Instead of revolutionary banners they carried icons and portraits of Nicholas and Alexandra, and as they marched, they sang hymns of the Holy Orthodox Church.

The army met them at barricades thrown up the night before. Twelve thousand troops, infantry and cavalry, had been given live ammunition and told by their commanders that the marchers were planning to seize the Winter Palace, murder the royal family, and unleash a revolutionary bloodbath. The soldiers fired repeatedly into the unarmed crowd, sabering and bayoneting those who threw themselves down in an attempt to escape the bullets. Some two hundred were killed, including many children, and eight hundred more were wounded. Rutenberg hoisted the injured Father Gapon on his shoulders and escaped with him to a village outside Moscow.

The following morning, throughout the workers' quarters, a new song could be heard:

> Conquered in the East,
> Victor over Russia,
> Be accursed, cruel Czar,
> Steeped in blood!

"Bloody Sunday" altered the political landscape of Russia irrevocably. Gapon (who played a double game something like Azef's, but with far less consistency and skill) later declared that he had led the people into an almost certain massacre in order to rid them of their belief in a fatherly, benevolent czar. If that was his intention, he succeeded. Particularly in the cities, the events of January 22 completed the work of disillusionment begun almost ten years earlier when Nicholas and Alexandra danced after the tragedy at the Khodynka Field. The tempo of mass meetings and political demonstrations, strikes and rural uprisings increased markedly. The government began to veer wildly between concessions and repressive tactics, and the stage was set for the great mass explosion that the revolutionaries longed for.

The Revolution of 1905 (as it was known afterward) would soon connect the Socialist Revolutionary party to a genuine mass movement, compelling its leaders to reconsider the whole question of terrorism. In the immediate aftermath of Bloody Sunday, however, terrorism seemed an appropriate and necessary response. Following the massacre, the grand duke, more unpopular than ever, had moved again for security reasons and was now residing at the Nikolayevsky Palace inside the Kremlin. But its ancient walls were less protective than he imagined. Boris Moiseyenko found it relatively easy to park his shabby cab near the "Czar-Cannon," directly in view of Sergei's palace, while Kaliayev and Kulikovsky watched the Kremlin gates to determine the times and routes of his journeys. In the course of his work, Kaliayev made an interesting discovery: he found that by staring at a certain patriotic picture mounted on the wall of a church outside the Kremlin—a picture framed in glass—one could see a clear reflection of the entrance to the palace behind the Nikolsky Gate. These coordinated observations revealed a marked increase in activity at the palace entrance; unaware of his vulnerability, the grand duke was again taking his green-lighted carriage to parties and theatrical performances.

Boris Savinkov, alias "James Halley," managed to persuade several prominent Muscovites to discuss the details of Sergei's social schedule, but he did not yet trust these sources sufficiently to order an attack. It was the daily newspaper that settled the time and place of the attempt on Sergei's life. Early in February, the paper announced a performance at the Bolshoi Theater for the benefit of the Red Cross. The benefit, scheduled for Wednesday evening, February 15, was sponsored by the grand duke's wife, the Grand Duchess Elizaveta Feodorovna, sister of the czarina. It was virtually certain that Sergei would also attend—and Savinkov intended to make it his last earthly social engagement. He conferred again with his watchers, met separately with Kaliayev and Kulikovsky, and then went to Nijni-Novgorod to talk with Dora Brilliant.

About one week later, on Tuesday afternoon, Brilliant arrived at the Slaviansky Bazaar Hotel in Moscow with the makings of two bombs in her suitcase. She assembled the bombs in her room the following morning, wrapped them in a blanket, and settled down to wait. At seven o'clock in the evening, one hour before the scheduled performance at the Bolshoi, she handed the blanket to Savinkov at the entrance to her hotel. Savinkov's plan was simple (Azef, he thought, would have approved). Two roads, two bombs, two assassins. From the Nikolsky Gate, only two roads led to the Bolshoi Theater. On one he stationed Kaliayev, on the other Kulikovsky, both dressed in peasant garb. Minutes after accepting Brilliant's blanket, he stepped into Boris Moiseyenko's cab, and half an hour later he delivered a bomb to each man.

Kulikovsky walked to the entrance of the Alexandrovsky Gardens, cutting off one road to the Bolshoi, while the Poet took up a position in Voskresensky Square, the more likely route. Savinkov entered the Alexandrovsky Gardens and sat on a bench, waiting for the explosion. He was later to describe the scene in detail.

It was bitter cold. A storm was beginning. Kaliayev stood in the shadow of the city [council] doors, facing the dark, deserted square. Shortly after eight o'clock the Grand Duke's carriage appeared at the Nikolsky gate. Kaliayev recognized it immediately by its bright green lights. The carriage turned into Voskresensky Square, and in the darkness, Kaliayev thought he recognized the Grand Duke's coachman, Rudinkin. Without hesitation he dashed forward, straight across the path of the carriage. He had already raised his hand to hurl the bomb. But suddenly he perceived that in addition to the Grand Duke there were also in the carriage the Grand Duchess Elizabeth and the children of the Grand Duke Paul—Marie and Dmitri. Kaliayev let his hand fall and withdrew. The carriage stopped at the entrance of the Bolshoi Theater.

No one had noticed Kaliayev in the dark square. Still carrying his bomb wrapped in its blanket, he walked over to the Alexandrovsky Gardens, where Savinkov was waiting. "I think I have done properly," he said, trembling with excitement. "How can one kill children?"

If the history of terrorism can be said to have its high points, this was surely one of them. Some commentators have portrayed it as a case of Kaliayev's humane instincts triumphing over his ideology—but it was the ideology itself that was, in this sense, humane. "How can one kill children?" The rhetorical question reflected the Organization's thinking, always closer to that of the old-time People's Will movement than that of modern revolutionaries or statesmen. Lenin was right to call it a philosophy of "single combat." A few carefully targeted villains were to be eliminated; the innocent (including children of the ruling class) were to be spared. Even with respect to this principle, however, Kaliayev was no absolutist. Perhaps, killing the grand duke was a goal so important that one *could* justify sacrificing his niece and nephew to achieve it. Standing with Savinkov in the park named for another tyrant, he offered to submit the issue to the group and to abide by its decision; if the comrades asked him to, he would throw the bomb into the carriage when the family left the theater. Savinkov rejected the suggestion out of hand, as did the others immediately afterward. Dora Brilliant spoke for the group: "The Poet did as he should have done."

During this post-battle discussion, Boris noticed that Pyotr Kulikovsky, the newest member of the squad, did not look well. He was silent and pale and seemed utterly exhausted. Nevertheless, Savinkov decided to make a second attempt on Sergei's life quickly, before a sense of failure could sap the terrorists' courage. Moiseyenko suggested the date: Friday, February 17, just two days after the Bolshoi Theater benefit. The grand duke had not driven to his office in the governor-general's palace since Monday, and Moiseyenko was certain that he would make the short trip across the Kremlin on Thursday or Friday. Attacking Sergei on Thursday was out of the question; the fighters obviously needed at least one day's rest before going again to war. On Friday, then, Brilliant would reload the bombs, and Savinkov would deliver them to the two throwers. Kaliayev was to attack the carriage first in the Senate Square. Kulikovsky, standing outside the Kremlin on Tverskaya Street, would hurl his bomb if the Poet's failed to explode, or if the grand duke were wounded but not killed.

On Friday, at one o'clock in the afternoon, Savinkov again received the blanket-wrapped bombs at the Slaviansky Bazaar Hotel and entered Moiseyenko's cab. The cabman had very bad news: Kulikovsky had decided that he was unfit for terrorist work and had left the city. Moiseyenko volunteered to replace him, but Savinkov declined the offer. Since Moiseyenko was a cabdriver, his arrest would expose the Organization's methods to the police, endangering the operations in St. Petersburg and Kiev, as well as future terrorist campaigns. Savinkov considered becoming the "second man" himself, but decided not to do so. (He later stated that he did not wish to compromise James Halley, the Englishman who had given him his passport, but it seems more likely that he simply was not prepared to go into combat on such short notice.) The choice was therefore clear: either Kaliayev would attack the carriage alone, or the attempt would have to be postponed.

A few minutes later, the Poet entered the cab to receive his bomb. Informed of Kulikovsky's defection, Kaliayev insisted upon going through with the operation. Savinkov argued briefly with him, urging postponement. What if he were captured before throwing the bomb? What if the bomb proved to be a dud? "Listen here, Yanek," Savinkov pleaded. "I do think it would be better to have two men. Imagine, if we fail! What then?"

Kaliayev's reply settled the issue. "Failure is out of the question. If the grand duke appears, I will surely kill him. You may be certain of that."

Without further discussion, the Poet slipped the bomb under his peasant's cloak, kissed Savinkov good-bye, and walked over to a chapel outside the Kremlin. There he paused, gazing as if entranced at a glass-framed picture on the chapel wall. He remained standing before the picture for several minutes, then turned abruptly and walked back at a measured pace past the Museum of History, through the Nikolsky Gate, and into the Kremlin.

The white carriage was just pulling into the Senate Square. Kaliayev ran forward until he was almost upon it and hurled his bomb. He was blinded by light and stunned by a sound too loud to comprehend. The carriage was demolished; windows shattered throughout the Kremlin. The explosion tore Sergei's body apart, decapitating it and severing one arm and leg entirely from the torso. Somehow, Kaliayev remained standing. "Despite all my precautions to the contrary," he later wrote, "I remained alive. . . ."

When the smoke lifted I found myself standing before the
remains of the back wheels. I remember that wood splinters
struck my face; my cap was torn off. I did not fall but turned
my face away. Then, about five feet away, near the gate, I
saw crumpled pieces of the Grand Duke's clothing and a
nude body. Ten feet further, beyond the carriage, my cap.
I walked over, picked it up, and put it on. I looked around.
All my clothes, torn by splinters, were tattered and burned.
Blood streamed from my face, and I understood: impossible
to escape. . . .

Kaliayev was seized by police agents and driven off through the
Kremlin in a cab. As the cab moved off, he shouted, "Down with
the damned czar, long live liberty! Down with the damned government, long live the Socialist Revolutionary party!" He was
booked at a police station and taken to the Yakimansky prison,
where he fell immediately into a shocked sleep.

Savinkov heard the enormous thump of the explosion on the
Kuznetzky Bridge, where he was to meet Dora Brilliant at a pastry
shop. He found her, and the two conspirators joined the large crowd
hurrying toward the Kremlin. In the thick of the crowd they heard
Moiseyenko calling, "Here, *barin,* a cab!" They climbed in with
relief. Moiseyenko turned the horses away from the Kremlin, driving
at an easy pace toward the railway station. When he announced
that Sergei was dead, Brilliant broke down, sobbing and moaning,
"We killed him . . . *I* killed him . . . *I* . . ."

At the same time, Elizaveta Feodorovna, the grand duchess, was
screaming at the crowd gathered around her husband's shattered
remains. "Aren't you ashamed to be staring here? Go away! Go
away!" Her footman ordered the bystanders to take off their hats,
but no one would do so. For about thirty minutes the gawkers stared
and chattered grieflessly. Officials milled about while police stood
by. Then a squad of soldiers appeared, pushed the crowd away, and
roped off the spot.

Several days later, Elizaveta went to meet her husband's assassin in prison. Since Kaliayev had been transferred to Butirky prison, the unusual encounter took place in his cell in the Pugachev Tower. "I confess," Kaliayev wrote of this meeting, "we looked at each other with a certain mystic sensation, like two mortals who happened to have remained alive—I, accidentally; she by the will of our organization, by *my* will, for both I and the organization deliberately sought to avoid unnecessary bloodshed." Apparently, the deeply religious grand duchess hoped to give her husband's assassin the opportunity to repent. She told him that they met as two human beings rather than as political figures and that God would forgive him. She gave him a little icon and told him, "I will pray for you."

Kaliayev misinterpreted this gesture, seeing it as "a symbol of her recognition of my victory, a symbol of her gratitude to fate for saving her life, and of her repentance for the crimes of the Grand Duke." He also made a serious tactical error, although a goodhearted one: while maintaining that his conscience was clear—he had done his duty and was willing to pay for his deed with his life—he apologized profusely for causing her grief. Elizaveta afterward informed the press that Kaliayev, crushed by guilt, had repented of his sin. He answered with a furious personal letter: "I emphatically protest against the application of political criteria to my personal sympathy with your sorrow. My convictions and my attitude to the ruling dynasty remain unaltered, and I have nothing in common, in any aspect of my being, with the religious superstitions of slaves and their hypocritical rulers. . . ."

This was true, yet the Poet's character *was* as religious, in its way, as the grand duchess's. In May, on the day that he was hanged at Schlüsselberg Fortress, he told the priest who offered to hear his confession that he was a believer outside the church. God existed for Kaliayev, but he was a god of revolutionary justice, demanding both the destruction of tyrants and the expiatory sacrifice of their destroyers. To the members of the Council of State who condemned him to death at a special session of that body, he announced, "I rejoice at your verdict. I hope you will have the courage to carry it out as openly and as publicly as I executed the sentence of the Socialist Revolutionary party. Learn to look the advancing revolution straight in the eye!" To his comrades Kaliayev wrote even more revealingly:

My whole life seems to me like a fairy tale, as if everything that has happened to me had been with me in premonition from childhood and grew within the recesses of my heart until it burst forth in a flame of revenge for all.

The flames of revenge burned brightly that summer. In July 1905, as revolutionary winds swept the country, a small, neatly dressed man appeared at a reception for Count Chuvalov, the mayor of Moscow. He joined the receiving line, and when the mayor turned to greet him, drew a pistol and shot him four times in the chest. The assassin offered no resistance when arrested. His name, he declared, was Pyotr Kulikovsky, and he was a member of the Socialist Revolutionary party.

Kulikovsky, the "fourth man" who had fled Moscow on the day of Sergei's assassination, had returned to the scene of his great failure. The Moscow military tribunal now empowered to try cases of terrorism sentenced him to die, but the sentence was later commuted to imprisonment for life at hard labor. With his deportation to Siberia, Kulikovsky disappears from history; yet with one shot, the little intellectual from Baku had redeemed his soiled honor. Apparently, he *was* fit for terrorist work after all.

SEVEN

The Walls Close In

ON THE DAY FOLLOWING Sergei's assassination, Azef brought a stack of newspapers back to his Paris apartment. Together he and Luba read the reports and commentaries, of which that of the English *Daily Telegraph* was the most dramatic. "Once more the red star of tyrannicide shines darkly in the somber Russian sky," wrote the editorialist.

> [Sergei] was killed instantly by one of those fatal bombs which the Russian conspirators prepare so skillfully and aim so well. . . . [Sergei] was a tyrant in the old sense of the word, one of those whom history and tragedy paint in darkest colors. The great words of St. Augustine are still true today: "When justice is cast aside, the rulers are no better than brigands."

The German *Die Zeit* was more dispassionate, but no less approving. "Those who play so bloody a role in history as did [Sergei] must always be prepared for a bloody end. [Czarism] should not wonder if its disasters evoke no sympathy in anyone." The Swiss *Peuple de Genève* described the killing as "the people's answer" to the massacre of Bloody Sunday, while *L'Humanité,* the voice of the French Left, thundered: "It must be admitted that the secret judges pronounce their sentence over tyrants without mistake. Who would venture to defend von Plehve? Who would dare to mourn [Sergei]? The Grand Dukes have removed themselves from the laws of humanity. . . ."

Azef might have reveled in this applause, but his moment of satisfaction gave way almost immediately to a bout of severe anxiety and depression. Auntie Ivanovskaya, who came to his apartment in Paris during this period to see his wife, recalls catching sight of him lying on a couch in an inner room looking ill and frightened; Lubov told her that Yevno had been talking about giving up the struggle and taking his family to live in America. It was not at all what one would have expected of the triumphant Eagle. Azef seemed almost paralyzed and had to be persuaded to leave for the victory celebration and meeting of party leaders called by the Central Committee in Geneva.

At least in retrospect, the causes of this mysterious malaise are not difficult to diagnose. To begin with, the explosion in the Senate Square had detonated another "bomb" inside the government. A few days after the assassination, Azef's police control, Leonid Ratayev, told him an astonishing story. While the Moscow police were still collecting pieces of Sergei's shattered body, Governor-General Trepov had stormed into Police Director Lopukhin's office, shouted one expletive—"Murderer!"—and left without uttering another word. The meaning of this was ominously clear. Trepov had been the arch-conservative grand duke's principal ally, a position that had already earned him a high place on the Fighting Organization's list of targets. His outrage reflected the suspicions of the reactionaries at court, many of whom believed that the Secret Police had become a tool of liberal-leaning officials bent on liquidating the extreme Right. Trepov might have accused Lopukhin of negligence in the performance of his duties, but he preferred to believe that he and

Ratayev had plotted with the terrorists to have Sergei assassinated. This charge was unfounded, but considering the relative independence of the police and the fogs of intrigue that swirled throughout the Romanov court, it did not seem far-fetched.

As Azef had foreseen, Trepov demanded an exhaustive investigation. Badly frightened, Director Lopukhin had departed immediately for Moscow to conduct his own inquiry; bureaucratic heads, especially those associated with the Moscow police, were sure to roll. But there was worse news still. Trepov, now exercising near-dictatorial power in the capital, had conjured up an old demon. He had recalled Pyotr Rachkovsky from his Parisian retirement and had appointed him special commissioner to the Ministry of Internal Affairs.

Rachkovsky! Here was a figure that even Azef might dread. Like Azef, he had begun as a police agent working among terrorists, but when his dual role was discovered, he joined the government openly and rose quickly to the position of director of the Secret Police's foreign operations. For almost twenty years this formidable figure reigned in Paris, the world's premier center of intrigue. His agents penetrated Russian émigré and student organizations, collaborated with the French police, and engaged in a series of terrorist provocations designed to discredit the radical movement in the West. On his orders, the "anarchist" Yagolkovsky blew up the Liège Cathedral in Belgium. The spymaster amassed a small fortune on the French stock exchange, hobnobbed with France's political elite, and even meddled in the affairs of the Russian royal family. At last, however, he made a serious political mistake. In 1902 he dispatched a report to St. Petersburg highly critical of "Phillipe," a charlatan who was acting as spiritual advisor and fortune-teller to the superstitious Czarina Alexandra. Nicholas II was furious. Von Plehve, who had always hated Rachkovsky, seized the opportunity to have him dismissed and appointed Ratayev to replace him. Finally, at von Plehve's request, Lopukhin drew up a long bill of particulars charging him with incompetence and corruption and leaked the document to St. Petersburg insiders.

An old proverb says, "If you attack the king, you must kill him." Rachkovsky was a dangerous man who would surely avenge himself, if he could, on his humiliators. At the moment, his influence was limited to St. Petersburg, where Trepov had placed him in a position to oversee the local police, but his presence signaled the beginning of a new struggle for control of the intelligence bureaucracy—a struggle far more dangerous to Azef than the official investigation of the assassination. Although Lopukhin was now sniffing the ground in Moscow, Azef could be fairly certain that his inquiries would leave the Organization—and himself—untouched. The Secret Police agents who had been shadowing the Moscow party committee knew nothing of Savinkov's assassination squad, and the indomitable Kaliayev would maintain his silence, if necessary, up to the gallows. But Lopukhin's failure to discover an "enemy within" would probably end his career, and if he followed Zubatov into retirement, the network of government officials that Azef manipulated so deftly would very likely collapse with him.

The political coloration of this group was "social monarchist." Officials like Lopukhin and Ratayev shared the conviction of their old mentor, Zubatov, that the secret police could play a relatively independent role in Russian politics, balancing between the revolutionary organizations outside the government and the reactionaries within. This notion of autonomous police work (the equivalent, on the government side, of the SRs' "autonomous terrorism") was made to order for an operator like Azef. But now his complaisant sponsors were threatened with political extinction. Not only did General Trepov and his friends hold them responsible for Sergei's death, they also blamed the "Zubatovists" for the disorders triggered by the assassination—a vast, confused uproar that was threatening to assume the character of a popular revolution.

Ironically, it was Azef, the opponent of mass terror, who had unwittingly reawakened the people. For unlike earlier Organization attacks, the killing of the Grand Duke was no isolated incident. On the contrary, it revived the movement of popular dissent temporarily stilled by the bullets of Bloody Sunday. In the wake of the explosion

in Senate Square, strikes and stormy street demonstrations, several
of them led by the SRs, broke out in half a dozen cities. Then, one
week after the assassination, Mukden in far-off Manchuria fell to
the Japanese with the loss of one hundred thousand Russian troops,
and the wave of protest swelled anew. The government temporized,
permitting "respectable" opposition groups (that is, the moderate
liberals) to meet and agitate openly, but this only added fuel to the
fire. The local assemblies debated forcing a constitution on the monarchy. Students turned their classes into political rallies. Instances
of spontaneous terrorism multiplied, and opposition organizations
leaped ahead in numbers and influence. Russia's workers and peasants had not yet risen en masse, but one could feel the earth start
to tremble.

Against this background, "Zubatovism"—the idea that the government could play the puppeteer with revolutionary groups, using
secret agents to manipulate them at will—was fast becoming ridiculous. The only type of manipulation that interested men like Trepov
and Rachkovsky was that which led by the shortest possible route
to the annihilation of the opposition. At the same time, on the
revolutionary side, the prospect of a mass uprising was discrediting
the notion of "autonomous terrorism." Why spend months equip-
ping a small band of heroes to kill a few tyrants when the people
themselves were on the threshold of an explosion that might sweep
away the whole rotten structure? At this point, neither General
Trepov nor the SRs knew that Father Gapon, the chief instigator
of Bloody Sunday, was another of Zubatov's protégés. But they
understood very well—as did Azef—that in a real revolution there
could be no room for "men in the middle."

Lying on his couch in Paris, Azef must have felt the walls closing
in. In St. Petersburg, the militant reactionaries were threatening to
scrap his entire government network. In the streets, militant revolutionaries were beginning to bypass his terrorist organization.
Steadily, his room to maneuver was being reduced. If the nation
continued to polarize, Azef would confront the choice that he had
been fleeing ever since his student days in Germany: the choice

between czarism and socialism. On the one side, the czarist elite with its antediluvian ideas and anti-Semitic terror squads; on the other, the armed masses, shouting for a freedom they were utterly incapable of sustaining. Rule by czarists or by revolutionary despots—confronted with these alternatives, what could a true individualist do? He could . . . take his family to America!

Azef's anxiety was well-founded. The walls *were* closing in, but not as quickly as he had feared. By the end of February, he had overcome his initial feelings of panic and helplessness; Switzerland, not New York, was his next destination. Arriving in Geneva, he found Viktor Chernov and the other comrades in a state of fervid anticipation. They congratulated him warmly on his latest victory, but already their attention was turning away from terrorist heroics and toward the coming revolution. Boris Savinkov, who arrived a few days later, was appalled to discover that the Central Committee that had just elected him to membership was now discussing the dissolution of the Fighting Organization. At a certain point, he was informed, mass terror would replace autonomous terror, and control over all the party's activities, military as well as political, would pass into the hands of the Central Committee. This point, Chernov made clear, had not yet arrived. Nevertheless, the question that now occupied the SR leadership was not whom to target next for assassination but how to intersect the mass movement. Should the party limit itself to passing out revolutionary leaflets and organizing strikes? Or should it proceed immediately to put weapons into the workers' and peasants' hands?

This question had been placed on the agenda by none other than Father Gapon, who had been brought to Geneva by his SR contact, the engineer Pyotr Rutenberg. Since Bloody Sunday, the charismatic but unstable priest had come to consider himself the predestined savior of the Russian people. After a brief flirtation with the Social Democrats, who rejected him as an unprincipled demagogue, he was now bidding for a leadership role with the SRs. One meeting with Gapon was enough for Azef, who immediately branded him shallow and untrustworthy. Others, including

Savinkov, were impressed despite themselves by his personal authority and oratorical power. The SRs admitted Gapon to the party, but denied him a position of leadership, whereupon he left for London to pose for photographs, give interviews, and negotiate the sale of his autobiography.

Shortly afterward, Gapon withdrew from the party, but the issue he had championed—arming the masses—remained at the center of attention. A majority of the Central Committee voted to establish a separate organization, headed by Rutenberg, to acquire weapons abroad and distribute them in Russia. In the spring of 1905, word came from Kony Zilliancus, a Finnish revolutionary leader, that a group of American millionaires had contributed one million francs for this purpose on condition that the weapons be distributed to all major revolutionary organizations without discrimination. In fact, this "contribution" was a gift of the Japanese government, which hoped that its use would further disrupt the Russian war effort in the Far East. Knowing nothing of this, the SR Central Committee accepted a portion of the money, setting aside one hundred thousand francs for the use of the Fighting Organization and turning the rest over to Rutenberg.

The result was a famous fiasco. In the summer, Rutenberg and several SRs went to England, where they purchased a steamer called the *John Crafton*. They loaded it to bursting with weapons and explosives and hired a Swedish crew to sail it to Finland and the Baltic coast, but the ship ran aground on a sandbar in the Gulf of Bothnia. The crew unloaded a small part of the cargo and buried it on several nearby islands. Then, fearing discovery, they blew up the rest of it with the ship. Some idea of the size of this shipment may be gathered from the fact that the cache buried on the islands and later discovered by Finnish frontier guards included 9,670 rifles, 720 revolvers, more than 500,000 rounds of ammunition, and 200 pounds of explosives. During the great strike wave of 1905, some of these weapons found their way into the hands of Finnish revolutionaries, but the Japanese plan to arm the Russian masses foundered with the *John Crafton*.

The real beneficiary of the Mikado's largesse, as it turned out, was the Fighting Organization. Azef used the terrorists' share of the "American gift" to establish a chemical and explosives laboratory in Villefranche, a small town on the French Riviera. There, in a more modern and secluded version of Marc Schweitzer's Paris lab, his brother Vladimir worked with a new group of Organization recruits to make bombs . . . and to train terrorists. The group at Villefranche now included three new members who were to become part of the Organization's core: Leo Zilberberg, a brilliant twenty-five-year-old mathematician; his outspoken wife, Xenia; and a quiet but absolutely determined young woman named Rachel Luriye. From nearby Nice, Mikhail Gotz kept watch over the operation, playing grandfather to this latest branch of the terrorist "family." The existence of the Villefranche laboratory was one piece of information that Azef never shared with his police superiors, not even when they began to demand new proofs of his loyalty to the czarist cause.

Through the first days of March, Azef waited impatiently in Geneva for news of Marc Schweitzer and his small army of terrorists in St. Petersburg. He was wagering heavily on Schweitzer's success, for if the chemist's plans bore fruit, both Grand Duke Vladimir and Governor-General Trepov would join Sergei Romanov in whatever hell was reserved for deceased czarist tyrants. *That* blow would solve a number of problems. At best, it might prove fatal to the autocracy, paving the way for a relatively quick transfer of power to the liberals and moderate SRs. At the very least, it would eliminate the entire leadership of the reactionary party, saving Azef's friends in the bureaucracy and keeping all his options open. The news arriving from the terrorist squad in Kiev was bad but inconsequential. The inexperienced comrades there had abandoned their attempt to kill Governor Kleigels; Jacob Borishansky had scattered his small group and had gone to join the far more important campaign in the capital. Azef approved of this decision. But day followed day, and still there were no headlines announcing either Schweitzer's arrest or Vladimir's assassination.

Azef soon had enough of waiting and more than enough of the endless political debates in Geneva. He dispatched Savinkov to Nice to visit the ailing Mikhail Gotz and to inspect the new laboratory in Villefranche. Then he returned to Paris to see his family and confer with his increasingly gloomy supervisor, Leonid Ratayev. The investigation of Sergei's assassination was continuing, Ratayev reported, but the heart had gone out of it. Police Director Lopukhin had returned from Moscow empty-handed. His resignation was expected momentarily; according to Moscow insiders, Trepov had already asked the czar to appoint Lopukhin's old nemesis, Rachkovsky, to replace him. Furthermore, there was evidence that Rachkovsky had entered into a strange alliance with the liberal-leaning Count Witte to purge the Secret Police of "unreliable elements" and consolidate both men's return to power. Ratayev, whom Rachkovsky would surely consider an "unreliable element," was frantic with worry. Clearly, it was time to produce new evidence of his and Azef's usefulness to the House of Romanov.

As always, Azef was prepared to pay the necessary price. The assassination of Sergei must be followed by a betrayal of the SRs—preferably, from Azev's point of view, a betrayal of the Fighting Organization's opponents in the party. Fortunately, the conference just concluded in Geneva had again provided a suitable target. Following Father Gapon's advice, a number of party members had volunteered to round up weapons in Eastern Europe for transshipment to Russian worker and peasant associations. Azef knew that two of these militants, Mikhail Vedenyapin and Vassily Troyitzky, had gone to Bulgaria, where local revolutionaries were prepared to provide them with a large quantity of ready-made bombs and a method of transporting them into Russia. With Ratayev's blessing, Azef took the overnight train to Bulgaria. He met with the two party men and their local comrades, familiarized himself in detail with their plans, and congratulated them on their work. Then, before leaving the country, he telegraphed Ratayev, giving him all the information needed to mop up the group and cut off the supply of weapons from Bulgaria. A few days later, Vedenyapin was arrested at the Russian border. Guards were stationed at all entry points, but fate simplified the work of the police: on March 19, 1905, an accidental explosion destroyed the Bulgarian laboratory and its arsenal, killing two of the comrades.

Another accidental blast, however, proved a serious blow both to Azef and to the Organization. He learned the whole story on his return to Geneva at the end of March.

In St. Petersburg, Tatiana Leontyeva, the young socialite who had joined the Organization in Paris, had quickly gained access to the society of privileged young people who clustered about the Romanov court. As she had promised, she provided Marc Schweitzer's terrorist squad with accurate information about the movements of various high officials about the capital. In addition, at Schweitzer's request, she agreed to guard a large quantity of dynamite that had been hidden in her apartment on the theory that this was the last place the Secret Police would think to search. In January, following the massacre of Bloody Sunday, Leontyeva presented Schweitzer with an astounding proposal: she offered to kill Nicholas II single-handedly. The czar was to appear at a court ball early in February. Young aristocrats charmingly dressed as peasant girls would sell flowers at the dance, with the proceeds going to charity. Why not take revenge then and there for the massacre of the workers? Leontyeva would simply hide a pistol or bomb in her flower box; no one else need be directly involved. After several days of agonized indecision, Schweitzer gave his consent . . . but the ball was canceled and the scheme came to naught.

This tale surprised Azef. Schweitzer's coolness and self-discipline were legendary. How could he have approved an attack on Nicholas II—the ultimate terrorist act!—that had not been sanctioned by either the Central Committee or the Organization? What made him think that the strict rule *against* killing the czar had been relaxed? Bloody Sunday must have affected the chemist greatly—or perhaps Schweitzer was another version of Boris Savinkov, a man capable of serving brilliantly in a secondary role, but unfit for overall command.

This impression was strengthened by a second instance of confused improvisation. In January, the group of street watchers tracking the unpredictable and elusive General Trepov discovered that they could far more easily calculate the daily movements of the new minister of justice, Nikolai Muraviev. They therefore proposed Muraviev as a candidate for assassination. In this case, Schweitzer felt it necessary to ask permission of two Central Committee members then in St. Petersburg, Auntie Ivanovskaya and Nikolai Tiuchev, but both rejected the suggestion. The justice minister was a figure of secondary importance. Killing him would be a diversion from the main business at hand and might well expose the squad to a government counterattack. Schweitzer abandoned the attempt, so it seemed, but a few days later, he changed his mind and authorized an assault by two bomb throwers on Muraviev's carriage. Fortunately for the minister, one would-be assassin, claiming that he was being shadowed, disappeared the night before the scheduled attack. The other arrived at the appointed time, bomb in hand, but was unable to make his way through heavy traffic to the target. Shortly afterward, Muraviev resigned his position, never realizing how close he had come to surrendering it involuntarily.

Finally, official piety presented Schweitzer's terrorists with an irresistible opportunity to fulfill their original plan. The court gazette announced a memorial mass to be celebrated on March 14 at the Peter and Paul Cathedral. The object of veneration would be the "Czar-Liberator," Alexander II, who had been assassinated thirty-four years earlier by the terrorists of the People's Will. Virtually the entire government leadership was scheduled to attend: General Trepov, Grand Duke Vladimir, Internal Affairs Minister Bulygin, the lot. What could be more fitting than to turn their memorial service into a bloody tribute to the heroic fighters of 1881?

Schweitzer designated four targets: Trepov, Vladimir, Bulygin, and Bulygin's ultra-reactionary assistant, Pyotr Durnov. Attacking them simultaneously would pose technical problems, but the squad leader had the essentials in hand: a sufficient number of attackers (the squad had now grown to some twenty members); enough dynamite; and a simple, workable strategy. On each of the roads leading to the Cathedral Schweitzer would station at least two bomb throwers. The attacks would take place as the officials made their way to the service; no use desecrating the Cathedral or killing innocent bystanders. Some of the attempts might flounder, but the odds favored at least a partial success. With a little luck, March 14 would provide the czarists with several new reasons to hold a memorial mass!

By March 10, Schweitzer's plans were complete. He made all the necessary assignments and said farewell to each comrade individually. All that remained was the final assembly of the bombs. Schweitzer was living at the Hotel Bristol, where he had established his identity as a Scottish chemical engineer. Unwilling to entrust anyone else with the task of fabricating the bombs, he had turned his suite of rooms on the hotel's second floor into a laboratory. He worked at night, handling the dangerous explosives with a delicacy born of long experience . . . but late on the night of March 11, something went wrong. An enormous explosion awakened the city. Room 27—the chemist's suite—was entirely destroyed. Three rooms nearby, an adjacent restaurant, and the shops located below Room 27 were wrecked. Across the street, thirty-six windows on the facade of St. Isaac's Cathedral exploded. The street and St. Isaac's Square were showered with debris. The following morning, among the shards of glass, the boards, tiles, and bits of furniture found in the square, policemen discovered several human fingers. The rest of Schweitzer's body had vanished entirely in the blast.

Years later, a czarist general and key intelligence officer named Aleksandr Spiridovich wrote an epitaph for the young terrorist:

This was a man gifted with a vast spirit, an energetic character, and a will of iron. Considering terrorism the principal method of action of the party, he gave himself entirely to this task, not just in theory but in practice, as an educated chemist.

Azef might have added that, with Schweitzer's death, the Fighting Organization lost its most admired member—a courageous, even-tempered comrade whose animosity toward the czarist system bore no trace of juvenile rebellion, egomania, or self-hatred. Over-conscientiousness was his undoing. Clearly, Schweitzer had taken too many tasks on his own shoulders; his own fatigue, an enemy more insidious than the police, betrayed him. Azef mourned him privately. To the surviving comrades in the capital he sent an urgent message: avenge Schweitzer by killing Trepov. This brutal and efficient officer was now the primary threat to the Organization (and to Azef's career). His reactionary views, far more potent than those of any grand duke or cabinet minister, would shape the government's response to the current social crisis. Let the comrades therefore concentrate all their efforts on assassinating General Trepov.

Even as he dispatched the messenger to St. Petersburg, however, Azef felt his hopes decline. If the redoubtable Schweitzer had not been able to organize a victory, how could lesser figures hope to do so? Boris Savinkov urged him to go to the capital to take charge of the operation himself, offering to play the lieutenant's role. But Azef's well-developed instinct for survival told him to steer clear of St. Petersburg. Although he had given the police no infor-mation—not even a judicious hint—that might lead them to the surviving members of the group, he could well imagine the frenzy of inquiries and new security measures that the explosion itself would trigger. And there was something else, something funda-mentally . . . *unsound* about the situation in the capital. Too much had already gone wrong there. So, Azef temporized. He would go to St. Petersburg eventually, he told Savinkov, but not yet. Not yet.

———

Even in this mood of foreboding, Azef was as unprepared as any of his comrades for the announcement that appeared two weeks later in the reactionary paper, *Novoye Vremya*. Referring to the recent disaster suffered by the Russian army in Manchuria, the newspaper hailed what it termed "the Mukden of the Revolution": the capture of virtually the entire Fighting Organization apparatus in St. Petersburg! Eighteen terrorists, including the veterans Ivanovskaya, Dulebov, Moiseyenko, and Jacob Borishansky, had been arrested and were now in jail. Enough evidence had been seized to make the outcome of any trial a mere formality. Of the entire squad formerly commanded by Schweitzer, the only name not mentioned in dispatches was that of Dora Brilliant. Brilliant must have succeeded in escaping the police net; the others, invaluable comrades all, were lost.

Azef went immediately to Paris to extract additional details from Leonid Ratayev. What he learned alarmed him as much as did the arrests themselves. Sixteen members of the squad had been seized in lightning raids made throughout the city on March 29 and March 30. The Organization's mock coachmen were captured with their cabs and its mock peddlers with their wares; all their false identities were obviously known to the police. On the first day of the raids, police agents had burst into the squad's safe houses and seized caches of weapons, documents, and propaganda. Tatiana Leontyeva's apartment, one of the first houses searched, yielded enough fulminate of mercury for three large bombs, as well as nineteen blank passports, three false passports, and a slip to a safety deposit vault containing parts for six more bombs. On the second day, the police arrested Jacob Borishansky at the Petersburg-Warsaw train station, calling him by his false name, "Podnovsky." In one of his suitcases they discovered a Browning pistol with its serial number filed away. In the other they found a bomb weighing four and one-half pounds. Boris Moiseyenko was taken with his Browning inscribed with the Organization's slogan, "You will be repaid according to your work." Utterly surprised, no one had offered any resistance except a young army officer named Trofimov, who fired at the arresting officer but missed his target.

Azef listened to these recitals with his usual impassivity, but the question that rang in his ears like an aftershock was *How did the police know?* The raids could not have been organized without accurate inside information, that is, without the help of a well-informed agent. But the information, he well knew, had not come from him.

Could the Secret Police have "turned" a member of Schweitzer's squad? According to Ratayev, two relatively untried terrorists recruited by Schweitzer, Markov and Bassov by name, had been arrested late in January and held incognito for two months. The evidence seized with them (including a pistol and a letter from Schweitzer) made it clear that they were members of the Fighting Organization and that they were to participate in some sort of action in the capital. Undoubtedly, they had been subjected to a more-than-thorough questioning at the Peter and Paul Fortress. But after toying with the hypothesis of a traitorous Markov or Bassov, Azef dismissed it. Both men were novices, new members who had no sooner joined the group than they were arrested. They knew nothing about Leontyeva's dynamite cache, nothing about Jacob Borishansky's return to the capital or his nom de guerre, nothing, really, of the key facts relied upon by the Secret Police in carrying out the March raids. If they *had* been spies, Azef understood, Markov and Bassov would not have been arrested in January; they would have been left at large.

No . . . the traitor had to occupy a higher position in the party or the Organization than either of these new recruits. One of Schweitzer's old comrades, then? But this also was most unlikely, since any spy within the inner circle of terrorists would have broken the chemist's cover and revealed the location of his dynamite laboratory before the explosion at the Hotel Bristol. Why wait until two weeks *after* the explosion to close the net on the remaining members of the group? Logic dictated that the source of information was someone at liberty in the capital during the latter part of

March—someone familiar with the identities and activities of the terrorists, but not close enough to the Organization to know Schweitzer's cover name and address. Ratayev's information (and his lack of it) corroborated this theory indirectly. Even now, in mid-April, the Secret Police's picture of the St. Petersburg squad was incomplete and, in some respects, erroneous. The police had not yet learned the identity of the man blown up at the Hotel Bristol. Moreover, they had announced the capture of "Boris Savinkov," evidently confusing Savinkov with Boris Moiseyenko.

It seemed clear, then, that the spy was *not* one of the St. Petersburg group. In Azef's view, the traitor would not be found in the ranks of the terrorists at all but elsewhere in the party. He *knew* the members of the Organization, but the party. . . . More a milieu than an organization, it was a hodgepodge of diverse personalities representing a broad spectrum of views—a collection of noisy politicians, as Azef might have put it, who agreed on little other than the importance of the "land question," the need for some sort of revolution, and the unfitness of others to lead it. In Lenin's colorful phrase, it was a "political swamp"—an environment quite suitable for ambiguous, subterranean creatures like Azef himself. Even leaders like Chernov and Gotz, whose strength of character was beyond question, demonstrated remarkably poor judgment when it came to choosing their comrades. Had they not offered a position to that transparent adventurer, Father Gapon? Azef, at least, had won their confidence by organizing assassinations, but others had been made privy to lethal secrets without passing any test at all.

The key to the puzzle, Azef decided, must be Rachkovsky. Who else but the old wolf would have the motive and the power to plant another infiltrator in the party—someone close enough to the Central Committee to ferret out the names and locations of Schweitzer's terrorists? Given the primitive state of the SRs' internal security system, the idea was sickeningly feasible. Azef grew more certain of it when Nikolai Tiuchev, the Central Committee member serving as liaison between the party center and the group in St. Petersburg, returned to Geneva and added one important detail to the information at his disposal. On March 27, he reported, someone had called him on the telephone—a male voice, quite unfamiliar—and had declared, "Warn everybody! All the rooms are infected!" Before Tiuchev could question the caller further, the line had gone dead. He had immediately alerted Ivanovskaya, who was then acting as group leader, but she was not feeling well and brushed the warning aside.

This story, later confirmed by Ivanovskaya, eliminated Tiuchev as a suspect. It also pointed strongly toward the police as the source of the warning as well as the "infection." As Azef knew, a silent war was now under way between the established officials loyal to Lopukhin, Ratayev, and their friends and the new men appointed or preferred by Trepov and Rachkovsky. He was also aware that, among the thousands who served the Secret Police, there were radical sympathizers who admired the SRs' peculiar combination of "soft" ideology and "hard" action. Yes . . . he would bet his life on it: a dissident police official—a party sympathizer or an enemy of Rachkovsky's or both—was warning Tiuchev that the St. Petersburg operation had been blown. This could only mean that Rachkovsky was striking at his old enemies using the methods he knew best: infiltration and provocation.

Another spy in the party! Somewhere in Russia, perhaps even now making his way toward Geneva, Rachkovsky's mole was busily at work, asking "innocent" questions, making useful suggestions, demonstrating his "good faith" to the comrades. If the reactionaries suspected Lopukhin and Ratayev of double-dealing, Azef—their man on the Central Committee—might also be under suspicion. After all, he had not prevented the assassination of Sergei, nor had he warned against the conspiracy recently discovered in St. Petersburg. On the other hand, these "failures" were consistent with the role he had carefully constructed for the Secret Police. The police believed him to be a source of reliable information about the Central Committee and the Fighting Organization, but he was not considered an active member of the Organization and certainly not its leader. According to Ratayev, Azef's recent exposure of the "Bulgarian connection" had apparently won him some credit with the group around Rachkovsky. Evidently, the new chiefs' suspicions of him were closely balanced by their need for his services.

For the moment, Azef concluded, he was safe. But Pyotr Rachkovsky was as ruthless as he was patient. If he *had* put his own man into the party, Azef's risks would increase geometrically the longer that the spy remained at large. This threat he found strangely energizing, for it clarified the three urgent tasks that now lay before him. Rebuild the Fighting Organization. Establish direct relations with the new Secret Police chiefs. Find Rachkovsky's spy, if he still remained active, and kill him.

Now it was time for his return to Russia.

EIGHT

On the Trail of a Traitor

APRIL 1905. Never before had the spring thaw in Russia brought with it such a heady mixture of expectation and uncertainty. The nation, half-awakened, paused as if after a long hibernation. Change was on the wind, but whether the coming season would bring all-destroying revolution or mild reform, violent reaction or peaceful reconciliation, victory in war or defeat at Japanese hands, no one could confidently say. Inside Russia, the pace of rebellion had slackened. The news was now of successful police raids and prosecutions, not new strikes and demonstrations. Even so, there was a sense widely shared that events beginning with Bloody Sunday had altered the landscape in some fundamental way. For the time being the streets were quiet, but behind closed doors radical groups representing a dozen ideologies laid plans for a stormy summer. Outwardly confident, the government took this plotting seriously, especially since nationalist agitators from Poland to the Caucasus were once again stirring popular hopes for independence. Beyond the Empire's borders, meanwhile, the Russian fleet under Admiral

Rozhestvensky was steaming through the China Sea to relieve the czar's huge conscript army, which still lay bogged down in Manchuria.

It was a time when almost anything might happen—a propitious time for a man like Azef, who prepared to return to his homeland after a year's absence with the excitement of a boy going on vacation. Nothing so whetted his appetite for intrigue as the sense of multiple possibilities. He had been glad enough to leave Russia the previous summer, after von Plehve's assassination had raised Comrade Valentine to the rank of a terrorist legend, and to remain abroad while the czar's uncle Sergei followed the insufferable minister into oblivion. But now he could hardly wait to return. Having abandoned the hunt for Sergei's killers, the Secret Police would be avid for hard information about the plots now taking shape across the country to organize mass rebellion. Very well—Azef would give them more information than they could handle! But the same seething undercurrent of revolt that so obsessed the government would surely net him several first-class terrorist volunteers: just what he needed to rebuild the Fighting Organization.

His first task—not an easy one—was to convince Leonid Ratayev to authorize the proposed trip. His police supervisor did not share Azef's enthusiasm for a tour of Russia's revolutionary centers; the risks of the project, he insisted, far outweighed its advantages. His old enemy and new chief, Rachkovsky, grew more powerful every day. He and General Trepov had already driven Police Director Lopukhin from office, having first filled the air with rumors of his "involvement" with terrorists. Undoubtedly, they had also marked Ratayev for political extinction. What if the reactionaries decided to strike at him through his principal agent? If Azef returned to Russia to spy on the SRs, it would be an easy matter for Rachkovsky to have him arrested in the company of known revolutionaries and to charge both men with playing some sort of double game. The ruthless spymaster would not even hesitate to expose Azef to the party if this favored his intrigue against the "Zubatovists." Everywhere he looked, Ratayev saw danger.

Azef responded to this with calm logic. Obviously, the proposed trip entailed certain risks. Undoubtedly, Rachkovsky was a dangerous enemy. But so long as the government's principal concern was the threat of an armed uprising, the Secret Police could not afford to lose their top agent in the Socialist Revolutionary party. The regime had good reason to fear the growing movements of rebellion among the Finns, Poles, and other oppressed nationalities. Azef would therefore return via Geneva, where a conference of radical nationalist groups convened by the SRs was now beginning, and where the Central Committee was formulating plans for the coming "hot summer." Rachkovsky would find his reports *most* illuminating—a foretaste of the information that his visit to Russia would supply. Naturally, all his reports would be sent via Ratayev, who alone would know his itinerary, and who could feed his new superiors such information as would keep them dependent on both men. This might not secure Ratayev's position, Azef admitted, but the more valuable his reports proved, the more difficult it would be for Rachkovsky to discredit him.

Ratayev had little choice, finally, but to agree. At his suggestion, the General Electrical Company would send "Engineer Azef" on a tour to inspect power plants in Kiev, Odessa, Saratov, Kharkov, Nijni-Novgorod . . . the very cities in which the SRs were laying the groundwork for mass terror. Azef made arrangements for Luba and the children to spend the summer on the coast of France. Then he returned to Geneva to meet with the dissident nationalists and the SR Central Committee.

No surprises there: preparing for a mass uprising was now the party's major activity. All other efforts were subordinated to the tasks of organizing and arming the people for the coming confrontation. New party branches were authorized and new printing facilities pressed into operation. Alliances were contracted with a heterogeneous assortment of nationalist groups. Personnel and funds were committed to strengthen the SRs' Peasant Union and to organize workers along the nation's new railway system. And—most vexing to the terrorist chief—the Central Committee approved the formation of local fighting organizations both in the cities and in rural districts. Of course, Viktor Chernov informed him, the work of *the* Fighting Organization would continue for the time being, but its allocation of funds would fall far short of the large sum recommended by Azef and Savinkov. With the whole Empire about to explode, the Organization obviously could not hope to maintain its near-monopoly of violence. Wasn't the People's Revolution, after all, what every comrade had been working for?

Azef chose not to argue the point. The idea of arming Russia's peasant masses horrified him, as it did many other liberal opponents of the regime. The Organization's activities were surgical operations; they aimed at excising reactionary leaders so that reasonable men could guide Russia into the modern world. An uncontrolled mass upheaval, by contrast, would be a pogrom writ large—a period of vulgar and chaotic bloodletting that was certain to end in a dictatorship either of the Right or the Left. That woolly-minded intellectuals like Chernov could control such a hurricane was no more conceivable than that the "Black People" of the villages could rule Russia by themselves. These convictions, reinforced by Azef's appetite for dangerous adventure and personal influence, would enable him to betray the "People's Revolution" without a moment's bad conscience. His firm intention was to sabotage the organization of mass terror so that the work of individual terror could continue.

Azef reported immediately to Ratayev, conveying detailed information about the party members dispatched to Russia to organize mass terror and to aid the rebellious nationalities. Arrests based on this information were made even before he left Geneva. Rachkovsky would be a fool, indeed, to endanger such an agent while the threat of a general revolt still hung in the air. Then, having secured his right flank, Azef moved to strengthen his left. Before leaving for Russia, he met at length with his chief lieutenant, Boris Savinkov. The buccaneering poet, no more interested than his chief in a large-scale rebellion, was in his customary state of furious outrage at the insult offered to the "honor" of the Fighting Organization by an ungrateful Central Committee. The Organization must be rebuilt

quickly, he argued. Before the party eliminated its funding altogether, it must carry out another notable assassination. Once again,
Savinkov suggested Governor-General Kleigels of Kiev as a target,
and this time Azef consented, although whether he wanted Kleigels
killed or merely wished to give Savinkov some temporary occupation
is not at all clear.

In any event, he did not give Boris much to work with. Savinkov's assassination squad was to consist of Leo and Xenia Zilberberg, Rachel Luriye, and a young Jewish couple that Savinkov
had recruited himself some months earlier: Aaron Shpaizman and
Mania Shkolnik. But Leo Zilberberg, clearly the outstanding personality among the new members, was not to take a direct part in
the operation, since Azef wanted him saved for future campaigns,
and his wife and Rachel Luriye were to be used only to hide and
assemble the weapons. Savinkov accepted these conditions. The job
was simple; he could handle it easily with the new recruits. In mid-
May, Azef wished his lieutenant Godspeed and sent him off by a
circuitous route to Russia. A few weeks later he would begin his
own many-purposed homecoming.

Savinkov arrived in Kiev at the end of May 1905, picking up
the members of his squad and the makings of several bombs en
route. Predictably, however, the campaign against Kleigels soon
turned to farce. Week after week, relying chiefly on Shpaizman and
Shkolnik, the squad hunted the governor-general—but although
Savinkov and Zilberberg frequently caught sight of their quarry
while walking in the city, their two street watchers were unable to
account for his movements, and, indeed, often seemed at a loss to
account for their own. Shpaizman disappeared for days at a time.
Shkolnik was not at her post because she was "ill." He missed
appointed meetings, then announced that Kleigels was too small a
fish to assassinate. She requested permission to throw the bomb
herself without any help from her partner. Late in June, Mania
revealed that Aaron did not want her to have anything to do with
the assassination and that he was threatening to prevent her from
participating, if necessary, by force.

Love, it seemed, was proving more potent than duty. Thoroughly frustrated, Savinkov went to Kharkov to confer with Azef, who advised him that the attempt was useless. "Nothing will come of this," declared his chief. "We must put an end to the whole business." Still, Azef had not *ordered* him to terminate the operation. By now, killing Kleigels had become something of an obsession with Savinkov, who wanted to demonstrate his own capacity for independent leadership. In July, therefore, after establishing a likely time and place for an attack on the governor's carriage, he made one last effort to inspire his two "soldiers" to finish the job. Savinkov might have saved himself the trouble. Twice he arranged a rendezvous with bombs for Kleigels, and twice Aaron Shpaizman refused to appear for the appointment. Leo Zilberberg begged to be allowed to throw the bomb himself, but Savinkov's orders were clear; he was bound to refuse the request. Recognizing at last that the campaign was hopeless, he disbanded the group and went to join Azef at their prearranged meeting place in Nijni-Novgorod.

Whatever Azef may have thought of Savinkov's generalship he kept to himself. He expelled both Shpaizman and Shkolnik from the Fighting Organization, whereupon (as happened quite often) the two lovers resolved to redeem their honor with one heroic deed. In January 1906, acting on their own, they threw bombs at Governor Chvostov, ruler of the city of Chernigov. Shpaizman's weapon failed to explode, but Shkolnik's wounded the governor fairly seriously. The sentences imposed by a court-martial reflected a "gallantry" toward women that was not fated to last much longer. While Mania's act of violence earned her twenty years at hard labor in a Siberian prison camp, the ineffectual Aaron was immediately hanged.

Azef's business, meanwhile, had proven far more profitable than Savinkov's, thanks in large part to the crew of the battleship *Potemkin*. In June, not long after his return to Russia, the men of that warship mutinied in the Odessa harbor on the Black Sea, setting off a series of naval mutinies that were savagely suppressed. Subsequent street battles in Odessa pitting striking workers against the police and the pro-government, anti-Semitic gangs called the Black

Hundreds took some two thousand lives. The revolt in Odessa did not immediately trigger a mass uprising in the industrial centers, but it did provoke a great outburst of provincial strikes and peasant violence that drove the regime to new excesses of repression. The army mobilized its elite troops. Thousands of workers and peasants were shot or sabred, and the revolutionary movement began to arm in earnest.

Azef found the chaotic situation perfectly suited to the achievement of his two chief purposes: the betrayal of revolutionaries and the recruitment of terrorists. His tour of major cities produced a rich trove of information for transmission, via Ratayev, to Rachkovsky. In such-and-such a location, weapons were being stored by the SRs for later distribution to striking workers. In another, an illegal printing press was being used to whip up opposition against the local military authorities. A Peasant Union (naming its leaders) had been formed by the party in Kursk. A new railway workers union was being organized in Rostov-on-Don. The Armenian *Dashnak* movement was preparing to ship pistols into the Ukraine along the following route. . . .

What Azef did not report, of course, was the success of his own recruitment drive. By the time he arrived in Nijni-Novgorod for his scheduled conference with Savinkov and other members of the Organization, he had discovered six new recruits capable of meeting his exacting standards. Three of these—Pyotr Ivanov, Aleksandr Kalashnikov, and Boris Vnorovsky—were intellectuals. Two, Ivan Dvoinikov and Fedor Nazarov, were workers. And Anna Yakimova, the sixth new member, was a name well known both to revolutionaries and to the police. A former member of the People's Will, Yakimova had been condemned to death for participating in the plot against Alexander II. Her sentence was commuted to twenty years in prison, which she served, and life in exile, from which she had escaped to join the Fighting Organization. An outstanding recruit, indeed—but although the group in Nijni-Novgorod awaited her arrival for several days, she failed to appear. Azef smelled trouble. He ordered the comrades to make preparations for a possible attack on Baron Unterberg, the governor of the province (good practice, in any event, for the novice members), and went immediately to Moscow to meet Yakimova.

The meeting took place in Filipov's restaurant and pastry shop, one of Azef's favorite haunts. The experienced Yakimova had delayed her trip to Nijni out of a sense that she was being watched. One glance around the restaurant told Azef that her fears were well-founded: several out-of-place strangers had their table under clumsy observation. Quickly, he questioned her. Who knew that she was in Moscow? Nobody, she answered, except several members of the SR Central Committee. Which members? She did not know; she had met a number of them for the first time in Minsk, and names were not used. What had she told them? Only that she had been recruited to the Organization by Comrade Valentine, and that she was scheduled to meet with Valentine and Pavel Ivanovitch (Savinkov) in Nijni-Novgorod.

Abruptly, Azef informed her that the meeting in Nijni was canceled. She should disappear for a while and meet him three weeks later in the town of Vladimir, not far from Moscow. As he left Filipov's, he was not surprised to discover another group of men in ill-fitting suits following him at a pace, and on the train back to Nijni he was certain that he was still being watched. But of course! By meeting with Yakimova, Azef had made himself more "interesting" than ever to the Secret Police and—unless he acted quickly—entirely vulnerable to Pyotr Rachkovsky. Clearly, he would have to turn the old terrorist over to the police. But what troubled Azef as the train rolled northward was neither the invisible presence of police surveillants nor the fate of Anna Yakimova. It was a single question: How, exactly, had the Secret Police gotten on her trail?

In view of the general disruption in the country and Yakimova's changed appearance, it was unlikely that the police had tracked her from Siberia or stumbled upon her by accident in Moscow. No: the key must be her meeting in Minsk with unnamed Central Committee members. One of these, Azef concluded, was very likely

Rachkovsky's mole. The police agent responsible for the devastating arrests of March was probably a member of the SR Central Committee! Inwardly (and not for the first time) he cursed the party leaders whose pre-revolutionary excitement had led them to expand the Central Committee to include any number of relatively unknown and untested militants. At this point, Azef had no way of knowing who the mole might be—but, by god, he would locate him before he stumbled on Comrade Valentine's true identity! As soon as possible he would find Rachkovsky's spy and feed him to the Organization.

Arriving in Nijni-Novgorod, however, Azef kept these convictions to himself. Later, the comrades would take care of this high-ranking traitor; for now, the watchword was defense. His first words to the members assembled to discuss the campaign against Baron Unterberg were, "We are being shadowed." Without reporting his conversation with Yakimova, he informed the group that he believed he had been spied on both in Moscow and on the train. Savinkov, who had mapped out a plan to assassinate Unterberg, was inclined to minimize these suspicions. Everyone had these feelings from time to time; wasn't paranoia an occupational hazard of their trade? But two days later, both Azef and Leo Zilberberg reported being followed in the street, and Savinkov himself thought that he recognized a policeman from St. Petersburg at the Nijni-Novgorod fairground. Now Azef scattered the group without objection, dispatching several members, including Zilberberg and Savinkov, to St. Petersburg to renew the hunt for General Trepov. Then he sent two reports directly to Secret Police headquarters. In the first, he "revealed" that, while in Nijni-Novgorod, he had discovered a plot by the Organization to assassinate Governor Unterberg. In the second, he disclosed the time and place of his scheduled meeting in the town of Vladimir with Anna Yakimova.

Azef played his game with cool finesse. By discussing the plot against Unterberg, although in terms too vague to permit a clear identification of any of the plotters, he nullified whatever suspicions might have been aroused by his presence in Nijni during a period when, as the mole had no doubt reported, a meeting of leading terrorists was to be held. More important, he had performed a classic chess move: sacrificing a theoretically weighty but compromised piece while positioning others for an unexpected attack. While safeguarding his own comrades, including the new recruits, he had given the Secret Police the notorious Anna Yakimova. On the day appointed for her meeting with Azef, the police arrested Yakimova in Vladimir and quickly returned her to a Siberian prison camp. Azef had every reason to believe that he had once again turned potential disaster into victory—but an unpleasant surprise awaited him on his return to Moscow. A terse message from Ratayev ordered him to report immediately to St. Petersburg for discussions with the new Secret Police chiefs.

The message, Azef understood, meant trouble. Very likely, he would be questioned at length about the recent increase in terrorist attacks against politicians and police officials—attacks he was powerless to prevent. Traveling from city to city, he had established contact with a new generation of SR militants and radical nationalists, including leaders of the local fighting groups established (over his objection) by the SR Central Committee. These he had no compunction about betraying, but localized violence was now spreading far too rapidly to permit effective intelligence work or police intervention. In May, acting independently of the party center, the SR fighting group in Ufa had assassinated the governor of that province. In June, although the Moscow Secret Police arrested a number of SRs and confiscated a sizable cache of guns and ammunition, Pyotr Kulikovsky managed to escape from police custody and kill the mayor of Moscow. Then, during July, the local fighting groups had turned their attention to the police. They organized ten assassination attempts in provincial cities across Russia, killing three police chiefs, wounding four, and missing one target by chance when a well-aimed bomb failed to explode. Only two plots were exposed in time to prevent the terrorists from acting.

Rachkovsky and his cohorts would undoubtedly be frantic; the SRs had declared war on the security forces, and they were winning! Altogether, in the six months *before* serious mass violence began in the fall of 1905, their fighting groups assassinated sixteen chiefs of police or of gendarmes, seriously injuring eight more. They also killed four Secret Police agents posing as revolutionaries. Government agents were successful in exposing only a few of the thirty-odd conspiracies mounted between April and September, and terrorist acts in the rural areas were also multiplying ominously— a foretaste of the mass terror that Azef had warned would be the next stage in the SRs' campaign to destabilize the government.

On August 21, Azef arrived in St. Petersburg and went immediately to the apartment used for clandestine police interviews. There he received one of the great shocks of his career. He was not particularly surprised when a pale and shaken Leonid Ratayev informed him that he, Ratayev, had been dismissed from office. Azef knew that the internal affairs department had ordered a major shake-up of the Secret Police and that General Trepov had been given full authority to supervise the reorganization. He was prepared to see Ratayev fall, prepared even to be sacked along with him. But he was not ready to be introduced on the spot to his new control: Pyotr Rachkovsky himself. By secret order, Trepov had placed his old ally in charge of the Secret Police. Henceforth, Azef would be reporting directly to the top intelligence officer in Russia!

When Ratayev had left the apartment, Rachkovsky set immediately to business. Azef was not to be sacked; he was to be rewarded . . . and threatened. His new chief smoothly congratulated him on his fine work and informed him that, effective immediately, his salary would be raised to 600 rubles (in current terms, about $5,400) per month—the highest rate paid any secret agent—plus a more generous expense allowance. However, he insisted with unmistakable menace, it would be necessary for Azef to be of even greater assistance to the police than he had been in the past. Here, for example, were photos of a number of notorious terrorists. Did Azef perhaps recognize this one? (The photo was that of Savinkov.)

Or this? (Ekaterina Breshkovskaya's lined visage appeared before him.) Or these? Could he, perhaps, match these faces with names or aliases and current addresses?

Azef understood that the rules of the game had changed. For the first time, he was under the supervision of a man as experienced, disillusioned, and clever as himself—a police control, indeed! He was certain that Rachkovsky had no idea that he was the notorious Comrade Valentine, but Rachkovsky obviously knew that he had had personal contact with a number of the well-known terrorists whose photos now littered the table. How much had his mole on the Central Committee (for Azef was now certain that such a figure existed) told him? Rachkovsky's avidity for information about the Organization suggested that he was not getting much help on this subject from his new agent. Clearly, he needed Azef—but it was equally plain that he would not be blinded by trust in him or put off by evasions. Rachkovsky was therefore offering him, in effect, a new contract: if Azef would agree to inform on the Organization, he would be enriched. If he did not, he would follow Ratayev into retirement, or worse.

A new line had been drawn on Azef's moral and political map. Unhesitatingly, he crossed it. He identified Savinkov, Breshkovskaya, and several "civilian" party members by name and gave Rachkovsky their temporary addresses, as well as revealing the locations of the SR bomb factories in Moscow and Saratov. The next day, he collected several months' salary and expenses in advance and left in the evening for Saratov, accompanied by the chief of the department's investigation section, to assist in the capture of Breshkovskaya. Another squad of detectives left at the same time to arrest Savinkov at the address Azef had given them: a friend's estate in the country near St. Petersburg.

Interestingly, these betrayals produced few results. Not one important terrorist or party member was captured. A few minor arrests, the seizure of the two dynamite laboratories . . . these were the only victories that the police could claim in the wake of Azef's revelations. In part, the department's own bungling was responsible for this failure. Boris Savinkov escaped arrest when his host's gardener came running back to the house to report that detectives were roaming about the neighborhood and asking for him by name. He managed to return to St. Petersburg and escaped again to Finland after the police arrested a friend with whom he was staying on the assumption that the friend (who looked nothing at all like him) was Savinkov. In part, however, the paucity of results obtained in these raids may also be credited to Azef. The house in Saratov to which he led the police had long since been abandoned by Breshkovskaya. Moreover, the terrorists whom he did *not* identify, or about whom he provided useless information, included virtually the entire present membership of the Fighting Organization.

Clearly, despite Rachkovsky's pressure, Azef had again misled the police. Rachkovsky's rewards and threats had inspired him to make another chess "sacrifice": the surrender of Savinkov would secure the continued existence of the rest of the Organization. The rules of the game had altered, to be sure, but Comrade Valentine still had no intention of resigning.

In September 1905, Azef moved his temporary headquarters to St. Petersburg, where an Organization squad was continuing to pursue the elusive General Trepov. On September 8, intending to coordinate this campaign with the local SR party committee, he called at the home of a committee member named Rostkovsky and received another shattering surprise. Rostkovsky was extremely upset. That very morning, he reported, he had opened his door to a veiled woman who had handed him a sealed envelope, turned, and left without uttering a word. His own hand shaking, he offered the envelope, now opened, to Comrade Valentine. The letter inside was long, and Azef read it silently, his face emotionless. The Socialist Revolutionary party, it began, had been infiltrated by two spies. One was "a certain T——, a former exile"; the other, "the engineer, Azief, a Jew recently arrived from abroad." Both men, it continued, were "secret collaborators" of the police. The letter went on to provide precise summaries of certain information given to the police by these agents. It ended without a signature.

As always when threatened with extreme danger, Azef went ice cold. He raised impenetrable gray eyes to Rostkovsky's and said in a normal tone of voice, "T——, that can only be Tatarov. And the engineer Azief, that must be myself. My name is Azef." He left immediately with the astonished committee member staring after him.

That same evening, Azef met briefly with Pyotr Rachkovsky and gave full vent to his rage. How in god's name could this have happened? Was the department incapable of keeping a secret? Who could have leaked this information to the SRs? Rachkovsky apologized profusely. He had no idea who had written the letter, he replied, but Azef's brilliant response to it had undoubtedly saved the day. Telling the committee member, who knew only his party pseudonym, that he was "the engineer Azief" was masterful; such self-confidence could only increase the party's confidence in him. But the furious agent was not to be mollified by compliments. This must never happen again—*never!* (Rachkovsky muttered his agreement.) The leak from within the department must be investigated immediately. And whoever "T——" was, he must *not* be told of the letter. If the SRs needed to discover a police agent in their midst, by god, Azef would make certain that they found one.

In fact, the old spymaster was telling the truth; he did not know who had leaked this damaging information to the SRs. The source, it turned out later, was an experienced Secret Police officer named Leonid Menchikov. In a sense, Menchikov was the mirror image of Azef: a highly competent, well-trusted policeman working secretly for the revolutionaries. In 1887, after being arrested for revolutionary student activities, he allowed himself to be "turned" by the government and joined the Moscow Secret Police. It is uncertain whether his original intention was to turn police secrets over to the revolutionaries or whether he formulated this plan later, but for almost twenty years he had worked diligently at his job, rising slowly through the ranks while compiling a detailed private dossier on the use of spies and *provocateurs* by his masters. The dossier might have remained private had it not been for Rachkovsky, but Menchikov was a member of the "Zubatovist" group whose careers were being terminated by the new Secret Police chief. Seeing the handwriting on the wall, he compiled the "Azief" letter, gave it to his veiled courier, and, after a decent interval, resigned from the police.

Azef, who knew nothing of this, nevertheless had every reason to be alarmed. He had no fear that the Central Committee would believe the mysterious accuser—not when the subject of the accusation was Comrade Valentine, the assassin of von Plehve and of Grand Duke Sergei, founding member of the Socialist Revolutionary party and the soul of its Fighting Organization! Nor did he believe that Rachkovsky himself was the source of the letter. Why should the Secret Police chief expose both his agents in the party to the vengeance of the Organization? But the letter *must* be the work of someone in the department, and, without knowing Menchikov, Azef knew that there were any number of police officers like him: intriguers who, either out of sympathy for the Left or hatred for their employers, might well play a double game not unlike his own. Clearly, someone else in the government's employ, someone other than "T——," was watching his every move. Azef understood that the balance of risks had now tilted against him. As he left Rachkovsky's apartment, he resolved to put some distance between himself and the department. At least for the time being, he would consider himself a retired police agent.

A second resolution followed hard on the heels of the first: Rachkovsky's mole must die. For the accusatory letter had at least produced one satisfactory result. Azef now knew the identity of the other spy on the Central Committee. "T——" could only be the most recent addition to the SR leadership, Nikolai Tatarov, a nervous, inquisitive fellow whose activities on behalf of the party had already raised eyebrows on the Central Committee. The son of the arch-priest of the Warsaw Cathedral, Tatarov had been arrested in 1901 after some ten years of activity as a revolutionary agitator in Poland and Russia. He had been imprisoned for several

months in the Peter and Paul Fortress, and was finally exiled to
Irkutsk in Eastern Siberia for a period of five years. There he joined
the SRs and established a secret printing press for the party. In
January 1905, however, his sentence was cut short and he was allowed to return to St. Petersburg. The official reason given was the
illness of his father, the arch-priest, who had come to the capital for
treatment. Tatarov had immediately contacted the SR leadership in
St. Petersburg and had remained there through March, when the
devastating arrests of March 29–30 aroused Azef's suspicions of
another spy in the party. He then left for Odessa, where he was
first named a traveling agent and then a full member of the Central
Committee.

While in exile in Irkutsk, Tatarov had been seen several times
leaving the house of Count Kutaisov, the governor-general of Eastern Siberia, whose son was an old school chum of his. The freed
exile was now living rather luxuriantly in Paris, where he was
attempting to raise money for a new publication, a journal that
would be published openly in Russia in an effort to improve com-
munication between the party leadership in Geneva and the literate
Russian public. The idea was to skirt the czarist censors by publishing
anonymous, noninflammatory articles that would still convey the
gist of the SRs' thinking to an urban audience hungry for new ideas.
After some hesitation, the Central Committee had approved the
scheme, provided that Tatarov, who had little publishing experience,
accepted editorial direction from the party and reported all financial
contributions made to the journal directly to the Central Committee.

Oddly, or so it seemed to Mikhail Gotz, Tatarov had immediately placed advertisements for the new publication in the leading
Russian newspapers—notices prominently featuring the names of
well-known SRs like Gotz and Viktor Chernov. It seemed almost
as if he were trying to draw the censors' attention to the new journal
in order to kill it. Or did he, for unknown reasons, feel himself
to be invulnerable to official censorship? Even before receiving a
copy of the anonymous letter naming "T——" and "Azief" as
police spies, Gotz had become sufficiently concerned about Tatarov's

behavior to initiate inquiries about his fund-raising activities in Paris. According to party sources, the arch-priest's son had already spent a small fortune on the journal . . . *without* reporting any contributions to the Central Committee. Gotz had summoned Tatarov to Geneva and had asked him directly where the money was coming from. "From Charnolusky," he had replied, naming a wealthy backer of liberal causes well-known in St. Petersburg. According to Tatarov, Charnolusky had given him fifteen thousand rubles to start the new publication.

Gotz wondered about that but had put the matter out of his mind until the mysterious accusatory letter revived his suspicions. Now, in mid-September, he summoned Savinkov, Tiuchev, Chernov, and other party leaders to a meeting in Geneva to make a preliminary inquiry into the case. There was no question, they agreed, of investigating the accusation against Azef, which was doubtless intended to sow discord among the revolutionaries. But Tatarov . . . The Committee quickly agreed to dispatch Alexei Argunov to St. Petersburg to interview Charnolusky about his alleged contribution to the new journal.

Azef, meanwhile, also came to Geneva to discuss the letter with Gotz and to be on hand in case he were asked to testify before a committee of inquiry. His three-month tour of Russia had exhausted him, in any event, and he wanted to be reunited with his wife and children—preferably in the mountains, where he liked to recuperate after arduous journeys. He had been subject recently to annoying back pains and was feeling unusually tired. Gotz, far more seriously ill than his visitor, greeted the terrorist chief from his sickbed. He congratulated him on the success of his efforts to recruit new fighters and reassured him that no one on the Central Committee took the letter's references to "Azief" as anything other than a crude, slanderous provocation. He advised Azef to spend a few weeks in the Alps with his family—advice the latter gladly accepted.

Shortly after Azef left for the mountains, Nikolai Tatarov arrived in Geneva. He was immediately placed under surveillance by a three-man team headed by Savinkov. Argunov then returned from

St. Petersburg and informed a small but rapt audience of the results of his interview with the philanthropic Charnolusky. Charnolusky *had* seen Tatarov and had offered to assist him in editing the publication, but he had neither promised nor given him money. "Did he tell you that I gave him money? I wonder why!"

So did the Central Committee, which also wondered why Tatarov had given them a false address in Geneva—a hotel at which he never registered or stayed. At Gotz's initiative, the party leaders quickly appointed an official committee of inquiry to investigate the case further. Its members were Savinkov, Chernov, Tiuchev, and the old revolutionary (formerly a member of the People's Will group), Alexei Bach. A few days later, Tatarov, who had no inkling that he was under suspicion, announced that he was returning to Russia and invited the comrades in Geneva to a lavish farewell dinner in his honor. At the conclusion of the dinner, Chernov and Savinkov informed their perplexed host that his trip to Russia would have to be postponed. He was to meet the following morning with representatives of the Central Committee to answer some questions about his activities in Paris.

The meeting took place at the home of Josep Minor, a member of the Central Committee. Chernov began the questioning in a calm, almost easygoing manner. What about these contributions to the journal? Again, Tatarov claimed that Charnolusky had financed the publication, adding that an Odessa publisher named Citron had promised him additional financial support. After a few minutes of this, Chernov abruptly changed the subject—and his tone of voice.

"You say you are staying at the Hotel des Voyageurs. Under what name?"

"Plevinsky."

"What is your room number?"

"I believe it is twenty-eight."

"We have made inquiries. There is no Plevinsky either in Room twenty-eight, or, as a matter of fact, at the Hotel des Voyageurs."

"I made a mistake. I live at the Hotel d'Angleterre."

"Under the name of Plevinsky?"

"I have not registered yet."

"And the number of the room?"

"I don't remember."

"We have inquired at the Hotel d'Angleterre. You don't live there either."

Relentlessly pressed by Chernov, Tatarov finally blurted out a "confession." He had lied about his address, he said, because he was living with a woman whose name and address must be concealed "to protect her honor." Immediately, his inquisitor moved to another subject.

"Will you tell us what protection from censorship you have obtained for your publication?"

"I have been promised protection by a powerful official."

"Who is he?"

"A certain prince."

"We ask you to name him."

"Why? I said a prince. That's enough."

Again Tatarov was compelled to yield to the implacable Chernov. The protector in question, he admitted, was Count Kutaisov, the czar's chief representative in Eastern Siberia, whose house he had visited both in Irkutsk and in St. Petersburg. This was enough for Chernov, who now turned to direct accusation. "I must tell you," he intoned, "that you lied to us not only in concealing your address. Charnolusky never gave you and never promised you a single kopek. Citron's name you learned only three days ago . . . and you could not possibly have had any relations with him." Again, Tatarov admitted the lie. The money, he insisted, had come from his father, the arch-priest, who had borrowed it to aid his son. He had concealed this information because his father was a well-known opponent of the Revolution. Silence greeted this improbable allegation. By now utterly flustered, the defendant decided to pose a question of his own.

"But of what are you accusing me?"

"You know that yourself," replied Chernov.

"No."

Tiuchev broke in. "Of treason!"

The questioning of Tatarov continued, with interruptions, for several days. It established, among other things, that the arch-priest's son had possessed sufficient information about the Organization's work in St. Petersburg to have betrayed the comrades arrested in March, as well as several captured in June—assuming, that is, that he had been working for the police. But the Central Committee, ever-scrupulous in refusing to act on mere assumptions, declined to find him guilty of treason to the party. Without further evidence of Tatarov's involvement with the Secret Police, a death sentence was out of the question; all that could be done was to declare him unreliable and to suspend him from party work. Azef learned of this decision when he returned from the mountains. "Ridiculous!" he fumed. The credibility of the party was at stake. Clearly, the traitor should have been executed. "Are there ever any more definite proofs in affairs like this?" he asked rhetorically.

Azef's reputation for sagacity was soon given a further boost. After his hearing, Tatarov went back to Russia, where he wrote letter after letter to the Central Committee seeking to exculpate himself. He was unlucky enough to be there still in October, when an unprecedented wave of strikes virtually paralyzed the country, prompting the czar's more liberal advisors to recommend that the government grant several long-overdue reforms. The result was Nicholas II's Manifesto of October 17, offering the opposition a limited form of parliamentary consultation (the Duma), and releasing hundreds of political prisoners from jail. Among those released were the SRs arrested on March 29–30, several of whom told stories that made it clear they could only have been betrayed by Tatarov. Indeed, in at least one case, the foolish fellow had been spotted identifying a prisoner to the police at the Peter and Paul Fortress!

Tatarov's days were probably numbered in any event, but he now hastened his own downfall by accusing Azef of being "the real spy" in the party. Questioned by a close friend about his role in the March arrests, Tatarov responded by revealing for the first time that his sister was married to a police lieutenant. This informant, he claimed, had access to the files of the Secret Police—files that proved that Yevno Azef was a longtime secret agent who had betrayed all of the comrades captured by the police in March. This charge by a man obviously intent on saving his own skin infuriated the members of the Organization, Savinkov in particular. Lies, slanderous lies, insulting not only to Azef but to the entire Fighting Organization! How could an ordinary police lieutenant have gained access to Secret Police files? Why had Tatarov never informed the party that his brother-in-law was a police officer? How *dare* this confessed liar accuse the party's most effective terrorist of treason? Savinkov demanded that the Central Committee authorize Tatarov's execution. He offered to organize the assassination squad himself and lead it into battle. With little discussion, the Committee consented and appropriated funds for the operation.

For several months other events intervened, and little could be done to put the Central Committee's mandate into effect. Meanwhile, Savinkov mobilized an Organization squad consisting of four men and one woman, swore them to secrecy, and assured himself that they would execute the death sentence faithfully even though they had had no previous knowledge of the case. Finally, in February 1906, he called them to Helsinki, Finland, to prepare for the attack. The veteran Boris Moiseyenko, a member of the squad, was dispatched to Russia to find the condemned man, who had disappeared without informing the Central Committee of his whereabouts. Moiseyenko returned quickly with the news that Tatarov had gone to Warsaw and was now living there in seclusion with his parents. Initially, Savinkov had determined to leave Azef out of the planning in order (as he said) to spare him "all the worries involved in the killing of this *agent provocateur,*" but Azef willingly joined in the meetings called to discuss the technical aspects of the assassination. He suggested a scheme designed to spare Tatarov's parents the agony of seeing their son killed, as well as to avoid possible identification of the assassin by witnesses. The team should rent an apartment in Warsaw, lure Tatarov to a "meeting" there, and shoot him on the spot.

At the end of the month the entire squad, with the exception of Savinkov, descended on Warsaw. Savinkov followed in early March after the comrades had secured their apartment and obtained the weapons they needed. He went immediately to the Tatarovs' dwelling and spoke at length with Nikolai, who was obviously terrified. Savinkov assured the trembling man that the party had not yet reached a decision in his case and invited him to attend a meeting that evening to explain himself further to the committee of inquiry. Tatarov agreed to attend, but he arrived early at the apartment building, talked at length with the janitor on the first floor, and left the premises immediately. Clearly, he had discovered that the residents of the rented apartment were not a committee of inquiry. So much for Azef's plan! After discussing the matter with his squad, Savinkov concluded that Tatarov must be killed at his parents' house, preferably by a lone comrade unknown to him.

Fedor Nazarov, a metalworker by trade, one of the new Organization members recruited the previous summer by Azef, volunteered for the mission, and the rest of the squad left Warsaw. Nazarov waited for several weeks to allow Tatarov's terror to abate; then, carrying a pistol in one pocket of his worker's jacket and a sharp knife in the other, he rang at the Tatarovs' apartment. Nikolai's parents came out, eyed him suspiciously, and refused him entry, but as they stood on the landing arguing, Tatarov himself—a tall man—appeared massively in the doorway.

"I whipped out my revolver," Nazarov later recalled. "The old man struck my arm. I began shooting wildly. Tatarov threw himself upon me. So did the others. The mother hung on to my left arm and the father to the right. Tatarov himself held me fast to the wall and tried to twist the revolver from my hand. I held on to the gun, however, and Tatarov could not take it away from me. He tried desperately enough. 'Well,' I said to myself, 'I guess I'm caught.'

"I managed to push away the old woman and release my left arm. She fell down. With my left hand I reached my knife and plunged it into Tatarov's side. He let go of me, took two steps forward and collapsed. The old man continued to hold on to my right arm, however. I shot into the ceiling. 'Let go, I say, or I'll kill you.' The old man quit. I then walked over to Tatarov and placed a note in his pocket: F.O.S.R.P."

F.O.S.R.P.—the Fighting Organization of the Socialist Revolutionary party. The next day's newspapers carried a dispatch from Warsaw stating that the arch-priest Yuri Tatarov's son had been killed by an unidentified man who escaped after wounding the victim's mother with a knife. In fact, Tatarov's mother had been shot, very likely by two bullets that ricocheted when Nazarov fired at the ceiling. She recovered quickly, but despite the description of the assassin furnished by the parents and the note in Tatarov's pocket, the Warsaw Secret Police remained baffled. Why would the SRs' Fighting Organization have assassinated a member of the SR Central Committee? Months later, Mikhail Bakai, the official in charge of the investigation (and a man destined to play a significant role later in Azef's career), discovered that Tatarov had been a police agent reporting directly by telegraph to Pyotr Rachkovsky. This fact remained secret until, three years later, Prime Minister Stolypin confirmed it in a speech to the Duma. The police archives opened after the Revolution of 1917 disclosed that the priest's son had been paid a total of 16,100 rubles ($145,000) for his brief work as an agent. Azef's police salary did not amount to half that much in one year. But unlike the amateurish Tatarov, Azef was still alive.

NINE

The Days of Reckoning

IN OCTOBER 1905, Azef returned from his alpine vacation to
Geneva, where a passionate debate had erupted about the future of
the party's terrorist activities. Events at home were now attracting
worldwide attention; at last, the mass uprising so long dreamed of
had become reality. What had begun several weeks earlier as a
railway strike had grown, quite spontaneously, into a general strike.
In virtually every Russian city, workers left their factories and went
into the streets, students abandoned their classes, and shopkeepers
shut their doors. Public demonstrations, increasing in size and in
number, were violently dispersed, but violence could neither move
goods to market nor persuade Russian workers to return to their
jobs. The nation was paralyzed—so much so that powerful voices
in the government demanded that concessions be made before extremist groups could take control of the situation. The result was
the czar's Manifesto of October 17, granting the people a constitution
that promised a measure of self-government, including a consultative

parliament or Duma, and formal guarantees of freedom of speech, the right of assembly, and due process of law.

The question that agitated the SR leaders was whether, under these circumstances, to authorize continued terrorism by the Fighting Organization and local combat groups, or to throw all of the party's resources into political organizing. The debate began in Geneva and concluded at a meeting of the full Central Committee in Moscow. Led by Boris Savinkov, a majority of the Fighting Organization bitterly opposed the motion to suspend the armed struggle. Now, argued Savinkov, when the government's weakness was apparent to all—now was the time to strike decisive military blows. But the dominant view was that of the socialists, represented by leaders like Viktor Chernov and Mikhail Gotz. For them, the major issue was how best to organize the masses to take power. So long as the people were "asleep," heroic acts of violence were needed to awaken them and avenge their injuries; but if they were awakening, terrorism by a small group would only alienate them and make it more difficult for the party to lead them in the political battles to come. Their conclusion: Organization attacks should cease while the party came into the open to bid for leadership of the mass movement.

The same conclusion was drawn for somewhat different reasons by party leaders of more liberal bent, including Azef himself. In their view, terrorism was inadmissible in any system capable of protecting individual rights. During the debates in Geneva, Azef stated emphatically (as he had done several times before) that on the day a liberal constitution was adopted, he would cease being a terrorist. The point of terrorism, after all, was to bring down the autocracy and empower the people. If the people were freed to speak and organize openly, why should revolutionary groups interfere in this process at all?

These declarations by the party's leading terrorist surprised a number of comrades and dismayed Savinkov, but Azef repeated them again at the formal meeting of the Central Committee in Moscow. During one particularly stormy session, Chernov proposed a compromise aimed at satisfying both the party majority and the unreconciled fighters led by Savinkov: while terrorism should be suspended, the Fighting Organization could be kept "under arms" in case the struggle for a meaningful constitution failed. Azef immediately rose and declared that it was impossible to keep an inactive terrorist organization "under arms." "That is a mere phrase," he remarked scornfully. Then he added in an authoritative voice, ending the debate, "I will take full responsibility on myself. The Fighting Organization is dissolved."

Azef's public position accurately reflected his private views. If a government respecting individual rights were established in Russia, the terrorist chief would gladly fulfill his vow to become a nonviolent "legalist" and "evolutionist." He had no hesitation in telling the comrades that he considered himself merely an associate of the SRs—one who would leave the party if it refused to accept a liberal constitution. Now that the old system seemed to be tottering, there was a possibility that his political goals might be realized without killing any more government ministers. But Azef had other reasons for abandoning terrorist work, at least temporarily. The letter from Menchikov naming "Azief" and "T——" as informers had made him acutely aware of his vulnerability—so much so that, after his stormy meeting with Rachkovsky, he had broken off communications with the Secret Police chief and had told his old supervisor, Leonid Ratayev, that his work as a secret agent was at an end. True, the SRs had not even bothered to investigate the accusation against him. But if Azef launched a new terrorist campaign without renewing his relations with the Secret Police, Rachkovsky would realize that he had turned and would see to it that he was exposed to the SRs—or simply eliminated as an enemy of the state. On the other hand, if he reestablished relations with the police and began betraying the comrades once again, what other Menchikovs might not appear to denounce him to the SRs?

Clearly, the situation was too complex and uncertain to permit a rational calculation of risks. Better, Azef decided, to wait and serve the party quietly during this stormy autumn while the god of history decided whether or not the autocracy would survive. Late in October, he returned to St. Petersburg, where the Committee had established its headquarters. There he came to the conclusion that the revolution was unlikely to succeed. "We are far from victory yet," he told Savinkov. "There will still be a reaction." Nevertheless, Azef was caught up in the struggle to compel the czar to make good on his promises of October 17. Only one terrorist project continued to interest him . . . for obvious reasons. If at all possible, he told several of the comrades, he intended to organize the destruction of Secret Police headquarters by incendiary bombs.

As a result of the decisions made in Moscow, the SRs were now operating more or less openly in Russia. During November, the party hurled itself into mass organizing activity, which had taken a giant leap forward as a result of the formation of the St. Petersburg Council *(Soviet)* of Workers' Deputies. Led by the charismatic Social Democrat Leon Trotsky, the Council was an unorthodox but essentially democratic organization representing all major anti-czarist tendencies, but strongly influenced by the more militant workers. Despite their differences with the Social Democrats, the SRs participated actively in its work, taking advantage of the opportunity to expand their influence, already strong in the countryside, to the urban milieu. Their efforts were rewarded; in a matter of weeks, workers around the country were looking to the Council for leadership. At the same time, this experience further radicalized the SRs. The czar's October Manifesto had ended the October general strike and split the opposition: liberal groups called for social peace pending elections to the Duma, while socialists advocated more militant tactics. For once, Azef found himself siding with the Left. Making peace with the reactionaries would not conciliate them or open the door to constitutional government; it would simply permit them to nullify the promises of the Manifesto.

A second "political strike" was to be launched at the beginning of December in the hope that it would grow into an all-out insurrection. The SR Central Committee, having committed itself to help organize this strike, put Azef and Boris Savinkov in charge of the party's military committee. Their mission: to win soldiers and sailors over to the revolutionary cause and to make plans (with the engineer Pyotr Rutenberg) to support an armed uprising in the capital. Savinkov was delighted. He and his chief would make the czarist bastards pay for their crimes! Azef was less sanguine. He doubted that the armed forces would come over in large numbers to the revolutionary side, and, if they did not, there was little hope that a mass uprising would succeed. Nevertheless, he accepted his orders and went to work with Savinkov and Rutenberg. The three terrorists concocted a variety of schemes aimed at supporting an armed uprising, including plans to sabotage St. Petersburg's water, electrical, and telephone systems, to kidnap Prime Minister Witte, and—an idea dear to Azef's heart—to blow up the headquarters of the Secret Police.

All these plans misfired. The authorities moved decisively to smash the strike, which, to begin with, lacked the fervor and massive participation of the October shutdowns. At the urging of Aleksandr Gerasimov, the new director of the St. Petersburg Secret Police, the St. Petersburg Soviet was suppressed and its leaders arrested, cutting off the movement's "head." As Azef had anticipated, few soldiers or sailors proved willing to risk being shot as deserters or traitors. Moreover, the actions planned by his military committee were stymied again and again by the police. Gerasimov's men seized two dynamite factories established by Savinkov, capturing several comrades, including Dora Brilliant, who was to die two years later in the Peter and Paul Fortress after suffering a mental breakdown. The committee's plan to have members of the railway union blow up a strategic bridge connecting St. Petersburg with Moscow collapsed when the bridge was found to be surrounded by police guards. Similarly, Azef's other initiatives failed, "partly," Savinkov later wrote, "because some of the points designated for destruction were found strongly guarded, as if the police had been warned beforehand."

What, if anything, had Azef done to help frustrate the military committee's plans? Although the evidence on this point is ambiguous, it appears that he gave the police little assistance. On the one hand, he did attempt to renew contact with Rachkovsky by writing the Secret Police chief several letters. Although the content of these letters is unknown, and Rachkovsky never replied to any of them, it is possible that some contained information that could have proved useful to the government. On the other hand, Colonel Gerasimov, the new director of the St. Petersburg Secret Police responsible for all arrests made in the capital, later denied vehemently that he had received any information either from Rachkovsky or Azef that might have assisted him in crushing the uprising. There is no reason to doubt Gerasimov's word. Rachkovsky, considering the new man a rival, had declined to assist him, and Gerasimov had established his own network of agents in St. Petersburg, including several informers in the SR camp. Whatever tidbits Azef fed Rachkovsky were most likely a form of insurance against the failure of the revolution, which would force him to revive his dual career as a terrorist and spy. Azef's letters may also have been intended to insure him against a more immediate threat: that of physical "elimination" by the government.

The incident that probably convinced Azef to renew his relations with Rachkovsky took place in St. Petersburg during the first week of December. As he was walking to his apartment late one night, he suddenly found himself pressed between two burly men. He opened his mouth to speak, but found himself grunting as the men bumped him hard from either side. Knives flashed. "Dirty kike!" one man spat. "Red scum!" Azef fought back furiously, and the two thugs fled. Panting for breath, he inspected himself for wounds. His thick fur coat was slashed front and back, but there was no blood. The knives had not penetrated to his skin.

Azef returned to his apartment in a state of shock. Obviously, his assailants were members of the extremist right-wing organization, the Black Hundreds. On the one hand, he considered, the encounter might have been relatively "innocent." Given the Black

Hundreds' rabid anti-Semitism and Azef's Jewish looks, as well as his open association with the SRs, the gang members could easily have targeted him for assault on their own initiative, as they had so many other Jews and revolutionaries. But it was common knowledge that the leadership of the right-wing group was controlled by the Secret Police. Was Rachkovsky sending his former agent a "message"? Since there had been no other pedestrians on the darkened street and Azef had been unarmed, the attackers need not have fled so precipitously. Perhaps their assault had not been intended to kill, but only to warn. How like the Secret Police to engage in such a "frightening"! Azef dispatched several letters to Rachkovsky. Then he put Savinkov in charge of the remaining operations in St. Petersburg and left the city for Moscow, where rumors of an impending uprising were rife.

Two days later, the workers' rebellion that had not occurred in St. Petersburg took place in the shadow of the Kremlin. In Moscow, a general strike led quickly to barricades, armed attacks on the police and army, government reprisals, and the shooting of prisoners by the revolutionaries. It is unclear what part Azef played in these events—apparently, he advised the local SR leaders on military matters—but he appears to have supported the uprising wholeheartedly. The party as a whole played a significant role, particularly in the working-class Presnya district, the heart of the insurrection. Here workers armed by the Moscow Soviet fought pitched battles with the police and soldiers, and here the Revolution of 1905 met its defeat. Although thousands fought bravely, their movement was not well-coordinated, and the army did not join it. After two weeks of fierce struggle, the troops commanded by General Fedor Dubasov, the military commandant of Moscow, were joined by General Min's elite Semenovsky Guards and the Ladozhsky Regiment from Warsaw. After subjecting the quarter to a twenty-hour incendiary bombardment that virtually leveled it, these forces exacted a terrible revenge, killing some 1,100 men, women, and children.

The Moscow Uprising was drowned in blood. Similar uprisings in Kharkov, the Don Basin, the Caucasus, the Baltics, and Siberia were ruthlessly suppressed by troops loyal to the monarchy. Mass arrests and executions followed; the revolutionary parties were again driven underground. By January 1906, the reaction Azef had predicted had become reality, and his party was ready to renew its terrorist campaign.

In January 1906, sixty-four voting delegates and a score of observers met at the Hotel Touristen in the town of Imatra, Finland, to formulate the Socialist Revolutionary party's program for the next period of struggle. Despite the shattering reversals of December, the general mood of the conference was optimistic; at last, the Russian masses—in particular, the urban workers—had demonstrated their capacity for revolutionary action. Their defeat was tragic but unsurprising, since the insurgency had been limited for the most part to the cities, where less than twenty percent of the population lived, and had not won the army to its banners. As Trotsky later put it, "In December 1905, the Russian proletariat foundered . . . on the bayonets of the peasant army." Still, even isolated from the peasantry, without a plan, lacking coordinated leadership, and without efficient weapons, the workers had rocked the autocracy to its foundations. And the aftershocks of their actions were still making themselves felt.

Even as the delegates at Imatra debated, the country was further destabilized by the violent repression unleashed by a vengeful government on its own people. Each day brought reports of new czarist outrages and new outbursts of popular rage. In cities already seething with resentment against the army and police, pogroms organized by the Black Hundreds took thousands of Jewish lives, generating resistance among workers who could no longer be persuaded to blame all their troubles on the Jews. At the same time, whatever moral authority the czar had enjoyed in the countryside was dissipated by the "Punitive Expeditions" mounted by his army throughout rural Russia. Mutinies were reported in some districts, and sporadic acts of terrorism continued to frighten the landowning gentry. Many of the delegates were convinced that the urban uprisings were only a prelude to the massive peasant rebellion that would soon follow, very likely in the coming spring.

These expectations were shared, at least to some extent, by the government, which the czar had reluctantly entrusted to the reform-minded Count Witte. Aware of the potential for further trouble in the country, Witte alternated the stick of repression (wielded by the arch-reactionary internal affairs minister, Ivan Durnovo) with the carrot of a promised constitution. The czar's October 17 Manifesto, he declared, would be honored. Elections to a Duma, although based on an extremely restricted suffrage, would be held during the spring.

How should the SRs respond to this two-track policy? Should they continue to eschew terrorism? Or was it now time to emerge as a peaceful, legal party to contest the first national elections in Russian history? The debate revealed deep divisions in the party. One group of delegates advocated campaigning nonviolently on a "minimum program" of liberal-democratic reforms in order to increase the party's influence among the masses; later, the SRs could move to implement their "maximum" (that is, agrarian socialist) program. A majority of their comrades vehemently disagreed. Given the government's duplicity and bloodthirstiness, they declared, it would be suicidal to come out into the open. The party's main task was to prepare to lead the expected rural rebellion; uncompromising violent struggle, including a renewal of mass terror, must therefore be its main policy. A third tendency, represented by Boris Savinkov, found little comfort in either of these positions. In Savinkov's view, the Revolution *was* dead, at least for the time being. Under these circumstances, the party should return to its previous *modus operandi*: nonviolent political agitation by the "civilians" and carefully orchestrated terrorism by the Fighting Organization.

As usual in debates of this sort, Azef spoke very little. Underlying these strategic differences were a number of ideological questions that did not interest him and that the party, in any event, seemed incapable of resolving. In what sense was the Socialist Revolutionary party "socialist"? Should industry as well as the land be popularly owned? How could the need for central planning and authority be reconciled with the party's commitment to decentralization? Was liberal democracy a first step on the road to socialism or an obstacle to its achievement? The delegates papered over their disagreements by adopting a series of compromise formulas proposed by Viktor Chernov. They agreed, for example, to boycott the elections to the Duma and to return to a policy of "centralized terrorism," with the Fighting Organization playing the leading role, but to terminate the terrorist campaign as soon as a new mass uprising erupted or more democratic elections were held. Compromises of this sort gave the impression of unity, but even in the short run they could not hold the party together. Not long after the Imatra Congress, the moderates seceded to form their own aboveground organization, the Popular Socialist party. One year later, with the SRs campaigning for seats in the Second Duma and terrorism again at a standstill, the "Maximalists" would organize their own party to continue the violent struggle.

The results of the congress displeased even Azef. True, the Fighting Organization was back in business—but for how long? The terrorist chief understood that the party strategists had tied the Organization like the tail of a kite to the vagaries of government policy. They had abandoned terrorism, with his blessing, in October. Now it was to be renewed. After this, however, Count Witte and his friends would decide the issue. If they relaxed their repression and broadened the suffrage somewhat, the party would veer toward "minimalism" and would renounce terror; but if they withdrew these concessions, Azef would be expected to revive the Organization for a second time, or a third, or . . . Had he not argued in October that this was exactly what could *not* be done—that organized terrorism could not be turned on and off like some spigot? On the other hand, his own principles dictated that violence be directed only against autocracy, not against a representative government. At the close of the congress Azef was elected to the new Central Committee, but even as plans were laid for a new series of assassinations, he found himself dispirited and fatigued.

Two primary targets were designated by the party leadership: the minister of internal affairs, Ivan Durnovo, and Fedor Dubasov, the governor-general of Moscow who had ordered the destruction of "Red Presnya." If possible, said Chernov, the Organization should also consider assassinating General Min and Colonel Riman, perpetrators of the Moscow massacre, and Admiral Chuchnin, who had recently crushed a naval mutiny with great brutality. All these attacks, the Committee instructed, should take place *before* the convocation of the Duma in order to embarrass the government without attacking the new parliament itself.

Azef gratefully put the war of words behind him and gathered his forces in Finland, which since October had enjoyed freedom from Russian occupation. To the old members of the Organization, many of whom had recently been released from prison, he added some twenty new recruits, including Mikhail Gotz's brilliant younger brother, Abram; Fedor Nazarov, who was soon to kill Tatarov in Warsaw; Maria Benevskaya, a religious revolutionary of noble background; and Mikhail Sokolov, known as "the Bear," a leader of the Moscow uprising who believed only in terrorism. Azef appointed Savinkov and Boris Moiseyenko his chief lieutenants, established a bomb-making facility in the town of Terioki, and began the planning of the new terrorist campaign.

The method decided on was the old one: intensive street surveillance of intended targets by cabdrivers and peddlers; papers, passports, and safe houses to be arranged by an Organization representative; bombs to be manufactured and delivered at the appropriate time by the "chemical group." Azef put himself in charge of the plot to kill Durnovo in St. Petersburg and instructed Savinkov to supervise the effort to eliminate General Dubasov in Moscow. In late January, however, during one of the planning meetings, he startled his lieutenants by announcing his intention to resign as chief of the Organization.

"I am weary," he said without warning. "I fear I cannot work anymore. Think of it: I have been in this work ever since the days of Gershuni. I am entitled to rest." Savinkov and Moiseyenko were aghast, but Azef continued, "I am convinced, nothing will come of all this new work of ours. Again cabdrivers, cigarette peddlers, observations. It's all a lot of nonsense. I have decided to quit. 'Opanas' [Moiseyenko] and you will get along very well without me."

Both men protested. Azef resign? Impossible! If he carried out his threat to quit, they would refuse to accept responsibility for the Organization. Even if they were to accept, the other members would never follow them as they would their natural leader. "Very well," Azef finally declared, "have it your way. But in my opinion, nothing will come of our work."

This was an honest opinion, not a prophecy that Azef intended to fulfill by betraying the Organization. Although he continued to write Rachkovsky about matters of little importance, he told his police supervisor (now promoted to assistant minister of internal affairs) nothing about the plots against Durnovo and Dubasov. He knew, however, that the informer Tatarov had revealed the Organization's methods to the police, who would no doubt be keeping a close watch on cabdrivers and street hawkers in St. Petersburg and Moscow. Even so, at this juncture, Azef lacked the energy and spirit to concoct new methods. For one thing, his back was bothering him and he felt tired a good deal of the time. For another, he did not believe that the great peasant uprising predicted by the party would materialize. As in the old days, the terrorists would be acting essentially alone, and in St. Petersburg they would be up against a dangerous enemy whom he knew only by reputation: the formidable Aleksandr Gerasimov.

What difference did it make, in any case, if Durnovo and Dubasov were killed? There were more than enough czarist brutes to replace them. With little enthusiasm, Azef went about the business of positioning two independent teams of "watchers" in the capital, while Savinkov began the operation against General Dubasov in Moscow.

In February, Azef's energies were fired by a campaign of a different sort. The engineer Pyotr Rutenberg, a party member who had been a close associate of the revolutionary priest, Father Gapon, arrived at Azef's headquarters in Helsinki with a remarkable, infuriating story. Gapon, the hero of Bloody Sunday, a veritable icon to the Russian people, had turned traitor! For some time, rumors embarrassing to the party (for Gapon still proclaimed himself a Socialist Revolutionary) had been circulating about the priest's behavior. He had become a habitué of disreputable Paris nightclubs. He had been spotted gambling in Monte Carlo, surrounded by high-priced prostitutes. He was constantly drunk, and, it was said, would do anything for money. Now it appeared that these reports had been valid. A few days earlier, Rutenberg reported, Gapon had visited him in Moscow, where the engineer, who was wanted by the police, was in hiding. At first, Gapon talked wildly of new revolutionary schemes. He was in the process of establishing a new workers' organization that would arouse the entire country. Mutinies in the armed forces were being prepared. His followers were ready to assassinate the entire Cabinet, and he expected the Fighting Organization to help organize this new wave of terror. . . .

None of this made sense to Rutenberg. Gapon's manner was strange, his speech forced and artificial, and as he rambled on, he boasted that he had met several times with the Secret Police chief, Pyotr Rachkovsky. According to Gapon, Rachkovsky had become his "dupe"—a source of inside information that he would soon use to overthrow the government. Immediately, Rutenberg suspected that the priest had become a police agent. Acting on instinct, he declared that he was no longer interested in terrorism; he had become disenchanted with the revolutionary movement, he said, and needed money. Much relieved, Gapon then revealed the truth—at least, most of it.

He *had* met with Rachkovsky, who had wooed him with grandiose promises. The government of Count Witte wanted to begin a process of gradual democratization, but it could find nobody capable of leading the workers in a peaceful, constructive direction. Only Gapon had the reputation and the ability to become the true Leader of the People. If he would simply help the government to put an end to terrorism, promised Rachkovsky, no office would be out of his reach. Rachkovsky himself would soon retire, and Gapon might well be named his successor—head of the Secret Police, a perfect position for one who wished to lead both the regime and the masses into a new age of freedom! Intoxicated by these prospects, as well as by the offer of an unspecified but "huge" amount of money, Gapon had agreed to draw Rutenberg and, through him, the Fighting Organization into the police net. According to Gapon, Rachkovsky had then arranged for him to meet the new St. Petersburg Secret Police chief, Gerasimov. After that interview, said the priest, Minister Durnovo himself had approved the plan and authorized Rachkovsky to negotiate an agreement with him. He and Rutenberg stood to make a fortune—"tens of thousands of rubles"—by working with the police.

Rutenberg pretended to fall in with this scheme. In fact, he went immediately to Helsinki and told Azef the whole story. Azef's immediate reaction, Rutenberg later related, was that "Gapon should be killed like a snake. I was to arrange an interview with him, take him out to dinner, and after dinner, while driving back through a wood in a sledge belonging to the Fighting Organization, stab him and throw his body out." But as Azef himself quickly recognized, the matter was too complex for such a simple solution. Gapon's leadership of the Bloody Sunday march had given him the aura of a hero-saint; his portrait could be found everywhere in Russia from peasant hovels to bourgeois drawing rooms. His murder for political reasons would obviously discredit whichever group was associated with it—unless it could be done in such a way as to expose the priest as a police agent.

Here was a problem that Azef found interesting! The solution, he suggested to his colleagues, was to dispose of Gapon and his police control at the same time and place. If Rutenberg were to assassinate Gapon and Rachkovsky together, say, at a private meeting, no one would doubt that the revolutionary priest had crawled into bed with the most reactionary elements in the government. At a meeting with Rutenberg, Savinkov, and Viktor Chernov, Azef spelled out the details of his plan.

The main difficulty was to establish Rutenberg's credentials as a terrorist leader, so that Rachkovsky (whose files would not identify Rutenberg as an active member of the Fighting Organization) could be persuaded to attend a meeting to negotiate the terms of his betrayal. Now, the obvious target for a terrorist action in St. Petersburg—the real object of the operation supervised by Azef— was Minister Durnovo. With a certain glee, Azef suggested that Rutenberg tell Gapon that he, Rutenberg, was the leader of an Organization plot to assassinate Durnovo! The engineer could then substantiate this claim by *simulating* a conspiracy against the minister. Using a cabdriver to be supplied by the Organization (but not, of course, one of the drivers involved in the actual conspiracy), he would pretend to be observing Durnovo's movements. Rachkovsky's spies would report that Rutenberg was, indeed, the important terrorist he claimed to be, and this information, passed back to Rachkovsky, would set the stage for the double assassination. After a week or so of chasing Durnovo around the capital, Rutenberg was to inform Gapon that he was prepared to betray the conspiracy for an appropriate price. He would then lure the priest and Rachkovsky to a meeting to discuss terms and kill them both with a single bomb.

Savinkov declared that the scheme was far too complex to succeed, but Chernov and the Central Committee approved it. Rutenberg, although unused to this sort of deception, agreed unhesitatingly to carry it out. "I am not a youngster," he declared. "Whatever I undertake, I do." On March 10, he returned to St. Petersburg, where he met the cabdriver assigned to assist him and immediately began the sham "hunt" for Durnovo. At the same time, he informed Gapon that he was, indeed, directing the operation against Durnovo, and was willing to sell the conspiracy out for a great deal of money. Gapon, whose greed knew no bounds, reported these meetings to Rachkovsky and demanded that the government pay him one

hundred thousand rubles (close to one million dollars)—an unheard-
of sum—to secure his and Rutenberg's continued cooperation. Rachkovsky was convinced that the plot against Durnovo was genuine,
but he refused to pay this much. The matter was referred to Minister
Durnovo, who made a counteroffer of twenty-five thousand rubles,
and eventually Count Witte himself approved the bargain.

The one dissenting voice on the government side was Aleksandr
Gerasimov's. Gerasimov, who was an acute judge of character, did
not believe that Rutenberg would betray the Organization and considered Gapon an irresponsible fool. He advised against continuing
the negotiations, but to no avail, since both Rachkovsky and Durnovo
had taken the bait. Nevertheless, when Gerasimov learned that the
Secret Police chief had agreed to meet alone with Rutenberg on
March 17 in a private room of the Café de Paris (a preliminary
meeting requested by Rutenberg to convince Rachkovsky of his
"good faith"), he telephoned and advised him strongly not to attend.
Rutenberg was still a revolutionary, he insisted, and the meeting
might well be a trap. Rachkovsky wavered, then decided at the last
minute to stay home. The engineer waited in vain for him to appear,
not knowing that Gerasimov had stationed several armed agents in
the room adjoining the meeting place. After this, Rachkovsky refused all invitations to meet with him and Gapon, and in late March
Rutenberg abandoned the effort and returned to Finland to confer
with Azef.

Poor Rutenberg! Unknown to him, Azef had already begun a
brilliant, if cynical, improvisation and bore at least part of the responsibility for sabotaging the double assassination plan. The terrorist chief had no doubt that Father Gapon must die. Not only
was the wretched priest preparing to betray the Organization, but
he was much too close to Rachkovsky for Azef's comfort. According
to Rutenberg, Gapon had informed Rachkovsky some time earlier
that Azef was not just a Central Committee liaison with the Fighting
Organization, but a leading member of it—a revelation that would
explain Rachkovsky's failure to respond to his letters. The old spymaster's death would certainly be no tragedy, but to kill him now

along with Gapon would gain Azef little, whereas to save him might well give him the hold on Rachkovsky he had long been seeking.

The problem could thus be reframed: how to kill Gapon *without* killing Rachkovsky, but in such a way as to expose the priest as a tool of the police? By mid-March he had the answers. First, warn Rachkovsky that his life was in danger from Rutenberg. Second, convince Rutenberg to violate the orders of the Central Committee by killing Gapon alone. Third, ensure that, before meeting his end, Gapon confessed his crimes against the people in the presence of credible witnesses.

It is not certain that Azef warned Rachkovsky about Rutenberg's intentions before the meeting scheduled for March 17, which Gerasimov's own urgent warning derailed, but it is quite clear that his letters exposing the plot against his control began to arrive soon afterward, and that Rachkovsky took them seriously. So much for the double assassination plan! To Rutenberg, who was waiting in Helsinki for further instructions, Azef now gave the following orders: he was to invite the priest to a meeting at a villa near Ozerki, Finland, just across the border near St. Petersburg. Members of the party, workers who had marched with Gapon on Bloody Sunday and revered him, would be hidden in an adjoining room. Rutenberg and Gapon would discuss the terms and details of their plot against the Organization; the workers would hear everything, and Gapon would be executed on the spot. Azef took full responsibility for altering the mandate of the Central Committee. He offered to explain the situation to the SRs and gain their approval, to help select the witnesses (and executioners) to be used in the conspiracy, and to consult with Rutenberg up to the last moment about the details of the plan.

Rutenberg accepted the proposal and invited Gapon to come to Finland to work out the final details of their arrangement. On April 10, a party worker disguised as a cabdriver met both men at the Ozerki Station and drove them to the villa. Gapon's annoyance at having been compelled to attend another meeting made the engineer's task easier. No sooner had they arrived at the meeting place than the priest lashed out at him. "What are you dillydallying about? Twenty-five thousand is good money!"

Rutenberg replied that betraying his comrades gave him a bad conscience. He reminded Gapon that the terrorists would surely be executed if they were turned over to the Secret Police.

"Well, what of it?" replied Gapon. "It's a pity, of course, but we can't help that. You can't cut a tree down without splinters flying."

The conversation continued in the same vein until Rutenberg rose silently and opened the door separating the meeting room from the adjoining room. The workers, who had heard everything through the thin walls, hurled themselves screaming on Gapon. The priest fell on his knees, sobbing for mercy. "Brothers, forgive me! Forgive me for the sake of the past," he pleaded.

"Rachkovsky is your brother, not us!" came the answer. "You sold our blood to the police! . . ."

The enraged witnesses put a noose around Gapon's neck. Rutenberg could not bear the sight and left the room, crying, "He was once my friend . . . my god! . . . how terrible!" The workers threw the rope over an iron hook near the ceiling and executed him czarist-style, by slow hanging. Although Azef informed the police several days later that the priest had been murdered in the vicinity of Ozerki, it took the authorities thirty days to find the deserted villa with its grisly inmate.

Rutenberg's fate, although less horrible, was scarcely less tragic. The Central Committee, which Azef had *not* informed of the change in plans, was furious that Rachkovsky had been spared and its mandate violated. Witnesses or no, Gapon was still enormously popular; several years would pass before the SRs dared accept public responsibility for killing him. For the present, they disavowed the act. Rutenberg defended himself against a charge of disobedience by asserting that Azef had given him permission to kill Gapon even if Rachkovsky could not be eliminated. To Rutenberg's bewilderment, Azef vehemently denied the allegation; the engineer, he said, had acted on his own. As usual, an accusation against Azef was

taken as proving the bad faith of the accuser. Some comrades suggested that Rutenberg had had personal reasons for killing Gapon.
Others hinted that he had set the priest up for execution after the
two traitors fell out over division of their "blood money." Rutenberg,
who was not cut out for this sort of scurrilous infighting, resigned
from the party and dropped out of politics altogether.

Years later, the Socialist Revolutionary party journal published
a vindication of his actions, but the damage had been done. "I see
him [Gapon] as if in a dream," Rutenberg told Savinkov shortly
after the murder. "His swinging figure still haunts me. Think of
it, it was I who saved him on January twenty-second [Bloody
Sunday]. And now he is dangling from a hook."

Five days after Gapon met his death, Azef had his first encounter
with Aleksandr Gerasimov. The circumstances were unusual, to say
the least, and came close to ending the terrorist-spy's career.

Near the end of March, after Rutenberg had given up his bogus
conspiracy against Internal Affairs Minister Durnovo, the police
discovered evidence of the real conspiracy. Following the arrests of
the SRs one year earlier, the owners of livery stables housing horses
and cabs in St. Petersburg had been ordered to notify the police if
any driver behaved unusually or seemed to be something other than
the honest cabman he claimed to be. Few such reports were made,
and those that were filed generally proved useless. But one report
attracted the attention of Police Detective Titushkin, a capable officer
who had heard that the Organization might make an attempt on
Durnovo's life. Evidently, a certain young driver had stationed his
vehicle near the minister's house, refusing to move even when customers requested his services. The agents assigned by Titushkin to
watch him soon confirmed the detective's suspicions. The suspect
met frequently with two other cabmen and with a fourth man,
heavyset, well-dressed, not a worker, who was seen talking to all
three men and who seemed to be their superior. Titushkin observed
this figure himself and reported to Gerasimov that, while the identity

of the three drivers was unknown, the fourth man was certainly "our Filipovsky."

Puzzled and intrigued by this reference, Gerasimov called Titushkin to his office. Who, pray tell, was "our Filipovsky"? Titushkin explained that he had given the heavyset man this name because he was often to be found dining in Filipov's pastry shop. Several years ago, he related, during a roundup of suspicious characters in that restaurant, the chief inspector had pointed him out, whispering that he was a high-ranking secret agent who should on no account be arrested. Since that time, Titushkin had seen him frequently, often in disreputable company.

"Our Filipovsky"? A top secret agent *and* a member of a terrorist organization? Gerasimov's curiosity now mingled with suspicion and anger, since this gave every indication of being another detestable case of "private" spying. The young officer was a fierce opponent of the old Secret Police system, which officially forbade informants to join terrorist groups and revolutionary policy-making bodies but allowed officials such as Rachkovsky quietly to run their own personal agents as they pleased. He considered the system both inefficient and corrupt, as well as contributing to the vicious warfare between competing bureaucrats in the department. Far better, he thought, to permit talented agents to penetrate these groups at the highest levels—and then hold them personally responsible for the actions of "their" organizations.

"Our Filipovsky," indeed! If the director of the St. Petersburg Secret Police did not know this fellow, who *did* know him? Who, to be more precise, was running him? Rachkovsky, perhaps? Gerasimov immediately telephoned the assistant minister and put the question to him directly, but Rachkovsky denied all knowledge of such an agent. Gerasimov persisted: Was he absolutely sure? Could the fat man be known by some other name? Might he be an operative recently returned from abroad? Yes, Rachkovsky answered with some annoyance, he was sure. "Filipovsky" could not possibly be an agent of the department. As everyone knew, the Secret Police did *not* place agents in or near the Fighting Organization.

Immediately, the younger man smelled an opportunity. He had the means to uncover the truth of the matter himself and perhaps catch his superior in a damaging lie. On the evening of April 15, as Filipovsky/Azef was walking home after meeting with one of the cab drivers, two detectives seized him. Ignoring his anguished protests, they took him in a closed cab to Secret Police headquarters, where Gerasimov himself was waiting to interrogate him. Producing his official papers, Azef insisted that he was "the engineer, Anton Cherkas," but Gerasimov only laughed. He knew, he said, that the man known as Filipovsky was a longtime police agent who had somehow become involved in terrorist activity. It would be best, he advised without rancor, to make a clean breast of the matter. When Azef declined to answer, he continued, almost gently, "If you don't want to speak, you needn't. We are in no hurry. You will have time to think it over here. When you have made up your mind, tell the guard."

The detectives escorted Azef to a cell in the basement of the building. When the door clicked shut, panic seized him, and he sat on the prison cot for the better part of an hour with his head in his hands. But the fear soon passed; in the midst of this improbable storm he found his mind clearing. There was nothing like a real crisis to focus one's thinking. He looked about the cell with an odd feeling of detachment. He loathed being locked in, of course, but it was not nearly the nightmare he had sometimes imagined. As Gerasimov had said, there was time here to consider all the possibilities. On a table near the bed lay writing paper and a pen. Did they expect him to write a confession? Nonsense! He would do what he always did when the situation seemed impossible: he would discover how to turn it to his own advantage.

Clearly, he had been spotted talking to the new recruit, Pavlov. Perhaps Gerasimov's men had also seen him conversing with the other cabdrivers, Tregubov and Abram Gotz. But even if the whole observation squad had been arrested, his "soldiers" would maintain their silence. And if they did talk, what of it? Rachkovsky knew perfectly well that Azef had infiltrated the Fighting Organization.

In addition—thanks to the late Father Gapon—he was probably aware that his agent was playing a more active role in its affairs than that originally agreed upon. The old bastard might be angry about this, but since he owed his very life to Azef's close familiarity with the Organization's current operations, how angry could he be?

Furthermore, if anyone had a right to be angry, it was not Rachkovsky but he, Azef, an agent faithfully reporting to his supervisor month after month without one word of reply or paycheck to compensate him for the risks he was taking. What did Rachkovsky expect him to do during this period of silent rejection, break off all relations with the Organization? How dare he refuse to communicate with his agent and then permit him to be jailed? What did he intend to gain by subjecting Azef to this pressure?

At a certain point—he was not sure what time it was—the prisoner slept. He awoke refreshed and with a clear conviction that had escaped him in the panic and confusion that accompanied his arrest. Of course! It was not Rachkovsky who was responsible for his imprisonment but this new man, Gerasimov. And Gerasimov, it was known, was Rachkovsky's most dangerous rival. Suddenly, Azef saw a pathway opening before him. Clearly, he was being used as a counter in the complex rivalry between the brilliant young police official and his superior—a situation that offered any number of opportunities to a player like himself. If Rachkovsky had not ordered him arrested—if, as seemed likely, the idea were entirely Gerasimov's—Gerasimov was undoubtedly preparing to use him to embarrass and wound the old Secret Police chief. In fact, he would not have dared to arrest Rachkovsky's top agent unless his star were already in the ascendant and the old man's in decline. The object of this game, then, was to assist Gerasimov to weaken Rachkovsky and then to enter Gerasimov's service. But how to win the new chief's confidence? Clearly, he would have to demonstrate his usefulness by exposing certain activities of the Organization, but not, of course, all of them. . . .

Azef spent the rest of the day thinking. Then he slept well and took the next morning to complete his planning. Around noon he asked to speak with Gerasimov. "I am willing to be frank," he told the attentive official, "but I should like my former chief, Pyotr Ivanovich Rachkovsky, to be present."

Gerasimov immediately telephoned Rachkovsky. "We have caught 'Filipovsky,' the man we asked you about, Pyotr Ivanovich," Gerasimov said smoothly. "And just imagine—he says that he knows you very well and that he served under you! I have him here now, and he wants you to be present when he speaks." For a moment, Rachkovsky was speechless. Then, in an obvious attempt to minimize the damage, he replied, "How can it be 'Filipovsky'? It may be Azef." ("That was the first time," Gerasimov later recounted, "that I had heard that name.")

One hour later, Rachkovsky appeared in Gerasimov's private office. "Ah, my dear Azef," he said with a smile, "we haven't seen each other for a long time." In response, Azef unleashed the full power of his invective on the vulnerable assistant minister. ("I have rarely in my life heard such choice abuse," Gerasimov remembered later with obvious relish.) Attacking without letup, he accused his former supervisor of refusing to reply to his letters, cutting off his salary, ignoring his requests for interviews, and abandoning him to the "mercies of fate"—all this, even though his letters about the Rutenberg plot had undoubtedly saved Rachkovsky's life. Rachkovsky did not deny any of these allegations. He may have felt that to voice all his suspicions about Azef's role in the Organization would have subjected him, as Azef's control, to further criticism by Gerasimov. In any event, his reply was limited to questioning (and rather mildly, at that) the agent's participation in the plot against Durnovo.

Azef answered angrily, but in terms calculated to win Gerasimov's sympathy. His supervisor had assigned him to spy on the Fighting Organization, knowing well that this meant establishing intimate relations with the terrorists; then he had deserted him completely. What was he supposed to do during this period of cruel silence? Breaking with the Organization would have exposed him to terrorist retaliation as well as rendering him useless to the government. Therefore, Azef insisted, he had had every right to continue his "professional party work." Still, despite his abandonment by the department, he had continued to function as a loyal police agent. Already, at considerable risk to himself, he had saved the chief of the Secret Police, and there were others who could be spared the Organization's wrath . . . *if* he were to be reinstated. Rather than interrogating him like some common criminal, Gerasimov should pay him his back salary for six months—plus expenses!—and put him back to work.

This attack carried the day. "I myself felt a twinge of conscience about Rachkovsky's treatment of Azef," wrote Gerasimov later, "and was astonished that such incompetent people were at the head of the Political Department."

Astonished? Perhaps, but the skillful young bureaucrat had clearly put his rival in an indefensible position—one of the many blows that would bring Rachkovsky down when a new internal affairs minister, Pyotr Stolypin, was appointed to replace Durnovo two months later. Azef now moved quickly to cement relations with the sympathetic Gerasimov. To begin with, he named the cabdrivers who were hunting Durnovo: Pavlov, Tregubov, and Gotz. Sometime later, all three were arrested, tried for associating with the Fighting Organization, and sentenced to long prison terms at hard labor. Next, he revealed that the Fighting Organization had dispatched two terrorists to kill General Min and Colonel Riman. Dressed as young officers, they were to seek admission to Min's and Riman's homes and to shoot their victims, just as Stepan Balmashev had shot Minister Sipyagin five years earlier. Finally, with undisguised pleasure, Azef informed his astonished superiors that their agent, Father Gapon, was now hanging from a hook in a villa on the Finnish border.

After further conversation, Azef was released from police custody. His absence went unnoticed by other members of the Organization; since the police seemed to be everywhere, many of the comrades went into hiding for days at a time. Gerasimov made good use of his information. In addition to arresting the comrades involved in the Durnovo plot, he placed additional guards at the homes of Min and Riman with instructions to check the identities of all strangers seeking admittance and to turn away any visitors not personally known to them. As a result, one terrorist dressed as a naval officer was barred from Min's house and did not return. (Min was shot and killed four months later by a member of a new group of SR terrorists outside Azef's control.) Another of Azef's young recruits, disguised as an aristocratic army officer, was refused entry to Colonel Riman's house but came back for a second try and was immediately arrested. Meanwhile, police protection of Durnovo was increased to the point that it became impossible for the members of Azef's second observation squad even to catch sight of him.

Gerasimov was duly impressed. He submitted Azef's request for payment of his back salary to Durnovo, who approved a payment of five thousand rubles. Azef was reinstated as a Secret Police agent, but with two significant changes. While he was to work under Rachkovsky's nominal supervision, Gerasimov would be present at all their meetings, and the new rules of engagement would also be Gerasimov's. Azef now had official permission to work with the Fighting Organization, but he would be held personally responsible for its activities. And Gerasimov would protect him by agreeing not to arrest anyone with whom he was in close contact. He could use Azef's information to sabotage the Organization's plans in more effective ways, for example, by guarding suspected targets tightly, or by subjecting known terrorists to deterrent "frightenings." ("We had real specialists in this line," Gerasimov later remarked. "When following anybody, they almost breathed down the back of his neck. Only a blind man could fail to notice them.")

By calling on his resources of nerve and concentration, Azef had once more turned near disaster into a victory of sorts. He was out of jail; he was five thousand rubles richer (with a promise of salary increases to come); he had won Gerasimov's confidence; and, most important, he had positioned himself to continue his double game. For while revealing a great deal, he had hidden much more. He did not reveal the existence of the second squad hunting Durnovo—

a group of seasoned terrorists whose inability to zero in on their target had nothing to do with Azef's revelations. In fact, when their attempts to reach Durnovo were frustrated by police vigilance, they selected a more vulnerable victim and came very close to assassinating the minister of justice, Viktor Akimov.

More important, Azef said nothing about the plot to kill Governor-General Dubasov in Moscow, a campaign that he had discussed in detail with the comrades in Helsinki. Some ten days after his release from the Secret Police's jail, he asked Gerasimov and Rachkovsky for permission to visit Moscow on "personal business." Naturally, they granted the request, having no reason to suspect that the agent whom they had so recently terrorized—the coward who had just betrayed five of his comrades to the police—was about to attempt another assassination.

TEN

The Man Who Saved the Czar

IN THE MONTHS between February and April 1906, some twenty-five million Russians voted for the first time in national elections. Despite a boycott of the elections by the radical parties and strong efforts by the government to ensure that the "loyal peasantry" would cast the vast majority of votes, it was soon clear that the lower house of the legislature, the Duma, would be dominated by pro-democratic forces. The parties most successful at the polls were the liberal Constitutional Democrats (known as *Kadety*) and the moderately leftist Labor Group, and even the unorganized peasant representatives were considerably less loyal than the czarists had hoped. Before long, this experiment in limited democracy would prove a fiasco; early in July, after doggedly resisting the Duma's demands for constitutional democracy and land reform, Nicholas II would dissolve the body and send its members home. But when Azef left for Moscow at the end of April, the SRs were in a fever of excitement about the rising tide of democratic sentiment. Many party leaders regretted their election boycott, and virtually all agreed that the work of the new legislature must not be disrupted by terrorism. The opening of the Duma was set for May 10. Azef was therefore given just two weeks to strike a last violent blow against the old regime.

This was a difficult task, but not impossible. Although small in number, the Organization's Moscow squad was fiercely dedicated to terminating the career of Governor-General Dubasov, gravedigger of the Moscow Uprising. Dubasov, moreover, was not as elusive a target as Minister Durnovo had been. In a last-ditch attempt to liquidate the "invisible" Durnovo before the start of the Duma, Mikhail Gotz proposed that a suicide squad wearing coats lined with dynamite force their way into his house in St. Petersburg and blow it (and themselves) up, but the scheme was abandoned as impractical. Eliminating Dubasov would require no such desperate tactics. Boris Savinkov's Moscow group had been stalking him since March. On six separate occasions, expecting his carriage to take a particular route to or from the Kremlin, the terrorists had waited for it with bombs in hand. Each time their intelligence proved faulty and Dubasov escaped his hunters, but catching up with him seemed only a matter of time.

Shortly before Azef arrived in Moscow, Savinkov's squad suffered a serious setback. While Maria Benevskaya was unloading a batch of bombs, a dynamite explosion blew off several of her fingers, sending her to hospital and, ultimately, to prison. New security measures were adopted by the Secret Police; their plainclothes spies, it seemed, were everywhere. Under these circumstances, the newly arrived Comrade Valentine might easily have declared the operation impossible and canceled it. Instead, he set the date for another assassination attempt: May 6, the Empress Alexandra's birthday.

Why did Azef involve himself in such a risky adventure? He knew that if the attempt succeeded and Dubasov was killed, his police supervisors would suspect that the "personal business" he had asked permission to pursue in Moscow was more than personal. Even if there were no evidence of his complicity in the plot, Gerasimov's system required that an agent working with terrorists be held responsible for their actions. Clearly, if Azef did *not* expose the conspiracy, Rachkovsky and Gerasimov would be furious . . . but they still had no idea that he was the leader of the Fighting Organization. Gerasimov firmly believed that Boris Savinkov, not Azef, was the Organization's chieftain. Furthermore, no matter what Gerasimov thought, the government's hands would be tied. With the Duma set to open in a few days, the last thing the czarists wanted was a scandal of any sort, and revealing the existence of a police agent inside the Fighting Organization would obviously create a scandal of major proportions.

Azef was certain that, if necessary, he could manage his police superiors' suspicions. The Organization, on the other hand, would probably not survive another defeat. Since being reactivated in January, it had accomplished nothing. The campaign against Durnovo had come to naught; Azef himself had exposed the plots against Min, Riman, and Rachkovsky; and General Dubasov had so far escaped his executioners. Not a few voices on the Central Committee were already declaring (in terms similar to Azef's own despairing statements in Helsinki) that the Organization's day was done, and some had gone so far as to hint that its impotence was "more than accidental." Still, Comrade Valentine was not yet prepared to give up his career as a terrorist. He *needed* his life with the Organization, and his experiences during the December uprising had given him a particular desire to rid the world of the bloodstained Dubasov. He would place his bet, at least for this turn of the wheel, on the Organization.

On the morning of May 6, the Empress Alexandra's birthday, Dubasov would almost certainly attend a special religious service in her honor at the Kremlin. Working with Savinkov, Azef devised a new plan that seemed foolproof. Three terrorists—the Vnorovsky brothers, Vladimir and Boris, and Vassili Schillerov—would each occupy one of the three roads leading from the Kremlin to the governor-general's residence. They would be suitably dressed for the festive occasion, and each would carry in his hands a large package of candy tied with a ribbon. . . . Azef was scheduled to meet the three men for a final briefing on the evening of May 5, but he did not appear. Very likely, considering the risk he was running, he wished to avoid any possibility of being spotted in their company. As a result, however, he did not learn that some of the Organization's supply of dynamite had been found to be spoiled. The remaining dynamite had been used to manufacture two bombs, which were distributed to Schillerov and Boris Vnorovsky.

At about ten o'clock on the morning of May 6, the carriage bearing General Dubasov and his aide-de-camp, Count Konovnitzin, drove out of the Kremlin through the Troitzky Gate and onto Chernishevsky Lane. Vladimir Vnorovsky, who was standing at the gate, watched the vehicle pass helplessly. If only he had been given one of the bombs! As the horses turned onto Tverskaya Street, however, a man dressed as a navy lieutenant suddenly dashed through a line of palace guards into the street and ran toward the carriage. At a distance of a few paces, he hurled what appeared to be a large box of candy under the vehicle. The official report of the incident stated:

> Having fallen under the cab, the box created a deafening explosion and raised a thick cloud of smoke, the detonation of the explosion shattering windowpanes in the neighboring houses and showering the ground with debris. General Dubasov was hurled out of the shattered cab and was slightly wounded. Count Konovnitzin was killed. The coachman Ptitzin, thrown from the coach box, suffered minor injuries, as did several other persons nearby. The would-be assassin who hurled the bomb was found lying in the street, near the pavement, with crushed skull, without any signs of life. He was later identified as Boris Vnorovsky, of noble extraction, twenty-four years old, a former student of the Imperial University of Moscow.

The official account was accurate in all respects save one. Dubasov's injuries, while not fatal, required a lengthy treatment that terminated his public career. The comrades considered the operation a success, and the Central Committee agreed; the Organization's reputation and that of Azef as a terrorist leader were rehabilitated. Boris Vnorovsky left behind a letter to his parents that stated, in part, "Many times in my youth, I had the desire to end my life, but each time I banished the thought, knowing what sorrow my act would bring you. I remained alive and lived for you. Now I live for you, for the people, for the whole of mankind, and I now give my life not as a sacrifice to my shattered nerves, but as a means of bettering, as far as I can, the life of my country." The Fighting Organization published a proclamation taking responsibility for his act and noting that news of the attack had made millions of Russians happy. "Let this happiness," it continued, "be a consolation to the fallen comrade who did his duty to the last."

When Dubasov's carriage exploded, Azef was sipping coffee at his usual table at Filipov's pastry shop. A few minutes later the café was raided by a squad of policemen searching for terrorists. Azef was briefly detained, but the squad's supervisor, a veteran detective, recognized him as a secret agent and ordered him released. Several days later, the terrorist chief returned to St. Petersburg for the inevitable confrontation with Gerasimov and Rachkovsky.

Rachkovsky wasted no time. As Azef entered the meeting room, the old man shouted, pointing his finger at him, "That affair in Moscow was your doing!"

"If it was my doing," the agent replied tartly, "why don't you arrest me?"

The bluff was called. Azef improved his hand by asserting, in a tone of outraged innocence, that while he had had nothing to do with the attack on Dubasov, the real organizer of the conspiracy, according to a reliable source, was a woman named Zinaida Zhutchenko. The accusation stunned his accuser, for Zhutchenko—a member of the SRs' local group in Moscow, but not of the Fighting Organization—was herself a police spy reporting directly to the Secret Police in Moscow! Furthermore, she had recently told her police superiors (who immediately wired the report to St. Petersburg) that Azef had been named by party members as the organizer of the Dubasov plot. It was this report that had inspired Rachkovsky's opening blast against him. But now, Gerasimov wondered, where did the truth lie? Was Azef dissimulating? Did he *know* that Zhutchenko was a police agent? Could she have participated in the conspiracy, or at least failed to report it? Were *both* of them somehow involved?

How Azef learned about Zinaida Zhutchenko's secret role remains a mystery, but his strategy was entirely successful. Once again, he had outmaneuvered his otherwise canny employers. Years later, Gerasimov would admit in his memoirs that he *still* did not know who planned the attempt on Dubasov's life. Moreover, with the government about to face a hostile parliament, the police were in no position to reveal that not one, but two of their top agents were working with the most dangerous terrorist group in Russia. For the moment, at least, Gerasimov could take no action against Azef, but henceforth, he vowed, he would watch him carefully. Even more, he would now insist that Azef provide proof positive of his loyalty. He must betray the man Gerasimov believed to be the real leader of the Fighting Organization: the terrorist poet Boris Savinkov.

When Savinkov met Azef in Helsinki later in May, the adventurer was itching for action. Although the Duma was now in session, the SRs had not officially called a halt to terrorist attacks, and Savinkov was anxious to follow up the Organization's partial success in Moscow with a smashing victory elsewhere. Besides, he told Azef, it was time to try out some new techniques. The group's membership should be increased and new methods of observation implemented. A better communications system and more effective weapons were also needed, but the main thing was to strike soon, before the Central Committee made yet another mistake (as Savinkov saw it) and abandoned terrorism for useless parliamentary games.

Azef agreed with alacrity. "Pick whatever men you need," he responded, "and go to Sebastopol. We must kill Chuchnin." Admiral

Chuchnin, who had mercilessly put down rebellion in the Black Sea fleet, was in residence in Sebastopol, the fleet's headquarters. As both men knew, a previous attempt to assassinate him had misfired when one of the newer Organization members, Ekaterina Izmailovich, wounded him with a pistol shot but failed to kill him. The admiral was still high on the Organization's list of prime targets, but Savinkov was unaware—and Azef did not inform him—that the Central Committee had already decided to call off terrorist activity during the period that the Duma was in session and was only awaiting a formal meeting to announce this decision publicly. Savinkov quickly selected an experienced assassination team consisting of Kalashnikov, Dvoinikov, Nazarov, Schillerov, and Rachel Luriye. He left Helsinki, met with his squad in Kharkov and again in Simferopol, and arrived in Sebastopol on May 25.

Two other facts were also unknown to Azef's lieutenant. The first was that his chief had already revealed his travel plans, associates, and ultimate target to Rachkovsky and Gerasimov, who had the group closely watched all the way from St. Petersburg to the Black Sea. Gerasimov's plan was to arrest Savinkov in the South in order to divert suspicion from Azef. The second fact (of which Azef, too, was ignorant) was that the local SR party group in Sebastopol had decided on its own to assassinate General Nepluyev, the commandant of the town. On May 27, two days after the arrival of Savinkov's squad in the city, they put their plan into effect.

General Nepluyev was reviewing a parade when a sixteen-year-old boy, a party member named Nikolai Makarov, suddenly hurled a bomb at his feet. The bomb did not explode, but another carried by Ivan Frolov, an SR sailor, detonated in his hands, killing Frolov and six bystanders, and wounding thirty-seven others. Nepluyev walked away without a scratch. This disaster was ready-made for the Secret Police, whose agents were in the street at the time watching Savinkov, Dvoinikov, and Nazarov. The three terrorists, who had been mingling with the crowd in hopes of catching sight of Admiral Chuchnin, suddenly found themselves under arrest. They were jailed with young Makarov in the fortress of Sebastopol and charged with attempting to kill Nepluyev—a charge that the police knew to be false but that required a trial by court-martial and carried the death penalty. Kalashnikov managed to escape the police net, but was arrested several days later at the Finland Station in St. Petersburg. Only Rachel Luriye, the bomb maker in the aborted plot, managed to avoid capture.

The mood among the captured terrorists was exalted; they seemed almost to welcome the opportunity to die for their cause. The navy captain appointed to be their attorney—a sympathetic, although inexperienced fellow named Ivanov—informed them that they would not have long to wait. Their court-martial was set for May 31, and they were likely to be executed on the following day. Savinkov asked the navy lawyer to telegraph his family so that he could say good-bye to his wife, Vera, before he ascended the scaffold. Ivanov complied, and Vera arrived the day before the scheduled trial with her brother and a team of lawyers that the SRs had dispatched to assist in the defense. After an emotional reunion, Vera told her husband that Leo Zilberberg had also arrived in town. Over Azef's objections (for he had argued against committing scarce money and personnel to an improbable escape attempt), the Central Committee had authorized Zilberberg to undertake an effort to free the three prisoners.

It was on the same day, May 30, that the police discovered Nikolai Makarov's real name (all the terrorists had given false names to the court) and learned that he was only sixteen. As a result, his case was transferred to a civil court for an opinion on the right of the court-martial to try him, and the trial of the other defendants was postponed. Elated by this news, Zilberberg threw himself into action, using Vera Savinkov as a go-between for discussions with her husband. Zilberberg's first idea was to organize a mass attack on the guardhouse, the most secure section of the fortress, where Savinkov and his comrades were imprisoned. Since the guards were members of the Fiftieth Byelostock Regiment, many of whose members sympathized with the SRs, there was a chance that they would not resist an attack aimed at freeing the imprisoned activists. But the plan proved impractical, and the conspirators' hopes turned to an escape organized from inside the prison with the aid of sympathetic guards. Zilberberg and Savinkov had made some headway in gaining the guards' cooperation, when a new regiment replaced the Fiftieth Byelostock, and even this scheme seemed to evaporate. At the same time, the district court in nearby Simferopol ruled that Makarov could be tried as an adult by court-martial, and the trial of the terrorists was rescheduled for June 9.

Again, Savinkov and his comrades prepared for the inevitable guilty verdict and its all-but-certain sequel. But fate, in the form of the skilled lawyers sent by the party, intervened once more. On June 9, arguing that the court-martial could not take place until Makarov's appeal from the district court decision had been decided, they won a further postponement that promised to last well into the summer. Zilberberg and Savinkov went to work immediately on the Latvian soldiers who had replaced the Byelostockers as prison guards. Through a sympathetic guard named Israel Kohn, a member of the revolutionary Jewish Bund, they made the acquaintance of a soldier who was also an active SR: Vassili Suliatitsky, a member of the party's Simferopol committee. In mid-July, Suliatitsky managed to secure the position of guard supervisor. He spent the next two weeks working out the details of an escape plan and was ready by the end of the month to put it to the test.

From the guardhouse of the Sebastopol Fortress there was only one exit route possible. The escapee would have to proceed down a long, well-guarded corridor housing twenty cells, through an iron door that was always kept locked, and into the next section of the prison containing the washroom, a dark pantry, a watchhouse full of soldiers, and the officers' room. The main gate of the prison lay just beyond the officers' room. Given the great difficulty of running this gauntlet, it was clear that only one prisoner could make the attempt. Savinkov suggested drawing lots for the privilege, but Dvoinikov and Nazarov would hear none of it. Obviously, if anyone was to escape, it must be the man most vital to the Organization: Savinkov himself. At the last minute, fearing that the escape attempt would fail, Dvoinikov tried to dissuade him from going, but Savinkov was now committed to trying his luck.

At three o'clock on the morning of July 29, Vassili Suliatitsky entered his cell. Savinkov reminded the young soldier that, while he himself had nothing to lose by making the attempt, Suliatitsky was risking his life. "Yes, yes, I know," he replied. "Let's try." He handed Savinkov a revolver.

"What are we to do if the soldiers stop us?" Savinkov asked.

"The soldiers?"

"Yes. Suppose the guards recognize me?"

"Don't shoot at the soldiers."

"You mean, I am to go back to my cell?"

"No." Suliatitsky smiled. "Why go back to the cell?"

"But what?"

"If you meet an officer—shoot. If an ordinary soldier stops you—shoot yourself."

Savinkov agreed, and the two men embraced. Suliatitsky unlocked the door of his cell and led him down the long corridor past sleepy guards, muttering, "He's going to wash. Says he's sick." The soldier guarding the iron door was sleeping in his chair. Suliatitsky awakened him roughly: "Come on, you'll sleep later. Open up!" Then he followed Savinkov through the door to the washroom.

While the terrorist splashed water on his face, Suliatitsky checked to see that all was quiet in the watchhouse. He returned quickly and led his "prisoner" to the pantry, where he had concealed a soldier's uniform and knapsack containing a razor. Working quickly in the darkness, Savinkov cut off his mustache and donned the gray uniform. The two men exited the pantry, walked past several unconcerned guards, and entered the last space separating them from freedom: the watchhouse.

Some soldiers were sleeping in their bunks. Others were listening to one man read aloud by the light of a dim lamp. As several heads turned in their direction, Savinkov held his breath, but no one recognized him. He and his liberator proceeded through the vestibule and past the open door of the officers' room. Still unnoticed, they left the prison through the main gate. A guard immediately outside looked briefly at their uniforms and turned away. They strolled at a measured pace down the street, turned a corner, and came upon another guard—a sailor who had been stationed at that point by Zilberberg. The sailor gave Savinkov a basket of clothing. Suliatitsky handed him a certificate stating that he was a Latvian soldier on leave, and the two comrades walked quickly into the city.

Minutes later, their flight was discovered, and the commandant of the prison dispatched a squad of soldiers in pursuit. But Savinkov and Suliatitsky had already reached an out-of-the-way worker's house where Zilberberg was waiting. The three men embraced joyfully, changed clothes, and wrote an announcement that was widely distributed: "On the night of July 29, by decision of the Socialist Revolutionary party and with the cooperation of V. M. Suliatitsky, a volunteer of the Fifty-first Latvian Regiment, Boris Viktorovich Savinkov, a member of the Socialist Revolutionary party, was liberated from the main guardhouse of the fortress, where he was imprisoned." A group of local party members led the escapees through the mountains outside the city to a farmhouse owned by a revolutionary sympathizer, Karl Shtalberg. Here they spent the next ten days while Zilberberg arranged a method of getting them out of the country.

By now, the whole region was crawling with police and army units searching for the notorious Savinkov; railway travel was out of the question, and traveling the roads almost as risky. Zilberberg therefore decided on an escape by water—across the Black Sea to Rumania. He soon won the enthusiastic support of Boris Nikitenko, a former navy lieutenant who had given up his commission in protest after the suppression of the Black Sea mutiny. Nikitenko borrowed a single-masted sailboat from the Sebastopol Biological Station, stating that he would return it after a brief excursion. He then provisioned the boat and recruited two other leftist sailors to help crew it. At dawn on August 8, in a rainstorm, Savinkov, Suliatitsky,

Shtalberg (who had decided to become an active revolutionist), and Zilberberg boarded the craft in the mouth of the Katch River, and Nikitenko sailed it into the Black Sea.

With the Russian fleet maneuvering off Sebastopol, the government flag flying from the afterdeck proved more than useful. Nikitenko passed under the guns of the squadron flagship, and for the next three days the inexhaustible sailor piloted the small boat through heavy seas, steering westward toward the coast of Rumania. A severe gale during the final day threatened to put a watery end to the voyage. Finally, on the night of August 10, the sailboat made the port of Sulin, a little Rumanian town at the mouth of the Danube. The last leg of Savinkov's escape—two hundred miles of open sea—had been completed.

Savinkov made his way across the Hungarian frontier and then to Germany, where he planned to visit Mikhail Gotz. On arriving, he wrote a letter to General Nepluyev, the target of the Sebastopol party group's assassination attempt, stating that neither he nor the other Organization men had had any connection with that plot. "I ... cannot accept the moral responsibility for the death of innocent people and the enlistment of the minor, Makarov, in this terrorist act," he added. Dvoinikov, Nazarov, and Kalashnikov were acquitted of complicity in the conspiracy against the commandant, but they were found guilty of belonging to a secret organization having explosives in its possession and sentenced to prison at hard labor. Because of his youth, Nikolai Makarov also received a jail sentence, but in the summer of 1907, he escaped from the Sebastopol prison and went to St. Petersburg. There he completed his terrorist career. In September, he shot and killed the commandant of the St. Petersburg prison, and this time he was hanged.

Earlier than any of his comrades, Azef sensed that the era of "heroic" terrorism was drawing to a close. On the one hand, the prospects for a revolutionary uprising seemed increasingly remote.

While the people's representatives wrangled with diehard czarists in the Duma, the people themselves, worn out by fruitless violence, were returning to their normal pursuits. Spontaneous attacks on policemen, politicians, and public buildings still flared up around the country, but no mass upheaval loomed. On the other hand, Azef was certain, the old Russia was dying. Whether or not the socialists realized their dreams, political change—a general movement toward more liberal politics, freer thinking, and freer trade—now seemed inevitable.

Azef had always stated that, when the autocracy became a constitutional monarchy, he would cease being a terrorist. Thus when the SRs officially suspended the activities of the Fighting Organization at the opening of the Duma, the Organization's chief not only agreed with the decision, but argued that the revolutionary parties themselves might no longer have a role to play in Russian political life. As always, his views were closer to those of the moderate liberals than those of his own party. But if Azef occupied a position on his party's far right, the government itself was now moving somewhat to the left. In April, Pyotr Stolypin, destined to become Russia's most important leader before the 1917 Revolution, had replaced Ivan Durnovo as minister of internal affairs.

Appointed prime minister two months later, Stolypin combined ruthless opposition to all revolutionary groups with unusual political skills and "advanced" ideas about economic development. Like Azef, he believed that the nation's economic future could be secured by turning the peasants into capitalist farmers and eliminating restraints on commerce. The "Stolypin Reforms" represented the last attempt before war and revolution intervened to convert Russia into a modern capitalist state. At the same time, the new prime minister was a savage opponent of the radical Left. His willingness to hang revolutionaries by the hundreds added a new phrase to Russian slang: the hangman's noose became known as "Stolypin's necktie." One of his first acts was to dismiss Rachkovsky from office and to put the Secret Police under the exclusive control of Aleksandr Gerasimov.

For the next two years, this formidable trio—Stolypin, Gerasimov, and Azef—were to function (or so the government men thought) as a close-knit team.

The attempt on Dubasov's life had earlier shaken Gerasimov's none-too-solid faith in his agent, but by the time Boris Savinkov escaped from prison, the new Secret Police director had become one of Azef's strongest supporters. "In view of Azef's unsatisfactory explanations of the Dubasov affair," he later wrote, "all his reports were treated with great reserve. But as a result of the honesty, zeal, and precision with which he carried out the duties imposed on him, all doubts of him were soon dispelled." For the first time, Azef revealed that he was not only a member of the Fighting Organization but one of its leaders. Gerasimov welcomed this news, since he and the spy would now be in a position to paralyze the Organization's activities. Equally important, Azef had become an important source of information on the political activities of the SRs and other opposition groups—so much so that Stolypin himself frequently asked Gerasimov to solicit his opinions on matters of counterrevolutionary strategy. Gerasimov made it clear that he would hold Azef responsible for all future activities of the Fighting Organization; there were to be no more "unfortunate accidents." Then he raised his salary to one thousand rubles (in our terms, nine thousand dollars) per month.

For Azef, the pendulum had swung again. From 1902, when he joined forces with Grigory Gershuni to found the Fighting Organization, until the spring of 1906, when he sent his followers into battle against General Dubasov, his position as "man in the middle" had been weighted toward the Left. Much of this time, the government was in the hands of arch-reactionaries like von Plehve, Grand Duke Sergei, and Rachkovsky—men Azef was eager to betray, if, indeed, he did not have them killed outright. During these same years, his hopes for a liberalization of Russian society were vested primarily in the Organization. Therefore, while playing an active part as a police agent, Azef seemed more comfortable in the role of Comrade Valentine, and for several months during the Revolution of 1905, he abandoned police work altogether. Now, however, with revolution of any sort an impossibility and a relatively liberal regime in power, the balance of roles shifted. Now he would function as a police agent with a terrorist "sideline." His double game was not over—far from it. Before his career was ended, Azef would launch one more terrorist operation, and that an incomparably important one. But for the time being, he was Aleksandr Gerasimov's "man."

In July 1906, Prime Minister Stolypin dissolved the Duma. This sudden move enraged the Opposition; even the moderate *Kadety* urged their fellow Russians to refuse to pay taxes or accept military service until the czar called the assembly back into session. At the same time, with customary shrewdness, Stolypin announced that national elections for a new Duma would be held early in 1907. The SRs decided that when the time came, they would participate in these elections; for the present, however, the terrorist struggle must be renewed. For the third time, Azef allowed the Central Committee to reappoint him chief of the Fighting Organization. Its primary target, on orders of the Committee, was his new "client," the prime minister. Azef quickly reactivated the dynamite factory in Terioki and inducted fifteen new terrorists into the Organization. While participating fully in the planning of the Stolypin campaign, he was openly pessimistic about its chances of success. The old methods of terror, he reiterated, were no longer effective. The government's security measures had outpaced the terrorists' offensive capabilities. Until new methods (for example, remote-controlled mines) were adopted, there was every likelihood that the frustrations and failures of the previous spring would be repeated.

Azef had good reason to predict failure: he was now informing Gerasimov about every detail of the campaign. Gerasimov passed the information on to Stolypin and, with the prime minister's somewhat nervous consent, immediately put his new security system to the test. To begin with, Stolypin was ringed with an impenetrable wall of agents; his daily schedule was a closely guarded secret, and his movements in the city became entirely unpredictable. The observation teams dispatched by Azef rarely caught sight of their prey.

More often, they returned to report that they themselves were apparently under observation by police agents. When Azef's "soldiers" became impatient and asked to put some plan or other of their own into operation, he gave his permission—and then saw to it that Gerasimov's spies "stumbled upon" them seemingly by accident and disrupted their plans. As Gerasimov had promised, no arrests were made, but the Organization "was made to feel," as one observer remarked, "like a machine that is running at full pressure yet producing nothing of any consequence."

Ironically, these frustrations added to Azef's stature, since it was he who had predicted that nothing would come of the campaign. Still, discontent mounted on the terrorist side, and quarrels erupted both between members of the Central Committee and the Organization and among the fighters themselves. While some voices whispered that the police must be tapping a source of inside information, several of the younger terrorists suggested in louder tones that the problem was the bureaucratic, top-down method of command adopted by Azef and his intimates in the Organization's "Old Guard." These disputes became more embittered in August, when a group of Maximalists (militant SRs who had left the party in January to pursue terrorism on their own) threw several bombs into Stolypin's villa on Aptekarsky Island. The bombs blew a large hole in the building, killing the terrorists and a number of visitors and seriously injuring Stolypin's daughter, but the prime minister escaped unharmed. At Azef's insistence, the party condemned the attempt, but many of his comrades felt that even a misguided blow at Stolypin was better than none at all.

In September, having at last rejoined his comrades in Finland, Boris Savinkov was dismayed to discover that dissension generated by frustration had broken the Organization's usually solid ranks. Egged on by Azef, the returned hero went on the attack against the Central Committee, accusing the party leadership of failing adequately to support and finance the terrorist campaign. The Committee promptly passed a vote of confidence in the Organization and elected Savinkov to its ranks. But before these same party leaders, Azef took a far different position—one that had been approved in advance by Gerasimov. The Organization's methods, he argued, were outmoded and ineffective. Since time was needed to develop more modern weapons, the Fighting Organization should dissolve temporarily while he and Savinkov went abroad to study the latest techniques in mining and aeronautics.

Azef found it relatively easy to persuade most of his followers that this hiatus was necessary. After the bombing on Aptekarsky Island, Stolypin had moved into the Winter Palace and now seemed completely invulnerable. But the Central Committee, for once, refused to abandon the terrorist campaign. In a bold move designed to bring the quarrels within the Organization to the surface, Viktor Chernov summoned all its members to discuss the matter at a general meeting in Finland. There, after a stormy session marked by bitter disputes between the younger and older terrorists, the Committee agreed to dissolve the Fighting Organization and to accept Azef's and Savinkov's temporary resignations. For the first time, however, it approved the formation of new terrorist organizations directly responsible to the Central Committee itself.

Two groups were created, consisting for the most part of former Organization members who insisted on continuing the violent struggle. One, called the "Fighting Organization attached to the Central Committee," was commanded by Leo Zilberberg, whom Azef had asked to assume this position in order to preserve at least one source of information. Zilberberg's group was to continue the campaign against Stolypin and other targets in St. Petersburg. A second group directed by a female terrorist known as "Comrade Bella" (her real name was Lapina) was directed to kill General V. F. von Launitz, the commandant of St. Petersburg and a leading force in the Black Hundreds. Shortly afterward, the Committee recognized a third organization led by Albert Trauberg, a daring Latvian revolutionary known as "Karl." Renamed the "Flying Detachment of the Northern Region," it was assigned the tasks of assassinating General Pavlov,

chief prosecutor of the Military Tribunal, and Governor Gudima
of the temporary prison in St. Petersburg, a man notorious for his
cruelty to political prisoners.

Gerasimov was appalled to discover that his plan had misfired.
Instead of one Fighting Organization controlled by his agent, there
were now three groups of which Azef knew (or claimed to know)
nothing. Moreover, at this juncture, Azef's health failed. He developed a serious throat abscess and was hospitalized in critical
condition. When he recovered, he informed Gerasimov that he was
retiring, at least temporarily, from police service. He moved to
Alassio on the Italian Riviera, where Luba and the children joined
him, and there he remained for the rest of the winter, leaving his
villa only to indulge his taste for gambling in Monte Carlo and to
visit an inventor in Munich—a man named Buchalo—who had
developed a prototype airplane. He continued to correspond with
Gerasimov, but his assurances that nothing of consequence would
happen during his brief "retirement" were belied by the facts.

On January 3, 1907, General von Launitz was shot to death at
a ceremony marking the opening of the new Institute of Experimental Medicine. The assassin, one of Leo Zilberberg's "soldiers,"
put a bullet in his own head rather than be captured. Stolypin himself
was saved only because he heeded Gerasimov's warning (based on
the report of a local agent) to stay at home. Five days later, a member
of Karl Trauberg's Flying Detachment killed Chief Prosecutor Pavlov, and on January 30, another member of that group assassinated
Prison Governor Gudima. Stolypin demanded that the Secret Police
take more effective action against the terrorists, and a frantic Gerasimov telegraphed Azef, pleading for information.

It is not clear how much Azef knew about the plans for these
killings. Through intermediaries, he had remained in contact with
the Zilberberg group, and he may well have been informed about
the plan to kill von Launitz. If so, it is clear that he would not have
lifted a finger to save the notorious leader of the Black Hundreds.
Several months earlier, he had similarly "neglected" to inform his

supervisor of a plan sanctioned by the Central Committee to have the local party organization in Sebastopol kill Admiral Chuchnin. (The admiral was killed by the SR sailor Akimov in July.) After all, if the Fighting Organization were not directly involved, he could not be held responsible for every assassination, could he? Under pressure from Gerasimov, however, Azef finally provided the Secret Police chief with one important piece of information. The headquarters of the Zilberberg group, he revealed, was the Hotel Touristen in Imatra, Finland—the same hotel at which the SRs had held their party conference. Acting on this report, Gerasimov dispatched two agents, a man and a woman masquerading as students, to Imatra.

Heavy snow was falling when the two young people appeared at the hotel clad in ski clothes, claiming to be lost. The warmhearted proprietress—a party sympathizer—admitted them and permitted them to stay for several days, while the storm raged outside. The two travelers proved both amiable and entertaining; they sang and danced for the guests at the hotel and made friends with virtually everyone. When they departed, they took with them detailed descriptions of all the guests and left behind two new police agents: a maid and a porter whom they had convinced to assist them. Several days later, Zilberberg and Suliatitsky arrived by train from St. Petersburg. The "students," who were watching the railway station, pointed them out to the police, and two hotel workers whose loyalty they had purchased identified them as associates of von Launitz's assassin. The captured terrorists were tried by court-martial on this evidence alone, since to reveal that the Secret Police knew more about them would have indicated the presence of a spy in the Organization. Despite the weakness of the government's case, they were convicted in July 1907 of participating in the von Launitz assassination and executed.

Vassili Suliatitsky had, in fact, been waiting in evening clothes at the Institute for Experimental Medicine on the night of von Launitz's assassination. His job, had the prime minister attended the inauguration, was to kill Stolypin. Suliatitsky went to his death without revealing his true name or mission. He announced only that he was a member of the Socialist Revolutionary party. "All of us," he said at the end, "know how to die."

Leo Zilberberg, who had been a fine mathematician, spent his last days solving a difficult problem in geometry. He completed his paper in prison and asked that it be sent to the Academy of Sciences, but the police confiscated it. The paper (on the trisection of an angle) was finally published ten years later after the Russian Revolution finally overthrew the House of Romanov.

Azef's brief retirement ended in February 1907, a momentous month for him, the Socialist Revolutionaries, and the government. While the SRs mourned the arrests of Zilberberg and Suliatitsky, the tide of terrorism swelled anew. Scores of attacks across the country were attributed either to Trauberg's Flying Detachment, local SR fighting groups, or Zilberberg's former comrades, who had now come under the leadership of Boris Nikitenko, the daring navy officer who had sailed Savinkov to freedom. From his office in St. Petersburg, Gerasimov wrote Azef repeatedly, urging him to return to action. Without an agent on the SR Central Committee, the Secret Police chief felt that he was operating in the dark. Moreover, the party's second congress was scheduled for the end of the month, and the major issue to be discussed would be the SRs' participation in elections to the Second Duma. Not only Gerasimov but the prime minister himself wanted Azef to be in Finland when that congress opened.

Azef considered the invitation with mixed feelings. His health had improved, and he was restless in retirement, but the idea of returning to service as an police agent without the opportunity to participate in revolutionary activity was unappealing. If the SRs decided to contest the forthcoming elections, as they almost certainly would, they would not revive the Fighting Organization; and if he were not the Organization's chief, what would he be? A mere informer! The issue was settled, however, by the arrival of an unexpected visitor: Grigory Gershuni, looking entirely out of place in the warm Italian sun. Azef's oldest and best comrade, recently escaped from Siberia by way of Japan and America, had returned to action and wanted Azef to accompany him to the forthcoming party congress. *This* invitation Azef found irresistible. With Gershuni he had helped found the party and then the Fighting Organization. In addition to his almost legendary reputation, his old friend had brought a large sum of money with him, collected from American supporters of the Russian revolutionary cause. Surely, the two veteran fighters could find something worthwhile to do with it!

Azef informed Gerasimov immediately of his decision to return and left for Tampere, Finland, with his refound comrade. The delegates greeted Gershuni (nicknamed "Comrade Cabbage" in honor of his escape in a barrel of sauerkraut) with wild enthusiasm and elected him president of the congress. As expected, the assemblage voted down the "boycotters" and approved SR participation in the national electoral campaign. But they refused to renounce terrorism, resolving instead, as a provisional measure, to put all terrorist activities, "insofar as they have administrative and political importance," under the exclusive control of the Central Committee. Similarly, the congress banned private "expropriations" (an uncontrolled wave of robberies that had reached epidemic proportions in the famine-ridden countryside), but allowed the Central Committee to organize bank robberies at its discretion in order to fill the party's treasury. Azef reported on these matters in detail to Gerasimov, who was pleased to learn that his agent had been elected, along with Grigory Gershuni, Viktor Chernov, Marc Natanson, and Nikolai Rakitnikov, to the new Central Committee.

Gerasimov recognized, as did Azef, that the formula adopted by the congress with regard to terrorism represented the worst sort of compromise. On the one hand, the SRs' local combat organizations and bandit groups would *not* stop killing and robbing just because the Central Committee directed them to stop; the party had never succeeded in imposing this sort of discipline on its "locals." More important, if acts of "centralized" terrorism were to be authorized while the Duma was in session, the SRs would be handing the government a very large stick with which to beat them, assuming that some plot or other could be shown to be their handiwork. Within two months of the close of the congress (thanks to Azef) this is exactly what happened.

The plot in question was no ordinary conspiracy; indeed, it was shortly to become known throughout Russia as "the Conspiracy against the Czar." Azef learned about it in March, shortly after the congress ended. The veteran terrorist's party duties now had little to do with terrorism. Since the old Fighting Organization remained disbanded, he had been put in charge of party publications and assorted other initiatives (for example, he was promoting a scheme to flood the Russian market with counterfeit currency, although nothing came of the idea). Still, it was natural for Boris Nikitenko to seek his advice about a terrorist act that Azef had long considered taboo: the assassination of Nicholas II. Prior to the Revolution of 1905 and the violent government counterattacks of 1906, the SR leaders had believed that killing the czar would horrify and alienate the peasants, who still viewed their sovereign as a potential savior misled by bad advisors. But the events of the previous two years had deprived Nicholas II of his aura of sanctity; his claim to be the Russian people's "Little Father" was now transparently bogus.

The outlines of a plan to attack the czar had begun to take shape several months earlier under Zilberberg's direction. His young successor, Nikitenko, inherited the conspiracy, but lacked confidence in his ability to carry it off. Comrade Valentine himself should assume command of his organization, he declared, and lead the terrorists to their greatest victory. The suggestion snapped Azef entirely out of his lethargy. Of course, he would not assume leadership of the remnants of Zilberberg's group; in fact, he would betray it as soon as possible. But now the game could begin again in earnest—and for stakes that were finally worth playing for.

Azef had never intended to surrender his independence entirely to the police, and the dangers of doing so had recently become quite clear. Upon his return from Italy, a friendly comrade had informed him that a nosy left-wing journalist was asking questions about him. Vladimir Burtzev was the writer's name; his journal, *Byloe (The Past)*, was a respected source of information about the history of the Russian revolutionary movement. Apparently, Burtzev, who specialized in exposing government plots to infiltrate opposition groups, had received a detailed letter from someone in the Secret Police claiming that a top leader of the Socialist Revolutionary party was a longtime secret agent. Further investigation by Azef revealed the name of Burtzev's informant. He was Mikhail Bakai, the same police officer who had discovered the truth about Nikolai Tatarov's relations with the old spymaster, Rachkovsky. Bakai had informed Burtzev that Rachkovsky had had an even more important spy on the Central Committee—an agent known to the police as "Raskin." Indeed, he insisted, the mysterious Raskin had been systematically betraying the SRs for years and was still doing so.

While the journalist began a search for Raskin, Azef immediately reported this leak to Gerasimov, who promptly arrested Bakai and had him shipped off to Siberia. But the implication of these events was clear. Both his security and his political principles required that he carry out a major terrorist act. Now that the SRs had placed regicide on their agenda, Azef could undertake the ultimate campaign: the assassination of the czar. *That* would not only right the balance that had shifted too strongly in favor of the police, it would silence his critics on the Left forever.

The Zilberberg/Nikitenko plot, of course, was unlikely to succeed. Leo Zilberberg had befriended the son of the manager of the telegraph officer in the czar's palace, a fellow named Vladimir Naumov, who had agreed to help him discover the times that Prime Minister Stolypin and Grand Duke Nikolai (both targets of Zilberberg's group) visited the palace. Naumov also told Zilberberg about a Cossack named Ratimov, a member of the czar's personal guard who claimed to be a revolutionary sympathizer. Ratimov, he said, wanted to help the SRs mount an attack on the czar himself. If the Cossack were sincere, he was obviously in a position to provide

important assistance to the terrorists—but Nikitenko, who met with
him after Zilberberg's arrest, doubted his reliability. Chernov and
Natanson directed him to cultivate Ratimov and to plan for a possible
attack on the czar, but to take no further action while the Second
Duma was in session. This is how matters stood when Nikitenko
asked Azef to take charge of the operation.

In Ratimov, Azef smelled a rat. He told Nikitenko, quite rea-
sonably, that he could not assume the leadership of a campaign that
depended upon fighters he had not chosen. Then he informed Gerasimov that Nikitenko's group (giving its members' names) was
planning to kill Nicholas II at some time in the future using a
member of the Czar's Guard. He did not, however, name Ratimov;
if the ill-considered plot happened to succeed, he wanted to be in
a position to take credit for it! But it did not succeed, nor could it
have. In fact, the Cossack was an agent of the palace police commanded by the redoubtable Colonel Aleksandr Spiridovich. Spiridovich had instructed him to approach the terrorists with offers of
assistance in order to uncover the whole conspiracy.

Gerasimov, who did not know this, put Nikitenko under close
observation and, without Ratimov's help, soon discovered the entire
membership of his group. At first, since he lacked solid evidence of
conspiracy, he deferred arresting the terrorists, but it soon became
clear that he must either move against them or risk an assassination
attempt against the czar. Precisely at this point, however, Colonel
Spiridovich told him about his Cossack agent. Now Gerasimov's
strategy changed: the police could observe Ratimov meeting with
the terrorists and collect enough evidence of the conspiracy to justify
a full-scale trial. By mid-April, the government was prepared to act.
On the night of April 14, 1907, virtually every member of Nikitenko's group—twenty-eight terrorists in all—was arrested. Vladimir
Naumov, who lacked the iron will Azef always sought in his own
recruits, made a full confession, which he later attempted to retract.
Eighteen of those arrested were tried in August by court-martial.
All the defendants were convicted, and three men—Naumov, Ni-

kitenko, and a young terrorist named Boris Sinyavsky—were executed by hanging.

The government made good use of "the Conspiracy against the Czar." A large number of radical deputies, including thirty-seven SRs and sixty-seven Social Democrats, had gained election to the Duma and were using the assembly to castigate and embarrass the government. Immediately after the arrests, Stolypin's supporters in the parliament accused the Socialist Revolutionary party of plotting against the czar's life. To save the SR deputies from arrest and prevent immediate dissolution of the Duma, Chernov denied that the plot had been authorized by the party—a position that made it difficult for the defendants to make the sort of political statements they would have liked to make at their trial. Moreover, Chernov's maneuvers failed ultimately to save the Duma. In June, Stolypin accused a number of Social Democratic deputies of plotting a mutiny in the army, and on the basis of this "Conspiracy of the Social Democrats" dissolved the assembly. In fact, the alleged conspiracy was largely the work of another of Gerasimov's agents, who had arranged meetings between the deputies and some soldiers in St. Petersburg.

On the basis of this coup and the court-martial of Nikitenko's group, Aleksandr Gerasimov—now known as "the Man Who Saved the Czar"—was promoted to general and became the absolute master of the Russian Secret Police. As Azef had hoped, he attributed a large part of his great success to his faithful agent on the SR Central Committee, the man known to the police as Raskin. Azef was now trusted—absolutely—by the most powerful police official in Russia. It was time to play his final game.

ELEVEN

An Affair of the Heart

IN A LETTER TO his mother, the Dowager Empress Maria Feodorovna, Czar Nicholas II had "predicted" the dissolution of the Second Duma. "We must let them do something manifestly stupid or mean," he wrote complacently, "and then—slap! They will be gone." Now the Duma *was* gone, in part thanks to Azef, and Nicholas ruled a sullen and resentful populace through his chosen instrument, Stolypin. Meeting in Finland, the leaders of the Socialist Revolutionary party heard Grigory Gershuni argue that the czar had finally forfeited whatever sympathy the peasants might formerly have felt for him. The Central Committee agreed: it was time to kill the hapless monarch. Led by Gershuni, the Committee urged Azef to reorganize the Fighting Organization and take charge of the operation himself. He agreed. Then he immediately informed the Secret Police chief, Gerasimov, that the campaign against the czar was "on." He was ready to play the game of double betrayal as it had seldom, if ever, been played before.

To begin with, Azef set about the task of re-creating a terrorist organization that would be capable of assassinating the czar. In late August 1907, accompanied by Gershuni, he went to Switzerland and settled his family in the little town of Charbonierre. Then he met with Boris Savinkov in Montreux. Savinkov had spent the summer in Munich working with the inventor Buchalo on the plans for an airplane that could be used to drop bombs on Organization targets, but he had returned empty-handed; the "flying machine" would not be ready for some time. To Azef's surprise, Savinkov refused to join in the new campaign against the czar. Repeating his chief's recent arguments to the Central Committee—new weapons and techniques were needed, the Organization was too small for effective observation work, the police were too strong—he declared that he would not recruit members to join a group that he considered "doomed to helplessness." Azef, who knew—but could not say why—*this* plot might succeed where others had failed, bitterly accused his old lieutenant of lack of faith. Savinkov took his case to the Central Committee, which also rejected his views, then he spent the next eight months in Paris working on his novel about terrorism.

With or without Savinkov, Azef was determined to rebuild the Organization. In the novelist's place, he appointed Pyotr Karpovich, the young militant whose assassination of Minister of Education Bogolepov in 1901 had electrified the country and inspired the SRs to launch their own terrorist campaign. Azef and Karpovich recruited their "soldiers" carefully, focusing their attention on old revolutionaries whose loyalty and willpower were beyond question. They established a complex system to observe the czar's movements in and around St. Petersburg and considered a variety of possible plans of attack. This activity consumed virtually all of Azef's time, leaving the other terrorist projects sanctioned by the party to be carried out by Karl Trauberg's Flying Detachment.

In October, when the Central Committee placed this group under his and Gershuni's control, Azef did not tell Gerasimov that he was now in charge of all terrorist activities directed by the party center. It was vital to put some distance between the Secret Police chief and himself. In the first place, he was quite serious about killing the czar, a deed that he told his comrades would be the "crowning achievement" of his terrorist career. But considerations of personal security also dictated prudence. Mikhail Bakai, the police official who had told Vladimir Burtzev about the spy called Raskin, had recently escaped from his Siberian exile and had reestablished contact with the dogged journalist. Burtzev, in turn, had confided to several party members, including the terrorist leader Trauberg, that he suspected that Azef himself might be Raskin. Azef had little sympathy for Trauberg or his group, the holier-than-thou terrorists of the second generation. At the appropriate time, he would gladly betray them. For the present, however, he told Gerasimov that, while he had no direct connection with the Flying Detachment, he had heard that Trauberg's terrorists were planning to assassinate several high-ranking officials who had abused political prisoners.

In fact, Azef knew quite well, since he and Gershuni had approved the plans, that attempts were to be made to assassinate the minister of justice, the chief of the central prison administration, the military governor of St. Petersburg, and the military commander of the Moscow region! A number of these attempts misfired, but on October 28, Elena Ragosinikova, a member of the Flying Detachment known in the group as "the She-Bear," gained entry to the office of Maximovsky, the prison chief, and killed him with one shot of her Browning revolver. Gerasimov now demanded that Azef provide further information about the Flying Detachment. Still disclaiming any direct knowledge of the group's plans, he reported that Trauberg's people had been overheard discussing a plot to blow up the State Council—the conservative legislative chamber dominated by Stolypin's friends in the nobility. The police should beware, Azef said, of the journalists in the chamber's press gallery; one of them might be carrying a bomb in his briefcase.

Acting on this information, Gerasimov immediately took precautionary measures. No journalists were admitted to the press gallery without being thoroughly searched, and Trauberg's plot was frustrated. More important, Azef now provided his supervisor with a detailed description of Karl, adding that the group's headquarters were on the Finnish side of the border, close to Vyborg. This was exactly the sort of information that might be used by an energetic policeman like Gerasimov without in any way jeopardizing Azef's security. Gerasimov flooded the border region with plainclothes detectives, ordering that all Finnish railway stations near the border be kept under continuous observation.

Soon this activity bore fruit. The police traced several suspects to two apartments near the Kelomyak Railroad Station. With Stolypin's approval (since current laws prohibited police raids into "autonomous" Finland), Gerasimov ordered the flats raided, and on the night of December 5, his men burst in. In one, they discovered a photographic studio and a number of important documents, including a floor plan of the State Council. In the other, they captured a man and a woman whose names were unknown. Weeks later, while meeting with Gerasimov at his private residence (he was the only agent entrusted with the police chief's private address and telephone number), Azef casually remarked, "You are still looking for Karl, but you have had him in your hands for a long time already. You got him in Kelomyak."

It remained only to mop up the rest of the Detachment, which was now working under the direction of Vsevolod Lebedintzev, a brilliant mathematician, artist, and journalist who had gained a European-wide reputation under the pen name, "Mario Calvino." But this mopping-up was no simple matter, since Azef feared that further betrayals too soon after Trauberg's capture might put suspicious investigators like Burtzev on his track. Thus he did *not* at first inform Gerasimov that the Flying Detachment planned to kill both Grand Duke Nikolai and the minister of justice, Shcheglovitov, on New Year's Day, 1908. The Secret Police chief got wind of the plot from other agents, however, and persuaded the intended victims to remain at home on the holiday. For the next six weeks, the terrorists hunted their elusive prey, but without success. Finally, in February, Azef gave Gerasimov one further scrap of untraceable information: he had heard, he said, that one of the members of the

Flying Detachment was a former political prisoner named Anna Rasputina.

This scrap was all that Gerasimov needed. To his surprise, he discovered that Rasputina was living under her own name in St. Petersburg. After searching her apartment himself, he stationed two agents posing as students in the apartment next door. The agents kept track of Rasputina's visitors and followed her into the churches where the terrorists customarily met, whispering together in the pews. In a matter of days, all their identities were known to the Secret Police. On February 20, Gerasimov's detectives arrested nine members of the group as they waited in the street for the grand duke and the minister of justice. Three of them, including Rasputina and Lebedintzev, were carrying bombs, and three more, revolvers. Seven terrorists were quickly tried, convicted, and hanged. Shortly afterward, Karl Trauberg and three other members of the Flying Detachment mounted the same scaffold. The last terrorist group outside Azef's control had ceased to exist.

The list of Azef's betrayals had by now grown to a great length. To the party members betrayed in earlier years—most of them "civilians" whose crimes carried the punishments of imprisonment or exile—he had now added active terrorists, men and women like himself, who would almost certainly be executed if they were captured, unless they first killed themselves. This lethal list included his old comrades, Savinkov, Dvoinikov, and Nazarov, who managed by chance to escape the hangman, as well as those who did not escape: Suliatitsky, Zilberberg, Naumov, Nikitenko, Sinyavsky, Trauberg, and ten other members of the Flying Detachment. By the end of 1907, Azef's hands ran with blood—not just the blood of czarist tyrants and spies, but that of his own comrades and associates. The question that demands an answer is: What kind of man would commit these betrayals? What sort of person would turn those who trusted him over to the czar's executioners, and do so without hesitation or regret?

The simplest explanation—that the informer betrayed his comrades for money—is also the least satisfactory. Azef no doubt had that special attachment to money that many feel who have risen from poverty on the strength of their own nerve and cunning. Clearly, he was determined to avoid the poverty that had dogged his family's existence in Rostov-on-Don. But it is unlikely that the "Russian Judas" (as he was later dubbed) would risk his own life month after month, year after year, for cash rewards that he could have earned in far less dangerous ways. After all, he had been living the life of a secret agent for more than ten years before his salary became "respectable." One strongly suspects that financial gain, although one of Azef's motives, was an incentive of secondary importance.

Perhaps he was addicted, then, to risk itself, or to the sense of power that he must have felt as the "man in the middle," deciding who on each side would live or die. Earlier in his career, he may well have found both the danger and the centrality of his position intoxicating. But from the time that Gerasimov became his supervisor, the territory that he occupied—the no-man's-land between contending forces—began to shrink. By 1907, when his betrayals reached their apogee, Azef had virtually no place left to stand. His close association with Gerasimov and Stolypin seriously undermined his independence, intensifying the danger of his exposure by the Left. Azef understood that Stolypin, increasingly pressured by the Right, was not the man to "liberate" Russia. The terrorist-spy might have resigned with honor from both camps and joined his wife and children abroad. Yet he persisted both in betraying revolutionaries and in plotting against the State.

Why? One could speculate that Azef felt himself to be a soldier at war and that he had not surrendered his dream of a free, democratic Russia. One could note that his position as a "party of one" permitted him no permanent comrades. If giving up Savinkov meant positioning the rest of the Organization to eliminate General Trepov, Savinkov would be given up. If betraying the "Conspiracy against the Czar" at present meant assassinating the czar later, the executioner could have Nikitenko and his fighters. Even understood in these terms, however, Azef's character remains mysterious. One still wants to understand how a human being, in many respects quite normal, could insulate himself so thoroughly against normal feelings of human solidarity and loyalty. How could he maintain a position requiring a theoretically endless series of betrayals and do so with a comfortable conscience?

The answer must remain partly hidden: we cannot know with any certainty what Azef was thinking and feeling as he decided to surrender members of his own organization to the hangman. But the conviction grows, as one follows his course through an accelerating series of twists, turns, and betrayals, that this consummate actor, incapable of fidelity to anything but his own role, was a man deeply wounded in his identity. His primary rule was: put yourself in no one's power. And the corollary: let no one make you responsible for his life. Only a person feeling himself, in some fundamental sense, to be a *victim* of betrayal could betray others with such ferocious conviction. Only one doubting the reality of his own identity could treat others so consistently as chess pieces or as characters in a play.

How, then, does one become a "total actor," playing conflicting roles in such a way as to convince others—perhaps, even oneself—that each role is equally real? One answer is that such a person annihilates (to the extent he can) his original, family-based identity and adopts in its place a series of artificial personae, no one of which is more real to him than any other, and no one of which feels *entirely* real. By the time he left Rostov-on-Don, Azef had annihilated his identity as the son of Fischel the tailor. He would not be poor, nor would he live as a Jew. He would not be subject to other people's control. He would not be riven by "Jewish guilt"; and never (except when playing the *goyim* for fools) would he wheedle or cringe. Rather than existing for other people, Azef would make others exist for *him*—a victimizer, if need be, but never again a victim.

But if he were not to be the little tailor's son, who would he be? The answer—the discovery of which must have both dazzled and terrified him—was anyone he wanted to be. Having abandoned his original identity, Azef was free to become, quite literally, a "self-made man." To achieve the invulnerability he craved, however, he would have to be several people: a devoted husband and father for his family and a reckless *bon vivant* for his companions, a fearless terrorist for the SRs and a nervous, "mercenary Jew" for the Secret Police. Obviously, directing this theater of multiple identities would require the continual betrayal of those who knew him only in one role—the betrayal, that is to say, of almost everyone he knew. But betrayal would not seem unconscionable to one who did not identify emotionally with others or feel himself attached to them in any organic way.

Azef's extreme individualism, it seems certain, reflected a profound sense of detachment—not loneliness so much as aloneness: the sense of being a world in himself. Whatever its etiology and drawbacks, this feeling of self-containment must have carried with it enormous compensations. Within the world of himself, relying on no one, trusting no one, needing no one, he could be safe. Within that same self-bounded world, obligated to no one by ties of custom, law, or morality, he could be free. And within a "society" composed of multiple roles, gestures, and audiences that he alone had created, he could be powerful.

Or so he thought. Ironically, though perhaps predictably, the system that Azef constructed to secure these goals tended, over time, to enslave him. Did it strike him, as the pressures from all sides intensified, that rather than becoming anyone *he* chose to be, he was compelled to become anyone *they* wanted him to be? Did he understand that, even apart from these pressures, it was not free choice that prevented him from adopting a stable identity, but his own incapacity to reveal himself to others, to give them power over him—in short, to trust himself to them? To each of his publics he presented a different face, a mask concealing a private self that he may well have considered too monstrous or too banal to display.

And since his wife, Luba, was a member of a particular audience (she remained a devoted SR), there was no "neutral" person to whom he could reveal himself.

Who *was* Yevno Azef? Apart from his various *dramatis personae,* the private man seemed scarcely to exist at all. Yet he did exist— not a blank face; not (except in the effects of his actions) a monster; perhaps not even a figure capable of interesting future historians and biographers; but a person nonetheless. Only one situation could expose the human being behind the masks. What if someone else, a performer like Azef, were to recognize the private man and find him admirable . . . even lovable? Would he still require disguises then? Azef revealed himself to no one because he trusted no one. But what would happen to the elaborately staged drama that was his life were he to find someone worthy of his absolute trust?

Life, as we know, has a way of realizing such hypothetical questions. Exactly at the point that Azef's bloody game reached its climax, the faceless man fell desperately in love.

The source of this unexpected passion was Hedwig Klopfer, a young woman of impeccably middle-class background from a small town in eastern Germany. In December 1907, however, when Azef first met her, she was "*La belle* Hedy de Hero," the toast of St. Petersburg's fashionable cabarets, a singer and entertainer whose photo, *en décolleté,* appeared on picture postcards offered for sale in the clubs where she appeared. Tall and full-figured, the dark-haired girl was known to have been Grand Duke Kiril's mistress during the Russo-Japanese War—one of those women whose scandalous behavior in the officers' quarters inspired the commanding general in the Far East to ask for their removal on the ground that they were "demoralizing the troops"! Hedy put her notoriety to good use. Now she was a star in her own right and a fixture at the Aquarium, a popular St. Petersburg nightclub.

Conventionally raised and educated in Germany, Hedy had nevertheless left her home soon after completing school to make her fortune in Russia, which was then (1904) enjoying an economic boom. In St. Petersburg, where the young nouveaux riches had created a nightlife to rival that of Paris, she almost immediately found employment as a singer. There she became the flirtatious Hedy de Hero, and there the grand duke and his friends had "discovered" her. After leaving Kiril to fight his disastrous war in the Far East, she had made a triumphal tour of Russian cities, appearing in Moscow, Kharkov, and Kiev before returning to the capital. She had already won and lost a fortune—fifty thousand rubles invested in a fly-by-night Siberian gold mining operation. She had lived the gay life to the full, and when Azef came to know her, she was seeking another sort of existence more in harmony with her middle-class upbringing and her sweet, essentially innocent, personality. She wanted to put the past behind her. She wanted to be taken care of, as she put it, by someone "substantial." She wanted a faithful, understanding, protective, and virile "daddy" (her pet name for Azef) who could inspire her own capacity for fidelity and nurturance. In Azef, as it happened, she found exactly what she was looking for.

On the day after Christmas 1907, Azef watched Hedy perform at the Aquarium, had dinner with her, and spent the night at her apartment. This behavior was not unusual for him, at least when he was away from his family and out of the SRs' sight. Azef loved the life of the cafés and craved the generous, no-questions-asked intimacy offered by complaisant companions. Despite his homely features, women of all sorts were attracted by his energy, attentiveness, and generosity; the heavyset man was well-known to the managers of certain theaters and brothels from Paris to Moscow. But this meeting *was* unusual; he referred to it long afterward as the turning point in his life. When he met his inamorata, Azef was thirty-eight, but with the temperament of a man a good deal older. Like Hedy, he had lived long during the past few years. Like her, he found his past an increasing burden and was beginning to yearn for a fresh start in another locale. Perhaps even more than Hedy, he craved the company of someone exciting and worldly but also simple and trusting—a woman who would accept the man behind the masks for what he was.

Of course, he already had a family. Azef treated his wife, Lubov, with tenderness and undoubtedly deserved his reputation as an affectionate, even a doting, father. His first thought, upon setting out on some new campaign or adventure, was always to see that she and the children were comfortably settled somewhere out of the line of fire. He wrote Luba regularly and visited when he could. But the long periods of separation from his family had taken their toll. Luba bore these absences uncomplainingly; her husband, so far as she knew, was a revolutionary hero, and her family was far better cared for than those of most of the other comrades. She remained, as she had always been, a devoted supporter of the Socialist Revolutionary cause and a passionate enemy of the czarist regime. For Azef, however, this was the crux of the problem. His wife might have suspected that he was less than a faithful husband while on lengthy trips out of town, but she did not have the slightest inkling that he was an agent of the despised Secret Police. She loved him, but she did not *know* him. And he would not—*could* not—bear to face her with the truth.

Azef's affair with Hedy swept almost everything else from his mind; it began at top speed and never slackened. (As he wrote her near the end of his life, referring to their early days together, "From that time we have never separated.") There can be no doubt that, particularly in its first stages, the relationship affected his judgment. At the beginning of 1908, he spent every minute he could spare with her and was seen with her, despite her notoriety, at fine restaurants, theaters, and *cafés chantants*. Some of the St. Petersburg comrades whispered that he had spent a fortune on jewelry; others feared that Luba, now back in their Paris apartment, would get wind of the affair; and even Gerasimov felt it necessary to warn him that his behavior was attracting too much attention. Azef explained to the SRs that the wealthy clientele of the cafés were an invaluable source of information about the czar—an accurate statement, so far as it went, in view of the grand dukes' love of pleasure and entertainment. To Gerasimov he also gave a partially honest reply: he would retire permanently from police work, he said, just as soon as he had sabotaged the SRs' campaign against the czar. By summer's end, he hoped to be out of politics altogether.

It was some time before Hedy learned about Azef's double life. At first, he told her only that he was a businessman. He was married, he said, and was devoted to his children, but the marriage had become a formality, and he longed for a more satisfying relationship. In March, when it was clear that their affair was more than a brief infatuation, Azef suddenly asked her to travel with him to the West. He advised her to terminate the lease of her apartment and store her furniture. They would remain abroad for about one month, he announced; then they would return to Russia for a while, while he wound up his business affairs; and, after that, they would leave the country for an extended period—perhaps permanently. Hedy, for her part, did not require further explanations. If he wanted to leave the country, she would leave with him. If he preferred to keep his business affairs to himself, so be it. She was no more interested in the details of Azef's career than in continuing her own, and she had learned to let the past remain in the past. It was enough that he loved her and that he intended to live with her henceforth as husband and wife.

In fact, Azef's abrupt decision to travel abroad was prompted by more than romance. His chief lieutenant, Karpovich, had been arrested by mischance in St. Petersburg. Azef stormed into Gerasimov's private office; the arrest, he bellowed, obviously endangered his security. Karpovich must be released immediately! Gerasimov, who knew nothing of the matter, apologized, and Karpovich was allowed to escape; the guard traveling with him to prison left him alone at a restaurant in order to go to the washroom, and Karpovich simply walked out the door to freedom. Azef was not at all pleased by the transparent phoniness of this "escape," which might reawaken suspicions of him among the comrades. Clearly, it was time to prepare for his own exit—for a new life abroad that now seemed inconceivable without Hedy.

In mid-March, the couple traveled to Germany, where Hedy introduced Azef to her family as her fiancé. Then they toured for about one month, staying in the best hotels. During this period, Azef made several short trips on his own, very likely to scout out possible sites for his European retirement; he may also have begun depositing his considerable savings in various French and German banks. In April, the lovers returned to St. Petersburg and registered as a married couple at a good hotel. There they would remain until they left the country again in June. Again, during this interim, Azef left periodically on unexplained "business trips." By now Hedy may have suspected that his interests were unusually shadowy and complex. She knew that he sometimes came to her at night exhausted and worried, and that he would often awaken from nightmares in need of comfort. But it was not until the summer, when they were both back in Germany, that she learned more.

Still fearing to shock her and not wishing to reveal secrets that might expose her to personal danger, Azef revealed himself slowly. Hedy had noticed that he seemed to be on friendly terms with a number of important government officials. He explained that this was because, in addition to doing business with some of them, he had functioned as a confidential advisor to certain government agencies. Prime Minister Stolypin himself had often requested his opinion. . . . Yet, as was well-known, he was an advocate of personal freedom and an opponent of the reactionary, anti-Semitic elements within the regime. In August, he would be taking Hedy with him to London, where he would attend a conference of the Socialist Revolutionary party. He was also an important figure in this party and was still involved in certain affairs that, for her own safety, he could not discuss further. In any case, all these involvements had become too risky and tedious to continue. Soon—very soon—they would conclude, and he and Hedy would be free to make a new life together.

Azef need not have worried about shocking his sweetheart. Hedy's own past did not incline her to moralize about the compromises made by others. Her only thoughts were for his safety and happiness—for an end to the risks that made him nervous and the dreams that made his nights restless. She loved his public assurance and private needs, shared his *joie de vivre,* his appetite for new experiences, admired his business acumen, and appreciated his solicitude for her well-being and indifference to her past. And in her, Azef found the woman he had not thought existed: a person before whom it was not necessary to pretend. With Hedy, all disguises were discarded. No longer must he conceal his tastes for gambling and risky business ventures, his love of pleasure, or his contempt for the authoritarians of the Right and the Left. He could share everything with her, even his memories of a bitter childhood in the Pale of Settlement and Rostov-on-Don. In time, he would tell her so much about himself that, as he wrote much later, "You are the only one of all people who is close to me—so close that there is no longer any difference between us. I don't know where you begin and I end . . . and this is not just a phrase. . . ."

With Hedy, Azef was on the way to becoming what he most deeply needed to be: an individual with his own identity and an ordinary man. His letters to her are filled with childish endearments, and these are echoed in her own, barely literate prose. The ordinary details of a life without pretense made him happier than he had imagined he could be. There was no longer any question of reviving his old duplicitous career, any more than of rejoining his former family. The liaison with Hedy was permanent, as was his break with Russia and its government. Only one task remained—to end his career in style, with an act that might well immortalize him and that would certainly silence his enemies in the revolutionary movement. His real life could begin after he had terminated the czar's.

Azef's most successful assassination plans were carried out in two phases. In the first phase, which only he knew to be an elaborate diversion, he would focus the government's attention on a conspiracy organized by himself or by others—a plot created to be betrayed— and see to it that it was smashed. Then, when the police trusted him implicitly and their agents were off guard, he would implement the real conspiracy, and another czarist monster would disappear. Now that his target was the Supreme Monster—the petulant, vindictive, Jew-hating, Little Father himself—Azef saw no reason to alter his basic *modus operandi*. First, he would betray. Then, he would strike.

In April, when he returned to St. Petersburg with Hedy, allegedly to wind up his affairs, Azef provided Gerasimov with the details of two plots against the czar that he had organized himself. In exchange for this information, the Secret Police chief guaranteed that, in order to make Azef's position absolutely secure, no terrorist or member of the SR Central Committee would be arrested, and any such person "accidentally" taken would be allowed to escape, using methods more subtle than those employed in the case of Karpovich. Both plots could be frustrated, Azef explained, without the necessity for either arrests or police "frightenings." Since Czar Nicholas loved hunting and was relatively unprotected while in the field, he had positioned one terrorist squad in a village in the hunting district near the royal residence at Tsarskoye Selo. Members of the Organization had opened a tea shop there with the intention of attacking the monarch while he was hunting in the nearby woods. To stymie this plan, all that was necessary was for Gerasimov to persuade the czar to hunt this season in some other part of the Russian forest—a suggestion which, coming from the "Man Who Saved the Czar," Nicholas gratefully accepted.

The second conspiracy, far more complex, required more subtle countermeasures to avoid arousing suspicions of betrayal on the terrorists' part. The plan concocted by Azef and betrayed to Gerasimov was to kill the czar while he was traveling to the Estonian capital, Tallinn, for an important meeting with King Edward of England. For this campaign, Azef had organized a larger assassination squad with alternative plans of attack, depending on what route the royal train or yacht took to Tallinn and where the czar stayed during the talks. Arrangements had been made to blow up the train at one of several points that it might pass, to attack his yacht en route to Estonia, or, failing that, to assassinate Nicholas at the home of one of the Estonian barons who was expected to entertain him during his negotiations with the king.

With Azef's help, these plans came to naught, apparently for accidental reasons. The Organization chief himself intercepted a telegram from a sympathizing railroad employee announcing the departure of the czar's train from St. Petersburg and saw to it that his "soldiers" got news of the route too late to act on this information. Another train, which was to carry a terrorist bearing dynamite to Tallinn, was "accidentally" delayed. And Gerasimov persuaded the czar to remain aboard his yacht, *Standard,* rather than visit his friends in the Estonian nobility. Naturally, the yacht was guarded by destroyers and was invulnerable to attack.

Thus was the czar saved once again. Moreover, no untoward incident marred his diplomatic triumph at Tallinn. Stolypin, who had approved Gerasimov's countermeasures, and, of course, Gerasimov himself, were richly rewarded. So was Azef, who had secured Gerasimov's agreement not to interfere with an "expropriation" undertaken by the SRs in Charjui, Turkestan. The proceeds of this bank raid, approximately one hundred thousand rubles, were now in the Organization's treasury, a goodly part of which Azef planned to "expropriate" himself at the proper time. Gerasimov now had no objection when, in June, his agent came to bid him farewell. He was leaving Russia, Azef declared. His career as a police agent was at an end, and he would soon leave the Socialist Revolutionary party as well, but as a personal favor to Stolypin, he would send in such information as he could obtain on the activities of the Central Committee abroad. Gerasimov congratulated him on his fifteen years of distinguished service to the police—something of a record for secret agents—and promised to continue his salary, as a sort of pension, for as long as possible.

Azef may well have had mixed feelings as he left Gerasimov's residence for what he expected would be the last time. The two men had worked closely together for two tumultuous years. Gerasimov understood Azef well, up to a point, and the terrorist no doubt recognized elements of his own character in the Secret Police chief. Both were self-created figures, relying on their wits and will-power to forge unique careers in a time of rapid change and high risk. Both shared a contempt for ideologues, dolts, and bigots of all stripes, and found pleasure in the dangers of covert action. Moreover, politics aside, they seem to have liked each other. This may be one reason why Azef never considered mounting an attack à la Plehve against his supervisor, even though he could easily have done so. But if we can imagine Azef regretting, a little, his departure from Gerasimov, we can also imagine him chuckling at the surprise he was planning for his former control, and for *his* master, Nicholas II. As he gathered up Hedy at their hotel and climbed aboard the train to Berlin, Azef knew that there was another plot against the czar's life in the making—and that this one had a genuine chance to succeed.

In Glasgow, Scotland, a new warship—a cruiser called the *Rurik*—was being constructed by the Vickers shipbuilding company. The ship was one of the first of the new vessels built to replace those sent to the bottom of the Tsushima Strait by the Japanese navy. It was to be delivered to the Russian fleet at the end of the summer, and the czar would come aboard to review it when it arrived at the Kronstadt Naval Base near St. Petersburg. One of the ship's engineers, a dedicated SR and a member of the party's military committee named Konstantin Kostenko, had recruited several of the crew to the revolutionary cause. He sounded them out on their willingness to participate in an attack on the czar and reported to the Central Committee that an attempt on Nicholas's life could be made during his inspection of the cruiser at Kronstadt.

In May, Azef sent his lieutenant, Pyotr Karpovich, to Glasgow by way of Paris. There Karpovich picked up Boris Savinkov, who was quite willing to participate in this novel conspiracy, and the two terrorists arrived in Scotland just as Azef and Hedy were leaving Russia. They remained in Glasgow for six weeks, meeting Kostenko and the sympathetic members of the *Rurik*'s crew and working out a method of attack. In mid-July, Azef, who had left Hedy tempo-

rarily with her family in Germany, joined them, and the real planning began.

Savinkov and Karpovich had originally hoped to find several
sailors willing to shoot the czar when he came aboard the ship, but
there were, at first, no volunteers. Several men offered to assist in
preparing the attack, but none of them—not even a sailor named
Gerasim Avdeyev, who expressed great interest in the plot—considered himself capable of pulling the trigger. Therefore, the two
terrorists had conceived another plan that involved bringing an
Organization man aboard and hiding him in a tiny enclosure that
Avdeyev had discovered near the ship's steering room. Fed and
protected by the revolutionary crew members, the assassin could
make his way from this hiding place up a stairway to a location
that would permit him to blow up most of the upper deck (where
the review was to take place) with a bomb. He could do all this,
that is, if he could stay alive and well in a small enclosure for several
weeks, while the ship sailed from Glasgow through the North Sea,
the Baltic, and the Gulf of Finland to Kronstadt. The only alternative, it seemed, was to smuggle an Organization assassin aboard
at Kronstadt. But since the ship would be heavily guarded, and
climbing aboard at night seemed virtually impossible, this idea did
not appear promising either.

Azef dealt with the problem with customary decisiveness.
Through the helpful engineer, Kostenko, he received the permission
of the commander of the cruiser to visit the *Rurik*. The Organization
chief took a close look at the proposed hiding place and the stairway
to the upper deck, examined the ship's sides, discovered where
guards would normally be posted, and quickly came to the conclusion that the Savinkov/Karpovich plan was unworkable. There was
no alternative but to find a sailor willing to shoot the czar. Soon
after this, Avdeyev came to the terrorists' apartment in Glasgow,
and Azef told him the results of his inspection of the ship. Avdeyev,
who had not met Azef before, was taken aback by his ferocious
appearance and brusque manner, but nevertheless announced, "I
myself will kill the czar at the review. I feel I must do it, and I

will." At once, Karpovich and Savinkov attempted to dissuade him. Could the disciplined sailor really kill his Supreme Commander face-to-face? Could he maintain his silence and mental balance during the long weeks remaining before the ship arrived in Russia? Did he realize that he would almost certainly be executed for the deed, if he were not killed on the spot by the czar's guards? Avdeyev answered all these questions with dogged affirmatives. Then he demanded a revolver, and Azef nodded his assent.

A few days later, a second volunteer appeared—a signaler named Kaptelovich, who was also subjected to an inquisition and given a revolver. Before the *Rurik* left Scotland, both men wrote farewell letters, including photographs of themselves, which Azef kept in order to document the attempt. On August 13, Avdeyev wrote:

> Only now have I begun to understand myself. I will never be a propagandist. After serious reflection, I now feel that I can perform the task with which I have been entrusted. I am happy. I am like a cannon that has been loaded and is waiting to be fired. I am not made for wagging my tongue, for propagandist work, which is what they'd like to have me do on the ship. I feel that I have tightened hard the spring within me, and that I must not any longer interfere with it, if it is not to break.

On the morning of October 7, 1908, the crew of the *Rurik* stood stiffly to attention as Czar Nicholas II came aboard. A cool breeze ruffled the sea off the island of Kronstadt. Avdeyev was glad for the warmth of his sea jacket and for the way it covered the handle of the revolver whose barrel he felt pressing against his thigh. Nicholas, who fancied the navy above all other armed services, was impressive in his naval uniform. Lightly guarded, he began with a tour of the cruiser, examining every part of the ship from the bridge to the engine room. The czar asked knowledgeable questions, and officers leaned forward to catch his murmured comments. He observed an artillery exercise by the ship's gunners, then talked at length with the officers and sailors, and ended by reviewing the entire crew drawn up for his inspection on the upper deck.

At one point, the czar came face-to-face with the signaler, Kaptelovich, who stood frozen to attention as Nicholas caught his eye. A few moments later, he noticed the tall sailor, Avdeyev, and asked him to bring him a glass of champagne. Avdeyev did so, hardly able to breathe. Nicholas noticed his trembling hand and bestowed a kind smile upon him. After dining with the ship's officers, the czar saluted the crew and left, much pleased with the new addition to his fleet. Not a shot had been fired, nor had any other hostile move been made toward him. Azef's last and most ambitious conspiracy had failed.

But why? Two explanations, perhaps not altogether inconsistent, have been offered. According to Savinkov, neither Avdeyev nor Kaptelovich was ready for terrorist work. It was impossible for "a sailor, bound by iron discipline . . . in one month to overcome all qualms and embark upon a deed of the kind for which we had steeled ourselves only after years of painful questioning and hesitation." Savinkov considered it unfair to accuse Avdeyev of lack of courage. "He had had all too little time to overcome his hesitations, and he was compelled to do so under too great a strain. There was nothing remarkable in the fact that the 'spring' cracked." This interpretation is supported by the czarist police official, Spiridovich, who quotes Avdeyev as saying sometime later that his hand simply would not obey him. Perhaps the bearded man in the navy uniform who smiled upon him was too human to resemble the bloody tyrant of revolutionary propaganda. Or perhaps, as Spiridovich says, it was a combination of "military discipline and the prestige of the monarch that foiled the plans of Azef and his associates."

Another explanation is offered by Konstantin Kostenko, the SR engineer. For Kostenko, the key to Avdeyev's failure was to be found in the words of his farewell letter: "I am not made for . . . propagandist work, which is what they'd like to have me do on the ship." The *Rurik,* according to Kostenko, was a hotbed of revolutionary activity. The "they" in this sentence referred to a sailors' organization, dominated by Social Democrats, which was plotting an uprising aboard the cruiser that the conspirators hoped would trigger mutiny throughout the Baltic Fleet. Both Avdeyev and Kaptelovich were members of this group, and when their behavior aroused suspicions that they were planning some action of their own, they yielded and told their comrades the truth. Kostenko believes that the would-be mutineers demanded that they abandon the effort, since an assassination attempt, successful or not, would produce an investigation that would end the possibility of a coordinated uprising in the fleet.

Each explanation may contain a part of the truth. One can imagine Avdeyev and Kaptelovich listening not only to their own doubts and hesitations, but also the voices of their comrades aboard ship. Listening, but not necessarily deciding to abandon their mission of destruction until the last minute when the czar appeared to them in the form of a living, breathing man wearing a uniform not unlike their own . . . and smiling. In all likelihood, military discipline had little to do with their refusal to act. All sailors, from the *Potemkin's* mutinous crew to those planning to set the Baltic Fleet aflame, were subject to the same "iron discipline." What probably stayed Avdeyev's hand was simple empathy—a feeling similar to that which prevented Kaliayev from throwing his bomb when the Grand Duke's carriage passed by bearing his wife and the two children. Savinkov may have been right to say that Avdeyev was not sufficiently inured to killing to overcome this instinct of human identification.

Azef knew how to recruit terrorists who would kill adults face-to-face, but he had not recruited the two sailors. In fact, he had accepted their offers of service at a moment of great desperation. The investigative journalist Burtzev was now accusing him openly of treason to the Organization and the Socialist Revolutionary party. A successful regicide would have answered these charges in one blow. Now, whatever had been the cause of the sailors' inability to shoot the czar, their failure would cost Azef dearly.

TWELVE

A Matter of Credibility

BORIS SAVINKOV'S Paris apartment was an unlikely setting for a trial. As usual, Savinkov had rented a decent place in a quiet bourgeois neighborhood; the house on the Rue La Fontaine was as far as one could get from the "terrorist lair" of popular imagination. But this time, protective coloration had not been his primary motive.

Savinkov had not expected the apartment to be used for party business at all, much less as a revolutionary courtroom. Months earlier, exhausted by a long period of fruitless plotting, he had brought his wife, Vera, and his two children out of Russia to this quiet refuge. Here, he thought, they could finally enjoy a normal domestic life. Here he could digest the experience of the past five years and transmute it into prose. His novel in progress was entitled *Pale Horse,* a reference to the frightening sixth chapter of the Book of Revelation: "And I saw, and behold, a pale horse, and its rider's name was Death, and Hell followed him. . . ." In its pages, the soul of the terrorist became transparent. The novel would explain

Savinkov to himself and to the world—if only he could complete it. June and July had been consumed by his attempt to organize the conspiracy aboard the *Rurik,* and further distractions marred his return to Paris in August. For one thing, Vera was not happy with him, nor he with her. He was not the same man she had married before years of separation and struggle intervened. Then, he had been a dashing young poet, and she the daughter of the famous writer Gleb Uspensky. But now . . . could *any* love, romantic or domestic, survive a terrorist career? Eventually, he would answer this question in his novel, but first he must send Vera and the children back to Russia. It had probably been a mistake to bring them out in the first place.

And then there was this damnable business of the trial.

In August, while the SRs were holding their conference in London, the respected journalist Vladimir Burtzev had sent a letter to a delegate, an old party member named Alexei Teplov, directly accusing Yevno Azef of being an agent of the Secret Police. Burtzev had been airing this charge more or less openly for months, and despite the absence of any "hard" evidence against Azef, he had gained the support of a number of party members. In May, after he made similar accusations to members of the Central Committee, the latter were compelled to establish a "Commission to Inquire into the Rumors of Provocation within the Party." The Commission made a cursory investigation and concluded that, although there *was* evidence that the party had been infiltrated, "so far as Azef is concerned, the rumors of provocation have been shown to be utterly without foundation."

Burtzev's letter to Teplov, however, which was circulated at the London conference, was designed to force the Central Committee's hand. After a stormy meeting, the Committee decided to convene a court of inquiry to try the journalist for libeling Comrade Valentine. The charge against Burtzev was that, by disseminating false rumors about a member of the Central Committee, he had discredited the party and impeded its work. He would be given the chance to prove the truth of his allegations before impartial judges. If he failed, as Viktor Chernov confidently predicted, "Burtzev will be crushed. He will be compelled to repent before the court."

Savinkov considered the decision to conduct an inquiry insulting to the honor of the Fighting Organization. Obviously, these absurd accusations were not worth discussing. As he later wrote:

> I knew Azef as a man of tremendous willpower, strong practical mind, and great executive ability. I saw him at work. I saw his unbending consistency in revolutionary action, his devotion to the revolution, his calm courage as a terrorist, and, finally, his ill-concealed tenderness for his family. I regarded him as a gifted and experienced revolutionist and as a firm, resolute man. This opinion, in general, was shared by all comrades who worked with us, men and women of different character and temperament, the credulous and the skeptical, old revolutionists and youths. . . .

Why give the journalist a platform to spread his poison? The trial would simply feed baseless suspicions, and even a clear decision by the court that they *were* baseless would not end such rumors. Savinkov went to London to plead his case to the Central Committee, but Chernov and Natanson, as well as Azef himself, insisted that there was now no alternative to a hearing. Only a trial could silence Burtzev and his supporters. The court's impartiality and prestige would be guaranteed by appointing as "judges" three revolutionaries of international reputation whose decision all would accept. These were Prince Peter Kropotkin, the great anarchist theorist, now sixty-six and a veteran of countless revolutionary battles; Vera Figner, known in her youth as "the Venus of the Revolution," a member of the People's Will who had spent twenty years in prison for preparing the bombs that killed Alexander II; and Herman Lopatin, another veteran of the People's Will who had been imprisoned for eighteen years in the Schlüsselberg Fortress. Prosecuting the case against Burtzev would be Chernov, Natanson, and—if he agreed—Savinkov. The journalist would defend himself as best he could.

When the SRs' London conference ended, Azef returned to Paris with Hedy. Confident that Burtzev had no solid evidence against him, he proceeded to enjoy Parisian life with his sweetheart, who was now to be seen dining out or at the theater wearing a pair of expensive diamond earrings. Azef proclaimed himself "too disgusted to wallow in the mud which Burtzev is stirring up," and entrusted the defense of his case to Savinkov and his closest party comrades. His friends agreed that he should not dignify the hearing by appearing at it. At the same time, they advised, it would be prudent to send Hedy back to Germany for a while and to spend some time with his wife and children, who were staying for the summer holidays at a resort near Biarritz. A number of the comrades in Paris were somewhat puritanical, Savinkov explained, and did not approve of Azef's taste for pleasure or his attachment to a "notorious woman."

Azef agreed to leave Paris, but he could not remain separated for long from Hedy. At the beginning of September, he joined his family for a short holiday in the Pyrenees. Then he sent them back to Paris, where the school year was beginning, and summoned Hedy by telegram to Biarritz. Was Lubov aware, during this short interlude with her husband, that he had fallen in love with another woman? Considering Azef's behavior in Paris and her many friends there, it is hard to see how she could not have known. Did they discuss the matter? We do not know, but, in all likelihood, the subject that dominated their thoughts and conversation was the forthcoming trial of Burtzev, which, of course, was an inverted trial of Azef. Luba may have had knowledge of her husband's philandering. She may even have accepted it as a concomitant of his life as a revolutionary iconoclast. But she had no doubt at all that he was innocent of the vile charge of treason.

Equally certain of Azef's innocence, Boris Savinkov invited Vladimir Burtzev to Paris, hoping to convince the journalist to retract his accusations and forgo the trial. The two men, who had met previously and who admired each other's work, began by exchanging information. Burtzev told Savinkov about a number of interviews that he had conducted with policemen, former police officials, and spies—men with scores to settle against the czarist regime—in which they alleged that the SRs had been penetrated at the highest level by the secret agent known as Raskin. He reviewed the history of the party and the Fighting Organization, pointing to numerous failures and arrests that could only have been brought about by betrayal. The traitor, it was clear, must be someone on the Central Committee who was also privy to the secret plans of the terrorists.

That Azef was Raskin, said Burtzev, could be proved both indirectly, through a process of elimination of other high-ranking comrades, and directly, by a wealth of convincing, although circumstantial, evidence. For example, his police sources were agreed that the informer was both an engineer and a Jew. Furthermore, according to the disaffected official, Mikhail Bakai, Azef was the only member of the SR Central Committee on whom the secret police kept *no* dossier. Bakai also reported that on the same day in 1904 that Raskin identified a local SR leader to the Warsaw police, Azef was in the city visiting the same comrade. . . .

Savinkov, unconvinced, responded by telling Burtzev the whole story of Azef's career as a terrorist, including much that the journalist had not heard before. Surely, as a dedicated revolutionary himself, as a man whose word was respected throughout the movement, Burtzev would not wish to end such a career! How could he possibly accept the word of police officials and spies against that of a proven revolutionary fighter, the nemesis of Sipyagin, Obolensky, Bogdanovich, von Plehve, Grand Duke Sergei, Dubasov, and others too numerous to mention? Why, even now, the comrades were waiting for news of Azef's latest triumph: the assassination of the czar aboard the new armored cruiser, the *Rurik!* The journalist seemed troubled by this piece of news, as well as by Savinkov's easy dismissal of his carefully prepared evidence. He *knew* that his suspicions of Azef were justified, but he could see how feeble the evidence might seem to a tribunal impressed by Azef's reputation, particularly if the czar were assassinated in the meantime. Burtzev made up his mind to gather additional proof. He bade Savinkov a hasty farewell and left the next day for Germany.

Savinkov was satisfied. He wrote his chief a long letter describing Burtzev's evidence, and Azef responded with an even lengthier diatribe picking apart the case against him. (The journalist's information was, in fact, inaccurate at several points.) "I do not know what else Burtzev may have," Azef wrote.

> Viktor [Chernov] writes that Burtzev is holding in reserve some ultra-sensational "material" that he is keeping secret for the time being in hopes of astonishing the court. But what I know, by god, is that his charges won't bear scrutiny, and that every normal mind must cry out: "Bathe yourself in the mud, but don't dirty others!" I believe that whatever he is keeping secret is of similar quality. It can't be anything other than lies and slander. That is why it seems to me that the court will know how to put an end to this dirty business. And if Burtzev continues to shriek, he will remain the only maniac. . . .

The letter concluded in a temporizing vein:

> Of course, we demean ourselves by going to trial with Burtzev. It is unworthy of us as an organization. But things have gone so far that we must accept this humiliation. It seems to me that we cannot remain silent. You forget the extent of the publicity. However, if you judge it possible to dismiss the matter, I am ready to do so, too—unless it is too late. I am certain that the comrades will go all out to defend the honor of a comrade; that is why I am prepared to yield my own view of this and drop the idea of a trial. . . .
> One thing only I would ask: to be excused from attend-

ing the proceedings. I feel that this would crush me completely. Do what you can to spare me this, if possible. . . .

The Central Committee also might have wished to delay or to cancel the trial, but later in September it received an open letter, alarmingly set up in print, from Burtzev. "To the Central Committee of the Socialist Revolutionary party," it began. "For over a year, in my talks with certain leaders of the party, I have pointed out that the main cause of the arrests that have taken place throughout the existence of the party was the presence on the Central Committee of the engineer Azef, whom I charge with the most vicious treachery, unequaled in the annals of the Russian movement for liberation." Burtzev went on to accuse Azef of causing "the recent executions" (of Trauberg and the members of the Flying Detachment). Finally, he threatened that if the matter were not adjudicated by a court of inquiry, he would take his charges to the press.

Further delay was obviously impossible. The trial of Burtzev was set for the end of October in Paris. In the meantime, Azef waited in Biarritz for the news that Nicholas II had been assassinated at Kronstadt. When Savinkov wrote that the czar's review of the *Rurik* had occurred without incident, Azef was gravely disappointed but not panicked. Although the attempt had failed, he had the letters and photographs of Avdeyev and Kaptelovich in his possession: documentary proof that he had made an all-out attempt to kill the czar. Trusting his comrades to protect his interests in Paris, he traveled with Hedy to San Sebastian in the Basque country, and then on to Madrid, where he could forget the "dirty business" in Paris for a while.

While the lovers toured Spain, Azef's judges (technically, Burtzev's judges) arrived in Paris to hear the case against him. Initially, the court of inquiry met at a private library on the Rue Lhomond, but the sessions were soon moved to Savinkov's apartment. The novelist had arranged the spartan furnishings of his living room to accommodate the tribunal. A table was placed in the middle of the room, with three chairs behind it. Herman Lopatin, as official

chairman, sat in the center, flanked by Peter Kropotkin and Vera
Figner. Vladimir Burtzev, the accused, sat in an armchair to the
right of the judges' table, and to the left sat the accusers, representing
the party: Chernov, Natanson, and Savinkov.

The trial was to last more than one month. For some time, the
tone of the proceedings was relatively calm, almost as if the seven
revolutionary veterans were having one of their customary theoretical discussions. But this mood of amiable mutuality did not last
long.

Burtzev began with a lengthy report detailing at great length
the evidence he had already summarized for Savinkov. He began
in 1901 with the police raid on the party's printing press at
Tomsk—clearly the work of a spy inside the party—and proceeded
to discuss the arrests of party members made in the winter of 1902;
the accusations against Azef by the student, Kristianinov; the betrayal of Serafima Klichoglu's terrorist group in 1903; "Raskin's"
and Azef's simultaneous visits to Warsaw; the mass arrests of 1905;
the "Petersburg letter" accusing "Azief" and "T——" of being
police agents; the "Saratov letter" in which Bakai made similar
charges against Azef; the failed campaigns against Trepov, Grand
Duke Vladimir, Durnovo, Min and Riman, Rachkovsky, Stolypin. . . . By the time he arrived at more recent disasters, in particular
the arrests and executions of Zilberberg, Suliatitsky, and the members of Trauberg's Flying Detachment, Chernov, the lead "prosecutor," was on his feet, his high orator's voice bitterly sarcastic.

What was the source of most of Burtzev's information? Mikhail
Bakai—a man who became a Secret Police official by betraying his
former comrades in the Movement—a man whose word was worth
precisely nothing! What, exactly, *was* the date of Raskin's alleged
visit to Warsaw? (Bakai had been unable to provide it.) Why, if
Azef had betrayed Klichoglu's group to von Plehve, would he then
have had his "employer" assassinated? (Burtzev was unable to answer.) Did Burtzev deny that Azef had organized the attacks on
von Plehve, Grand Duke Sergei, Dubasov, and the czar, among
others? (He did not.) What evidence was there that he had had

anything to do with the recent executions? (There was none.) Who had the most to gain by equating Raskin with Azef and sowing discord in the ranks of the party? Why did Burtzev think that these police officials and spies had agreed to be interviewed by him? Had he never considered that, having failed to destroy the party and the Fighting Organization by other means, the government found a better way to do its work of destruction?

Burtzev's case was seriously damaged by this cross-examination. Chernov then went on the offensive, examining every piece of evidence for flaws and contradictions, throwing doubt on the credibility of Burtzev's sources, and highlighting Azef's outstanding career as a terrorist and revolutionary leader. Marc Natanson followed with an address questioning the journalist's motives and methods, in particular his willingness to discuss the case against Azef with private individuals and members of the party before bringing his suspicions to the attention of the Central Committee. Burtzev answered vehemently; the Committee, he said, had become the captive of its own elitism. Driven by bureaucratic instinct to defend one of its own against attacks by "outsiders," it had been unpardonably negligent in refusing to take the charges against Azef seriously. In reply, Savinkov made a long, eloquent speech demonstrating why the party had always defended Azef against accusations of this sort. He described his chief's career and their association in detail, concluding with a dramatic plea to Burtzev:

> I turn to you, Vladimir Lvovich, as a historian of the Russian Revolutionary movement, and I beg you, now that we have told you of Azef's achievements, to tell us absolutely frankly whether there exists in the history of the Russian Revolutionary movement, already famous for its Zhelybovs, Gershunis, and Sazonovs, or in that of any other country, a more brilliant name than that of Azef.

Up to this point, the judges had listened attentively, and for the most part, dispassionately, to the evidence and arguments presented by both sides. Neither Kropotkin nor Lopatin knew Azef. Both understood how difficult it was to obtain "hard" evidence of police spying, and both were inclined to believe that enough smoke, in cases like this, betokened some sort of fire. (Kropotkin later stated that, in his experience, repeated charges of spying made against some activist by diverse accusers over a period of years invariably proved to be true.) Vera Figner, on the other hand, had known Azef for a long time and admired him greatly. Occasionally, unable to contain her emotions, she glared at Burtzev or smiled approvingly at some sally of Chernov's. At the conclusion of Savinkov's speech, however, all the judges were visibly moved. Figner pointed at Burtzev and said angrily, "Do you know what you will have to do if your accusations are proved groundless? You will have nothing left but to shoot yourself for the harm that you have done to the Revolution!"

Burtzev, meanwhile, seemed to be struggling with himself. After several moments, he spoke in a flat, resigned tone. "I have the evidence of one more witness," he said with evident reluctance. The journalist explained that he had given his word not to use this testimony, and that revealing it publicly might very well cost the witness his freedom . . . perhaps even his life. Now, he continued, he saw that it would be necessary to break his promise—but he would do so only if all those present, both the judges and the SRs, guaranteed the absolute confidentiality of what he was about to reveal. The judges nodded their assent and Chernov snapped, "Yes, yes. Get on with it." Burtzev then told a story that transfixed his listeners.

"You are familiar, I assume, with the former director of police, Alexei Alexandrovich Lopukhin?" All the participants were, indeed, familiar with the former police director's career. They knew that, after Grand Duke Sergei's assassination, General Trepov had called him "Murderer" to his face, and his old enemy, Rachkovsky, had secured his dismissal. They knew, too, that Lopukhin now considered himself a liberal, and that his application for membership in the Constitutional Democratic party had been rejected because of his past association with the police. Burtzev explained that he had left Savinkov's apartment in September convinced that more evidence might be necessary to persuade the tribunal that the great terrorist, Azef, was also a great traitor. He learned that Lopukhin, whom he knew and had previously attempted to interview, was in Germany, and that he was scheduled to board the Eastern Express on September 25 at the Cologne Station, bound for Berlin and St. Petersburg. After leaving Paris, he therefore went directly to Cologne, intending to discuss the matter with Lopukhin.

Burtzev had watched the former police *wunderkind,* now an angry middle-aged man, board the Eastern Express. He took a compartment near Lopukhin's, waited until the train was well under way, and then stopped at the former director's compartment as if recognizing him by chance. Lopukhin welcomed him. The two men chatted about history and literature as they had done several times in St. Petersburg. Then Burtzev turned the subject of conversation to his journal, *Byloe,* which he was now planning to publish in Paris to avoid the Russian censors. He told Lopukhin that he was planning to expose an important police agent who had long played a double role as a top spy for the Secret Police and as leader of the SRs' Fighting Organization. When Lopukhin did not respond, Burtzev asked him the following question: "Will you allow me, Alexei Alexandrovich, to tell you everything that I know about this *agent provocateur,* about his activities in both revolutionary and police circles? I shall give you proofs of the double role he is playing. I shall mention the name by which he is known to the Secret Police as a spy in revolutionary circles, and also his real name. I know everything about him. . . ."

Lopukhin, who was asked only to listen, could not resist the bait. Burtzev launched into a description of Azef's activities, but *without* revealing the agent's name. Combining his own information with what he had learned from Savinkov about Azef's terrorist career, he told the story in such detail that, as Lopukhin later remarked, he was "amazed" at the extent of Burtzev's knowledge of Secret Police methods. The former police director listened without visible emotion to Burtzev's account of Raskin's early exploits, but when he came to the assassinations of von Plehve and of Grand Duke Sergei—the events that ended Lopukhin's career—his eyes widened, and he shook his head as if clearing his mind of cobwebs.

Of course! He had always known that there had been a plot to get rid of him masterminded by Rachkovsky, who soon afterward entered into an alliance with Count Witte. The agent called Raskin must have been working secretly all the while for Witte and Rachkovsky! In fact, Lopukhin concluded, he had probably assassinated von Plehve and the grand duke on their orders. After all, it was Witte who had proposed that the czar be assassinated by a "rogue" agent, and von Plehve who had deprived Rachkovsky of his position as head of the Secret Police's foreign affairs department. . . . To the end of his life, Lopukhin, who did not believe a mere spy to be capable of acting independently of his masters, adhered to this version of the story. But he had still not uttered a word to Burtzev. The latter, determined to provoke him to speak, now told him that Raskin was still active both as a terrorist and a spy, and that he had initiated a plot, which still might succeed, to assassinate the czar. If Lopukhin did not respond, the blood of Nicholas II, not to mention that of countless other government officials and revolutionaries, would be on his hands.

"You as director of the department," Burtzev pleaded, "could not but know the existence of this *agent provocateur*. As you see, I have now completely exposed him. I should like to beg you once more, Alexei Alexandrovich, to allow me to tell you now who hides under the pseudonym of Raskin. And it will only remain for you to say whether I am right or wrong."

Lopukhin did not wait for Burtzev's revelation. "I know nobody by the name of Raskin," he exclaimed, "but I have seen the engineer, Yevno Azef, several times."

As Burtzev uttered these words, the makeshift courtroom seemed to explode. Suddenly, everyone was on his feet shouting. "You gave Azef away!" cried Chernov. "You prompted Lopukhin!"

The old chairman, Herman Lopatin, walked over to Burtzev, put his gnarled hands on the journalist's shoulders, and looked into his eyes. "Give me your word of honor as a revolutionary that you heard these words from Lopukhin," he demanded. Burtzev began to answer, but Lopatin turned away, his eyes filled with tears. "What's the use of talking?" he said hopelessly. "It's all clear now!"

The trial continued, but in an entirely new atmosphere. The presumption of Azef's innocence had vanished. Vera Figner, who still clung to her faith in the Organization's chief, confessed that Burtzev's statement had "dumbfounded" everyone present. Chernov and Savinkov redoubled their efforts to discredit the journalist's testimony, but their arguments now fell flat. At one point, Savinkov asked Herman Lopatin directly for his opinion. "One would be quite justified in killing on such evidence," the chairman replied. Kropotkin was of similar mind. Referring to the traitor who had betrayed the People's Will organization some twenty years earlier, he declared, "Vera Nikolayevna Figner once believed Degayev, too!"

By now it was clear that key witnesses would have to be called to testify directly before the tribunal. The former Secret Police officer, Bakai, had already agreed to appear. He repeated what he had previously told Burtzev, weathered Chernov's cross-examination, and made a favorable impression on the judges. But the indispensable witness, obviously, was Lopukhin. With the consent of Azef's defenders, the tribunal dispatched Alexei Argunov to St. Petersburg to investigate Lopukhin's current relations with the Russian government and to persuade him, if possible, to come to Paris to testify in person. Early in November, the proceedings were temporarily adjourned, and Argunov left by train for Russia.

Azef, meanwhile, had been writing Boris Savinkov in terms that betrayed his increasing anxiety over the course of the trial. "Why question Bakai and witnesses living outside Paris?" he wrote. "However, I suppose you who are closer to the situation know better. I am sure you have the situation well in hand. I think I will take your advice and delay my arrival." Then, a few days later, ". . . much remains incomprehensible to me in this case. I am not criticizing, dear friend, but a great deal remains unclear to me. I suppose that my general frame of mind, my subjectivism, has something to do with it. I do want to be rid of this abomination, and, moreover, I am sick of this constant wandering."

Finally, when the court had adjourned, Azef sent Hedy to her family in Germany and hastened to Paris. He pumped Savinkov and other comrades for information. The participants, of course, were sworn to secrecy about the testimony concerning Lopukhin, but the rumor that there had been a mysterious "sensation" at the hearing had spread, and Azef was obviously interested in running it into the ground. Savinkov insists in his memoirs that he told his chief nothing about Lopukhin. Argunov also disclaims the role of talebearer, although he stopped to speak with Lubov Azef before leaving the city for St. Petersburg. Chernov, Azef's most vociferous defender, might also have been tempted to give his "client" an opportunity to defend himself against secret testimony. In any case, although it is not known who told Azef about Lopukhin's testimony, someone clearly did.

"When God wishes to punish anyone," Azef later wrote about his reaction to this news, "He takes away his reason." In a state of panic unprecedented for him, he told Chernov and Natanson that he was going away for ten days to visit one of his old friends, a party member who lived in Munich. He did go to Munich for a few days, but then—after announcing that he was leaving for Berlin—he took the train to St. Petersburg. At about ten o'clock on the evening of November 24, he presented himself at Lopukhin's apartment in Sergeievskaya Street. There he implored his old employer to save his life by recanting what he had told Burtzev, but Lopukhin would have none of it. He was convinced that Azef, in concert with his enemies in the government, had deliberately destroyed his career.

Finding himself stymied, Azef went the next morning to see Gerasimov. He threw himself upon the mercy of the police chief, recalled his long years of service to the department, and emphasized the embarrassment that the government would suffer if Lopukhin's allegations became public knowledge. Gerasimov agreed to help and then went himself to see Lopukhin. Revealing state secrets, he warned, could subject the former police director to criminal prosecution. Lopukhin, infuriated by this pressure, immediately wrote to several high-ranking officials, revealing that Azef and Gerasimov had come to see him and demanding protection against threats "which endangered his personal security." More important, he agreed to see the court of inquiry's traveling investigator, Alexei Argunov.

Argunov was one of the comrades who believed most firmly in Comrade Valentine's innocence. Together, he and Azef had helped found the Socialist Revolutionary party. He had been arrested by the Secret Police at the end of 1901 and was imprisoned in Siberia, escaping in 1905 to rejoin his comrades at the time of the campaign against Grand Duke Sergei. Argunov obviously had no idea that Azef had been responsible for his arrest. He had gone to Russia convinced that Lopukhin was involved in a government plot to destroy the Organization and the party—a scheme he was determined to expose. Instead, to his horror, he discovered definitive proof of his old comrade's guilt.

Lopukhin told the old revolutionary all he knew about Azef's dealings with the police—considerably more than he had told Burtzev. "The tale unfolded of Azef's activity," Argunov later remembered, "pressed with its crushing weight upon my brain. I wished to find but one weak spot and so tear asunder this ingeniously contrived mesh of evidence. But I failed to find a single false note or contradiction in his account. It breathed of truth." Lopukhin then revealed that both Azef and Gerasimov had visited him to pressure him to recant his testimony, and that he had written letters about these meetings to three government officials. (From another source, Argunov was able to get copies of these letters.) A shaken Argunov asked the former police director to repeat his testimony in London for the benefit of a revolutionary committee of inquiry, and Lopukhin promised to consider the request carefully.

Early in December, Lopukhin arrived in London. He met at

the Waldorf Hotel with Argunov, Savinkov, and Chernov, who found his story wholly convincing. But why did this former czarist official take the risk of coming to London to confer with known revolutionaries—an act that he must have realized was politically and legally dangerous? One explanation, later offered by a cousin of his, suggests that Lopukhin had been terrorized into participating in the Azef inquiry. More than one year earlier, his eighteen-year-old daughter, Varvara, then a student in London, had apparently been kidnapped by persons unknown, held for a few days in an apartment, and then released unharmed to her father, who came to London solely for the purpose of securing her freedom. If, as alleged by Lopukhin's cousin, the kidnapping was the work of SRs allied with Burtzev, this might explain why Lopukhin agreed to cooperate with them later on. There is, however, no evidence that this kidnapping (if that is what it was) was the work of the SRs, or that Lopukhin had any motives other than to repay Azef and Rachkovsky for old injuries suffered and to end the system of provocation, which he believed to be immoral and self-defeating. Lopukhin also seems to have believed that if his role became public, his old friendship with Prime Minister Stolypin would protect him.

Whatever his reasons for participating, the former official's testimony gave new impetus to the investigation. According to Lopukhin, Azef had come to see him on November 24. But Azef had told Chernov and Natanson that he would be in Munich on that date. Therefore, the party leaders dispatched Savinkov to Munich, where he met Azef's friend and learned that the terrorist chief *had* visited that city, but that he had departed, allegedly for Berlin, on November 20 or 21. The comrade also said that he had received a letter from Valentine, postmarked Berlin, on November 22. The Central Committee then instructed Chernov to interrogate Azef about his whereabouts during the period between November 20 and November 26. Azef responded by giving Chernov two Berlin hotel bills, the first of which was genuine, but the second was easily proved to be a forgery. In his unaccustomed panic, Azef had made an elementary mistake. The rooming house where he claimed to have stayed from November 22 until November 26 was managed by a man known by revolutionaries in Berlin to be an employee of the German police. And the description that the manager gave of his tenant bore no resemblance at all to Azef.

The proof was now definite: Azef had not been in Berlin on November 24, but in St. Petersburg, seeking to save his revolutionary reputation and his life. Comrade Valentine, the chief of the Fighting Organization, was also Raskin, the Secret Police's top spy.

The only question now, one would have thought, was how and when to kill the traitor. Boris Savinkov, whose moral universe lay in ruins, favored immediate execution. But of the fifteen or so leading party members assembled in Paris by the Central Committee early in January 1909, only four, Savinkov included, voted for immediate death. One member of the Central Committee, Marc Natanson, still thought that Azef might justify himself. The others, although convinced of his guilt, worried that a violent act against him on French soil would provoke official retaliation against the SRs residing in Paris. Most important, they feared that executing Azef summarily, without publishing the evidence against him, would generate internal warfare in the party. Chernov had already received a letter from Pyotr Karpovich in St. Petersburg threatening to "shoot the whole of the Central Committee" if it "dared to touch Azef." The party as a whole, it seemed, was not ready to accept a verdict of guilt rendered by its own leaders. Therefore, the Central Committee decided to interrogate Azef further with a view to extracting a confession from him. At the same time, Argunov was instructed to rent a secluded villa across the French border in Italy. At the appropriate time, Chernov and Savinkov would take Azef across the border and kill him.

Late on the evening of January 5, Chernov, Savinkov, and a third SR terrorist named Panov rang at Azef's apartment at 245 Boulevard Raspail. The interrogators carried no weapons; they had been forbidden to execute the traitor and had decided to go unarmed in case they were tempted to kill him on the spot. Azef admitted the three men and led them into his study. Sensing immediately that he was in serious trouble, he seated himself at a table near a window and asked, "What's the matter, gentlemen?"

Chernov handed him a document—the accusatory letter by Bakai—and asked him to read it. Then, speaking slowly and deliberately, he declared, "We have learned that on November 24 you were at Lopukhin's in St. Petersburg."

"I was not at Lopukhin's," Azef answered.

"Where were you?"

"I was in Berlin."

"At what hotel?"

"First, at the Fürstenhof, and then at the Kertch."

"We know you were not at the Kertch."

"How ridiculous! I was there."

"You were not there."

"I *was* there. But what kind of conversation is this? My past is my defense."

At this, Savinkov broke in. "You say your past is your defense. Very well. Tell us the details of the attempt on Dubasov."

Azef answered. His account of the Dubasov operation differed in some respects from the information provided by other participants, but the discrepancies were not serious. Savinkov drew blood, however, by inquiring about Azef's near-arrest at Filipov's restaurant immediately following the assassination attempt.

"You say you were in Filipov's pastry shop?" he asked.

"Yes."

"You were trapped inside the police cordon?"

"No."

"You told Argunov you were trapped but were released after showing the police a foreign passport."

"I did not tell Argunov that."

"So, Argunov lied?"

"No."

"So, you are not telling the truth?"

"No, I *am* telling the truth."

"Where is the explanation?"

"I don't know. . . ."

Now Chernov resumed the questioning, leading the rattled defendant into a tangled thicket of lies, evasions, and contradictions about his sojourn in Berlin and his trip (which he denied making) to St. Petersburg. Azef waited anxiously for a pistol to appear in someone's hand, but as question followed question on various subjects, he realized with a rush of relief that his visitors had not come to execute him but to persuade him to confess. Sensing weakness in his accusers, he went on the attack. Of course, he was confused, he declared. Who would not be upset, after so many years of service to the party, to be attacked so viciously by his closest comrades? "Viktor," he pleaded, looking Chernov in the eyes, "we have been such good friends for so many years. We worked together. You know me. How could you come to me with such vile suspicions?"

"If I came," replied Chernov painfully, "that means I had to come." The party chief urged Azef to make a clean breast of the affair. "Tell us frankly about your relations with the police. We have no need to ruin you and your family." The latter, however, had no intention of confessing. Instead, he promised to come to Chernov's apartment before noon the next day and to make a full explanation that would satisfy all the comrades present. "Very well," Chernov replied. "Tomorrow at noon," added Savinkov menacingly, "we shall consider ourselves free of all obligations."

Shortly before two o'clock in the morning, the interrogators left the apartment. For reasons that have never been explained, these experienced terrorists neither confiscated Azef's papers nor posted a guard outside his apartment; they simply went home to bed. Perhaps, even now, they believed that he would recognize the moral authority of the party and appear at Chernov's house the next morning. Or it may be that they wanted half-consciously to give him the chance to escape. Azef's flight would be tantamount to a confession, ending all doubt in the party as to his guilt—and it would also relieve his comrades of the duty to execute him immediately. In any case, the condemned man quickly packed a small suitcase, explaining to his terrified wife that he must leave to gather proof of his innocence before "they" killed him. He destroyed some of his papers, placed the remainder in his suitcase, and left one document prominently displayed on his writing desk: the farewell letter and photograph sent by the sailor Avdeyev before embarking on his quest to kill the czar.

At half past three in the morning, Azef kissed his sleeping children good-bye and rode with Lubov to the railroad station to board the first train to Germany. He and his wife embraced. Promising to return as soon as possible, he left her a forwarding address in Vienna. But his first stop was not Vienna; it was the little Saxon town of Friedrichsdorf, where Hedy had been waiting for him since the beginning of November. His political career was over, he told his lover, embracing her warmly. They would never be separated again.

THIRTEEN

The Final Gamble

AZEF'S FLIGHT gave one person, at least, cause to rejoice: Vladimir Burtzev was entirely vindicated. The Socialist Revolutionaries dropped their charges against him, and the court of inquiry later congratulated the journalist publicly on his "disinterested and audacious efforts to uncover the truth." Other parties concerned, however, were stunned by this implicit admission of guilt. A few days after Azef's disappearance, the SR Central Committee published the following notice:

> The Central Committee of the Socialist Revolutionary party wishes all comrades of the party to know that the engineer Yevno Filipovich Azef, 38 years of age (party names: "The Fat One," "Ivan Nikolayevich," "Valentine Kuzmich"), a member of the Socialist Revolutionary party since its foundation, elected several times to the party's central institutions, a member of the Fighting Organization and of the Central Committee, has been convicted of having entered into

relations with the Russian political police and is hereby declared a provocateur. Having disappeared before the end
of the open proceedings against him, Azef, because of his
personal qualities, is considered extremely dangerous to
the party. A detailed account of his activities as a provo-   .
cateur and further information about him will be published
shortly.

The Central Committee sentenced Azef to death in absentia.
Several weeks later, a party communiqué describing his career in
detail created a worldwide sensation. Articles on the "Azef Affair,"
many with photographs or drawings of the terrorist/spy and other
leading characters in the drama, appeared in newspapers and journals throughout Europe and North America. Many of these accounts
focused on Azef's personality, emphasizing the satanic character of
the man they now called the "Russian Judas." According to *The
North American Review,* for example, Azef was "an engineer by
profession, a libertine by nature, and a systematic destroyer of human
life by choice. His baseness and callousness, which knew no bounds,
excite universal horror and disgust." But the Azef Affair also provided the definitive exposé of the "Russian system of provocation,"
which was roundly condemned by writers and political figures
throughout the West. It served to reinforce the image of the czar's
government as a barbaric, police-ridden autocracy, and gave even
the Kaiser's regime cause to congratulate itself on its relative liberalism.

The tendency of these commentaries, which shaped the later
literature about Azef, was to picture the terrorist chief as a police
agent above all, and to underplay or ignore his independent motives
for attacking czarist officials. It was almost as if the Russian regime's
liberal critics had accepted the myth of Secret Police omnipotence.
No one wished to consider that Azef might have played a role as
independent of the government as of the SRs. Several journals suggested that he had been secretly controlled by a dissident faction at
the Russian court. Somewhat more judiciously, Herman Rosenthal

summarized the case for the readers of *The American Review of Reviews:*

> Azef, the all-powerful leader of the Russian bomb-throwing organization, was an *agent-provocateur* of the Russian Government. He entered the various secret committees and organizations of the revolutionists with the knowledge of the secret police, who paid part of the expenses of the plots laid by him against both sides, the government officials as well as the plotters, who in most cases acted as his tools. In this way the Russian Government became itself one with the bomb-throwers, and provoked the young Russian idealists to the crimes for which they were then shot or hanged by court-martial or even without trial of any kind.

In Russia itself, Azef's exposure exploded with more force than any Organization bomb. The czarist government, humiliated abroad, now found itself under attack from all quarters within the country as well. Again, it was Azef's role as a police spy rather than as Russia's most effective terrorist that fascinated most observers. The Social Democrats charged that, through him, the czar's henchmen had assassinated their own colleagues in order to justify their policy of violent repression. The Constitutional Democrats demanded a full accounting of the "extra-legal activities" of all the government's secret agents. And the conservatives were furious that the secret police had been used to rid the country of its most orthodox leaders. Compelled to respond to these charges in the Duma, Prime Minister Stolypin admitted that Azef had been employed by the police since his student days in Germany, but refused to apologize for making use of his services. For his own reasons, Stolypin, too, accepted the prevailing view that Azef had been a police agent at heart. He had nothing to say about alleged acts of terrorism, the prime minister declared, but he considered Yevno Azef to have been "a true servant of Russia."

Behind the scenes, however, Stolypin's government moved to

avenge itself against those responsible for this embarrassment. Its first victim was Alexei Lopukhin. Gerasimov's threats had not been empty ones; Lopukhin's trial was approved by the czar himself in order to make an example of government officials who dared "collaborate" with revolutionary groups. Against all the evidence, the former police director was accused of *belonging* to the Socialist Revolutionary party and aiding it in its work. His trial—one of the speediest on record—was nominally public, but the court prevented him from making statements that would have placed responsibility for Azef's treachery on his chief "protectors," Stolypin and Rachkovsky. (Lopukhin was also prepared to accuse the police, with the knowledge of these two officials, of fomenting murderous pogroms against the Jews.) Notwithstanding protests by opposition leaders and foreign representatives, the former police director was convicted and sentenced to five years' imprisonment at hard labor. Although his sentence was later reduced, he spent the next three and a half years in Siberian exile, regaining his civil rights only in February 1913.

Lopukhin was the official scapegoat for the Azef Affair, but no one who had been close to the "true servant of Russia" escaped unscathed. The rumor that Rachkovsky had used Azef to assassinate his political enemies ruined what remained of the old man's career. The once-feared Secret Police chief now became a police suspect, to be followed everywhere by the agents he once commanded. Even his house was searched, and he went to his grave an angry and disappointed man.

Aleksandr Gerasimov's fall was even more precipitous. Although Stolypin had promised to protect him, Gerasimov was suspended from office because of suspicions aroused by Azef's exposure. Months later, his reputation suffered irreparable damage when a young SR named Aleksandr Petrov assassinated Colonel Karpov, the new chief of the St. Petersburg Secret Police. Petrov, who had pretended to enter into the service of the police while in prison, had originally hoped to kill Gerasimov, but when arrested for the Karpov murder, he found another way to bring Gerasimov down: he stated that he had committed the assassination on his orders! So poisoned was the atmosphere by suspicion and distrust that Gerasimov—"the Man Who Saved the Czar"—escaped a court-martial only through the prime minister's personal intervention. In this way, Azef, who had hoped to revenge himself on his Secret Police masters by killing the czar, had his revenge after all. His exposure brought the Russian police system into international disrepute, eliminated its most talented administrators, and generated such distrust within the government that the department never regained its former prestige or freedom of action.

The effect of the Azef Affair on the SRs and the terrorist movement was, if anything, more profound. The Central Committee, under heavy attack for failing to investigate earlier charges against Azef and for defending him against Burtzev, submitted its collective resignation and was replaced. Vladimir Zenzinov, who visited the local party centers throughout Russia in the spring of 1909, found the SRs in utter disarray. This decline had begun even before Azef's exposure, for reasons having to do with Stolypin's double-barreled policy of repression and reform. Still, Zenzinov reported that:

> What was most intolerable was the sense of psychological breakdown that one felt during the meetings with the comrades and that shaped the atmosphere in which they were compelled to work. One had the clear feeling that Azef's treason had plowed a deep furrow in the psychology of the party workers. This was one of the most painful feelings that I have ever experienced during the course of my work for society.

In the wake of the scandal, the Socialist Revolutionary party split openly on the subject of terrorism. To some members, Azef's treason demonstrated the utter futility of small-group violence, while others (including Boris Savinkov) insisted upon "rehabilitating the honor of the terror." The party Council, siding with the pro-terrorist

forces, asked Savinkov to "re-create" a Fighting Organization composed of members of his own choosing, but the ex-lieutenant's efforts
to replace his old chief failed miserably. Three of the twelve terrorists
whom he recruited turned out to be police agents, and Savinkov
himself, exhausted and demoralized, spent the better part of three
years gambling with party funds and debauching himself in Paris.
He would not cross the Russian border again until 1917, when for
a short time he became deputy minister of war in the revolutionary
Kerensky government.

Of course, terrorism did not cease altogether after Azef's flight.
During the next two years, local SR groups mounted several attacks
on prosecutors and prison officials, and on September 1, 1911, a
former anarchist and police spy named Dmitri Bogrov, who claimed
to be an SR, gained access to the St. Petersburg opera house during
a performance attended by Stolypin and killed the prime minister
by shooting him in the chest. Writing for the *New York Times,*
reporter Herman Bernstein asked, rhetorically, who was responsible
for this assassination. "The real answer," he asserted, "is Stolypin
himself. Stolypin encouraged a system of spying and provocation,
the small Azeffs and the big ones developed during his regime, and
Stolypin himself defended in the Duma the archtraitor Eugene
Azeff, who plotted and organized the assassinations of Grand Duke
Sergius and Von Plehve." But this was the last terrorist act of any
significance before world war and revolution changed the face of
Russian politics altogether. As one commentator put it, referring to
the effects of Azef's exposure on the party, "In these circumstances,
the terror as a method of fighting became both politically and psychologically impossible."

And what of Azef? Trusting the effects of shock and of his
own flight to paralyze the Organization, at least temporarily, he left
Germany with Hedy and spent the first half of 1909 traveling with
her in Italy, Greece, and Egypt. The previous December, Gerasimov
had provided him with several passports, which he used freely,

changing them so often that Hedy found it difficult to remember her current name. Azef's photograph could be found in countless newspapers, and since both the Secret Police and the SRs might well be searching for him, he exercised great caution, checking the registers at the hotels where he and Hedy stayed for Russian names, and leaving if any other Russian guests were registered. On several occasions, Hedy later remembered, he would return home apparently shaken by some encounter with a suspicious person and insist that they move immediately to another city. Even so, she recalled, the trip was like a honeymoon. Their enjoyment of each other unabated, the couple traveled in style, resting at the best hotels, visiting the Greek islands, and marveling at the ruins of Egyptian Luxor. The summer found them touring the Scandinavian countries. Only in the autumn did they decide that it was safe to settle permanently in one place.

Their choice, somewhat surprisingly, was Berlin. Of course, Germany was Hedy's native land and (since his student days) Azef's second home. Both were fluent in German, and Azef had liked the country well enough to consider accepting a job there after receiving his degree. Furthermore, Berlin was on the way to challenging London's primacy as the financial capital of Europe. There a "respectable stockbroker" could find security, as well as the opportunity to prosper and enjoy the life of a cultured bourgeois gentleman. But Azef's new home was not only one of the world's leading centers of trade and culture, it was also the capital of an ambitious Great Power, a center of revolutionary agitation and political intrigue, a mecca for travelers and refugees of various nationalities . . . in short, rather a public place in which to become anonymous. It seems clear, then, that the decision to settle in Berlin represented another calculated risk. Not for Azef the sleepy sanctuary of some out-of-the-way retreat. He would make his life in this thriving city as "Alexander Neumayer, Merchant" and deal in time with the ever-present danger of hostile recognition.

If there were clouds on the horizon, they did not at first disturb the tranquil existence of Herr Neumayer and his devoted *frau*.

Azef's savings from his engineer's salary, his work for the police, and, very likely, the proceeds of his "expropriation" of Organization funds were substantial. After decorating his new six-room apartment in the fashionable Wilmersdorf neighborhood, adorning Hedy with clothes and jewelry, and setting aside a large allowance for her use, there still remained approximately 100,000 marks (over $400,000 in our terms) to invest in his new business. Hedy was delighted with their new home, which contained a grand piano on which she could accompany herself while singing. She and "Herr Neumayer" made influential friends, dined out often, and entertained liberally. His appetite for risk was satisfied by his professional activity as a stockbroker, at which he was successful, and by occasional gambling sprees at the casinos on the French Riviera. Although Azef had again assumed a new identity, it was no longer a mask. He *was* the merchant Neumayer, beloved by his Hedy, and for the first time in his life he was at peace.

For about one year this peace was undisturbed, except for worries about Lubov and the children, who had remained in Paris. Azef's affection for his family was not feigned. He felt a keen sense of responsibility for them, and had supplied Luba with funds for their support after leaving France. (He also wrote Gerasimov asking the police to provide for his family if he were killed by the SRs.) Shortly after his flight, his wife had written him an anguished letter urging him to establish his innocence quickly, since she and the children were already being treated as pariahs even by their best friends. After the story of her husband's career became public knowledge, however, it became clear that he would not return to her and that their marriage was at an end. Luba stopped trying to contact him, and Azef's letters to her went unanswered. Cut off from information about his family, he took a desperate step. Late one night (the date is uncertain, although it was probably in 1912), he visited her at their Paris apartment. According to Lubov, he offered her advice and money, whereupon, shaking with fury, she found the revolver he had left in the house, aimed it at him, and banished him from her home. That was their last encounter. Not long afterward, she left with the children for America.

While his wife remained in Paris, however, Azef used her as a conduit for information that he wished conveyed to the SRs. Beginning in the winter of 1910–1911, he wrote asking her to contact his old comrades and to tell them that he was now willing to appear before a party court. He had always acted in the interests of the Revolution, he said, and would convince the party leaders of this if he were given the chance to tell his whole story. If, in the end, the tribunal decided to execute him, he would save it the trouble by taking his own life.

Azef's motives for making this offer are unclear. On the one hand, he may have gotten wind of the fact that the revolutionaries had renewed their hunt for him. Acting on a rumor that the notorious traitor was in Berlin, a group of German and Russian Social Democrats led by the famous Marxist, Karl Liebknecht, had begun a systematic search for him, and Azef may have hoped that an offer to talk would at least prevent the SRs' death sentence from being carried out. On the other hand, even without knowledge of this particular danger, he seemed to have felt a growing need to have his case closed. His and Hedy's happiness could not be complete while he remained a fugitive. Sooner or later, someone would recognize him. Before a possibly fatal confrontation took place, he wanted the chance to present his own version of the "Azef Affair" to the public—especially to the revolutionary groups that sought his death.

That opportunity arrived in August 1912. Some weeks earlier, Azef had been a guest at a health spa near Nauheim, Germany, a resort he visited frequently despite the fact that Russian guests sometimes came there as well. One day in July, without his knowledge, he *was* recognized by a Russian who made a note of his Berlin address and gave this information to his old nemesis, the radical journalist Vladimir Burtzev. Several weeks later, he received a letter from Burtzev demanding a meeting. He would not inform the party of his whereabouts, Burtzev said, so long as Azef agreed to talk with him for the sake of the historical record. Azef replied immediately: "Your suggestion that we should meet coincides with my own long-standing desire that the truth about me should be told." Their encounter was set for August 15 in the Café Bristol in Frankfurt. But first, Azef sold his flat, stored his furniture, and sent Hedy back to her mother in Saxony. Burtzev, he felt, was a man of his word . . . but he had not survived this long by taking unnecessary chances. Who else might have learned his Berlin address or discovered the time and place of the meeting in Frankfurt? He made a new will leaving all his property to Hedy before leaving for his reunion with Burtzev.

These security precautions proved unnecessary. The journalist had come for a story, not an execution, and the world learned its contents several months later in an exclusive article that was widely published. The conversation—for the most part, a monologue by Azef—took place over the greater part of two days.

The ex-terrorist's story was designed to convince Burtzev's readers that he had been, at heart, a dedicated revolutionary, and that since leaving Russia he had had no further contact with the police. As far as it went, in fact, his tale made considerable sense. Azef stated that he had originally entered the service of the Secret Police while a student in Germany, but that, after meeting Lubov and the Socialist Revolutionary leaders, he had been converted to the revolutionary cause. The problem, he said, was that revealing his prior police connections would compromise him in the eyes of the comrades and end his career as a revolutionary activist. As a result, he decided to use his position as a police agent to facilitate the party's terrorist campaigns. He had hoped to accomplish such heroic deeds that his past could be revealed and, once revealed, forgiven. But each assassination campaign involved him more deeply with the police. Finally, he recognized that he could only tell the truth about his double game after he had committed the ultimate terrorist act: the assassination of the czar. Burtzev's campaign against him, however, had ended his own campaign against Nicholas II. "If it had not been for you," he told the journalist with a flash of anger, "I *would* have killed him."

Azef was at his most persuasive, and Burtzev took his explanation seriously, although certain aspects of the account puzzled him. He suspected that the double agent might be concealing certain facts, but, more important, he was astonished by his subject's lack of moral qualms when describing the betrayals of his party comrades. Azef's main theme was that his revolutionary strategy had worked: he had done enormous damage to the czarist regime while delivering only insignificant blows to the party. Holding his hands before him as if they were scales, he argued earnestly, "Do you think the two can be compared? What did I do? I organized the assassination of von Plehve, that of the Grand Duke Sergei"—here his right hand dropped lower, as if weighed down by these important victims— "and whom did I give to the police? Only Sletov, Lomov, Vedenyapin"—here his right hand rose slightly, illustrating the insignificance of these names. Burtzev began to object that he was overlooking a matter of principle; one simply could not weigh lives in this manner. But Azef stared at him as if astonished, and the journalist failed to complete his argument.

To Burtzev, this stare of incomprehension was evidence of Azef's essential amorality. The value of a life, it seemed, meant nothing to him. From Azef's perspective, however, Burtzev's objection was childish; it was his interrogator who did not understand the morality of terrorism. Of course, one could "weigh" lives! Wasn't that the essence of the terrorist project? The Central Committee declared that Minister X was worth killing, even at the price of several terrorist lives, because his death would advance the interests of the Revolution. But General Y was to be spared because the effects of his death would not justify sacrificing the life of even one revolutionary. Such calculations were made every day both by revolutionaries and by "statesmen" in power. Burtzev's objections, therefore, were not based on the value of human life (which, as a pro-terrorist writer, he must have deemed "weighable"), but on Azef's individualism—his failure to work exclusively for the SRs—

and on his willingness to "sacrifice" party members, without their knowledge, for the sake of the Revolution. To Azef, Burtzev's principles must have seemed purely sentimental. Why, after all, should some socialist fanatic's life be worth more than that of, say, Gerasimov? And what god had decided that only the Socialist Revolutionary party had the right to make such an evaluation?

Azef and Burtzev did not, therefore, find themselves on common ground. Still, through his interview, Azef succeeded both in publicizing his version of the story and in convincing the SRs that he was no longer dangerous to the party. Burtzev reported that Azef had apparently severed his relations with the Secret Police and that he was willing to make his extensive knowledge of police personnel and methods available to the party. He repeated Azef's declaration that he was willing to stand trial before a party tribunal and to accept its judgment, and presented him as a man who should either be tried by the SRs or left alone, but not executed outright like a common murderer.

Azef's strategy worked; the party decided not to pursue him actively, at least for the time being, and Burtzev kept his promise of confidentiality. Even so, Azef spent the next few months moving about Germany to throw possible pursuers off his track. During the winter of 1912–1913, the Balkan Wars brought him back to the Berlin Stock Exchange to take care of his investments, but he lived alone in the city, frequently changing his passports and addresses, and visiting Hedy when possible at her mother's house in the country. It was not until autumn 1913 that he felt secure enough to reestablish his household in Berlin. As soon as Hedy had found a new apartment and taken their furniture out of storage, the "Alexander Neumayers" resumed their interrupted lives.

Once again, all was well. Azef and Hedy were reunited, and for the first time he did not feel it necessary to look constantly over his shoulder. The SRs had clearly abandoned their campaign against him, and with wars raging throughout the Balkans, the Secret Police's foreign affairs department had better things to do than rake up old scandals by hunting him down. Moreover, the Balkan Wars had done Azef an additional favor: the price fluctuations they caused on the stock market made trading on the Berlin Exchange as interesting as gambling at Monte Carlo. Impressed by Russia's economic growth, and betting on a favorable outcome for Russian interests in the current wars, Azef invested heavily in Russian bonds. At one point in 1913, he was down 14,000 marks, but he soon made that sum back and more. Even the following year, when talk of a European-wide war reached a crescendo, his position seemed secure enough. War talk had been ceaseless in Europe since 1910. Either there would be no general war, Azef reasoned, or Russia would stay out of it. The czar's peasant army, which had been crushed by the Japanese ten years earlier, was hardly a match for the German war machine. Surely, the timid Nicholas II would not commit military suicide by challenging German power!

Azef was not alone in these sentiments. Even after the assassination of the Austrian Archduke Ferdinand and his wife at Sarajevo, there was no great rush by Berlin traders to liquidate Russian bonds. But one can imagine the gods laughing as the man who had once hoped to kill the czar staked his fortune on the rationality of the czarist government. When war between Germany and Russia broke out in August 1914, trading in Russian bonds was forbidden on the Berlin Exchange, and Azef lost almost his entire fortune. He conferred with Hedy, and together, the two adventurers decided to make a fight to maintain their standard of living. They liquidated Azef's remaining holdings, sold part of Hedy's jewelry, and opened a fashionable corset shop in her name.

Comrade Valentine a *corsetier!* What others might have deemed either a tragedy or a farce, Azef and Hedy considered a challenge. He kept the books and made the commercial decisions; she supervised the shop and did the selling; and the enterprise was immediately successful. Indeed, working as a team with his beloved wife (for that is how Azef thought of Hedy and presented her) gave him more pleasure than occupying his seat on the Stock Exchange. For the better part of one year, while millions perished in Europe's most savage war, fortune smiled on the "Neumayers." But the war would soon deliver Azef a blow from which he could not recover.

On the evening of June 11, 1915, Azef returned home trembling with anxiety and furious with himself. Against his better judgment, he had stopped for a drink in a café on the Friedrichstrasse, and a man there who seemed vaguely familiar had called him by his real name. "He recognized me," Azef told Hedy despairingly, "and now I am in for it. . . ." She attempted to reassure him, but he spent the evening going through his papers and burning most of them. Only a few documents, including the plans for an airplane drawn up in 1906 by the inventor, Buchalo, were preserved. On the following day, on their way home from work, he and Hedy were accosted by a man who turned back the lapel of his coat, revealing a police badge. Azef was arrested, charged with being an enemy alien dangerous to the security of Germany, and immediately thrown into Moabit prison.

But why? The obvious reason, or so it seemed, was that the German authorities, now at war, considered him an agent of the Russian enemy. For months, while Hedy struggled to keep their business going, Azef repeatedly petitioned his captors, insisting that he had long ago ceased working for the Russian government and demanding that they ascertain the truth by contacting responsible officials. But his petitions went unanswered. Meanwhile, the atrocious conditions of his imprisonment undermined his health. From June until Christmas 1915, he was kept in solitary confinement in a cold, damp cell, without the right to receive visitors, to converse with other prisoners, or to read the daily newspapers. (The cell was dark as well until October, when he was provided with a gas lamp that he was allowed to use until eight o'clock in the evening.) Fighting to maintain his mental balance, Azef kept his mind and spirit alive by reading books sent by Hedy and corresponding with her.

Azef's letters professed his great love for Hedy ("You are my

beloved—the only one interested in me. All around me is a desert.")
She answered, bewailing her loneliness and describing the financial
reverses that were beginning to impair their business. He replied
with anguish: "Your tears tear my heart apart." In a more sanguine
mood, he offered business advice: the war will be long and hard.
Hedy should order corsets in smaller sizes to reflect the effects of
wartime rationing! Perhaps for the benefit of the prison censors, his
letters also referred with increasing frequency to God and to the
lessons of "Christian patience" which he claimed to be learning. In
November, he sent Hedy "an entire table of applied morality" that
he had compiled for the use of businessmen like himself. "Write
only what you can put your signature to," a typical homily states,
almost as if he were lecturing his earlier self. "Do only what you
can talk about. . . . Don't despise people . . . pity them." Meanwhile,
he read Italian and French grammars, books on electrical engineering, novels, and studies of law and criminality. He asked Hedy
to send him only one work of philosophy, a favorite from his own
library (and hardly a work of Christian piety): Max Stirner's defense
of radical individualism, *The Ego and Its Own*.

By late November, Azef's hopes for an early release had vanished. In a state of panic, he addressed an urgent appeal to the
director of the Berlin police, asking that "his case should be investigated and that he should be set at liberty an innocent man." Again,
he insisted that for seven years he had had no contact with the
Russian government or with the Secret Police. The police director's
reply several weeks later astounded him. He had been arrested, it
appeared, *not* because he was considered a Russian agent, but because
the German police believed him to be an "anarchist" and a "dangerous terrorist"—a belief his previous letters had done little to
dispel. Azef responded immediately; obviously, he had never been
an "anarchist"! He had been a member of the Socialist Revolutionary
party, which he had joined on the orders of the Russian government.
Everything he had done in Russia he had done at the request of
the police. Did not the German government know of Stolypin's
speech to the Duma, calling him a "true servant of Russia"? "For

the past seven years," he wrote, "I have been living in Berlin as a peaceful merchant, removed from any politics, striving only to forget my fatal past and to earn my bread in a decent manner." When the police director remained unmoved, Azef sent Hedy to the Spanish Embassy to file an appeal for his freedom through the Spanish consul. But this appeal was also denied on the ground that he was "undoubtedly an anarchist, and moreover an upholder of the terror." Evidently, the authorities were prepared to keep him in prison until the war ended.

At Christmas, 1915, for unexplained reasons, the conditions of Azef's imprisonment improved. He was permitted to receive visitors and to read newspapers, as well as to travel in the city in the company of a guard. The opportunity to see Hedy again cheered him immensely: "My body is sick," he wrote to her after one visit, "but my soul is healthy." His physical condition soon worsened, however, and in April 1916, complaining of fatigue and excruciating back pain, he was transferred to the prison hospital, where he was again placed in solitary confinement. He would remain in the hospital for the next twenty months. Shattered by this reversal, Azef lost the ability to read and work. "I cannot work with my mind," he wrote Hedy in despair. "I cannot exchange a word with anybody for weeks on end." He slept constantly, unable to exercise, rousing himself only to write to his beloved. "I have already been without you for two years. It's too swinish for anything!"

By October, Azef had lost more than thirty pounds and could not walk without losing his breath. He had struck bottom. Now, forgetting the prison censor, he wrote of his fury at being unjustly imprisoned and his identification with those so disillusioned as to have lost all respect for humanity. Strangely, Azef's mental anguish seems to have been intensified by the *absence* of guilt for past deeds of violence; unlike Dostoyevsky's heroes, he was not conscious of any sin requiring expiation. He was driven even to compare himself to Lieutenant Alfred Dreyfus, the innocent French Jew victimized by an anti-Semitic plot. "The greatest misfortune that could befall anybody has come upon me—a misfortune that can only be compared with that of Dreyfus." Justice, he concluded, was a mere illusion. Hedy's plight no doubt contributed to his bleak frame of mind. With the corset shop out of business, she had sold the rest of her jewelry and was now existing on what little remained of the proceeds. Devoted as ever, she left her weekly ration of bread and cheese for Azef at the hospital and went to eat in a communal dining room.

Only one thing could revive the prisoner: the expectation of peace, and with it, of release. The Revolution of February 1917, which overthrew the czarist regime in Russia, at first left him unmoved, since the Provisional Government of Prime Minister Kerensky insisted on prosecuting the war. But as hopes for an armistice rose in the spring, some of his old optimism returned. He compared Russia with an unfinished building, expressing regret that he could not "help in the work of completing this building." Soon he was identifying the cause of the Russian Revolution with that of international peace. He quoted Tolstoy: "Russia will bring mankind peace. *Ex oriente lux.*" And in June, he declared, "Only revolutionary Russia is unselfish; peace does not yet rest on solid ground." Once again, Azef wrote Hedy long letters advising her how to invest her small income. In the autumn, food packages from the Red Cross and other charitable sources began to arrive, and he felt himself growing stronger. One package, in particular, fascinated him; an unknown woman in Moscow—evidently an intellectual—had mailed him dried flowers, tea, delicacies, and books! He never discovered the identity of this anonymous benefactor.

In Russia, Kerensky's failure to end the war with Germany had doomed his regime, and when Lenin's Bolsheviks took power in November under the banner of "Peace, Land, and Bread," Azef knew that his own liberation was near. One month later, peace talks between Germany and the Soviet regime began in Brest-Litovsk, Poland, and a temporary armistice was arranged, providing (among other things) for the release of civilian prisoners. Azef wrote his last letter to Hedy on December 10, 1917, and was released from the hospital just before Christmas. All told, he had spent two and a half years in prison, almost all of that time in solitary confinement. After embracing Hedy, he poured out his rage against the German government, which had imprisoned him not for being a Russian agent or a terrorist, both of which he had certainly been, but for being a danger to German security, which he most assuredly was not. Meaningless! And, as if this were not ironic enough, he owed his release not to his old comrades in the Socialist Revolutionary party, who had refused to take Russia out of a stupid, barbaric war, but to his bitterest enemies in the revolutionary movement, the Social Democrats (or, as they were now known, the Communists).

Azef's first thought on being released was to emigrate with Hedy to Switzerland, which had always been a place of refuge and rehabilitation for him. This proved impossible; the war was still raging in the West, and the Swiss frontier was closed. Furthermore, he needed a job, and, with his knowledge of the Russian language and Russian politics, the best place to find one was in the German Ministry of Foreign Affairs, which was currently conducting the Brest-Litovsk peace negotiations. How the former "enemy alien" obtained a post at the foreign ministry is not known, nor is anything known about what services he was expected to perform, but in January 1918, he did succeed in securing a position of some sort.

We may imagine that for a few months, Azef and Hedy were happy. But imprisonment had undermined his health, and his kidneys now gave him constant pain. In April, he went to the Krankenhaus Westend Hospital for treatment of acute kidney disease. On the seventeenth of that month he wrote Hedy that he was in such a bad way that he could not hold a pen long enough to write her a real letter. His condition deteriorated rapidly, and on April 24, at four o'clock in the afternoon, Azef died. His age at the time was not yet forty-nine.

Two days later, Hedy buried him at the cemetery in their old neighborhood of Wilmersdorf. She was the only mourner. For eight hundred marks, she obtained a respectable lot and a funeral ceremony of the "second class." But she decided not to inscribe a gravestone with Azef's name. Russians often visited the cemetery, she explained to a visitor, and it was best to avoid any "unpleasantness." On Azef's grave, there appears only a marker bearing a number: 446. But over the grave a rosebush flowers, planted by Hedy and tended by her as long as she lived.

Epilogue

THEY SAY THAT HISTORY is written by the winners. If so, this would explain not only why Azef's story disappeared from public consciousness, but also why his contemporaries' fates attracted so little attention following the enormous events of 1914–1921. What generations of revolutionaries had dreamed of accomplishing—the destruction of czarist power—was accomplished in a few years of incomparably bloody world war. Then, for a brief time, it seemed that Azef's old associates on the Left, the Socialist Revolutionaries and Constitutional Democrats, would become the rulers of Russia. But the October Revolution of 1917, which brought the Bolsheviks to power, and the subsequent Red victory in the Russian Civil War, made losers of all the Communists' competitors. SRs and *Kadetys,* Social Monarchists and Black Hundreds, revolutionary terrorists and Secret Police agents . . . all were apparently cast into the "dustbin of history" by the triumph of Lenin's party.

Even now that the categories of winner and loser have again been shown to be purely provisional, it takes some effort to recall that when the February Revolution overthrew the Romanov dynasty, the Socialist Revolutionary party was the largest political organization in Russia. Eight years earlier, the SRs had reeled from the impact of Azef's exposure as a double agent, but their loss of identification as "the party of the terror" eventually brought them more benefits than burdens. When the World War threw Russia into chaos, the SRs were able to compete with other revolutionary groups for mass influence without diverting their energies and funds to the pursuit of a private war against czarist officials. After the great mass uprising of February 1917 overthrew the monarchy, the party emerged as the most powerful revolutionary group in the countryside and a partner, with the Constitutional Democrats, in the new Provisional Government headed by Prime Minister Kerensky. Viktor Chernov was named Kerensky's minister of agriculture; Boris Savinkov served for a time as deputy minister of war; and Vladimir Zenzinov became one of the prime minister's close advisors.

At the same time, however, the loosely organized party had already begun to crack under the pressure of events. While the majority of SRs supported continued Russian participation in World War I, an influential minority adopted the "revolutionary defeatist" position advocated by the Bolsheviks. This split became irreparable when Lenin's party, promising to take Russia out of the war, made their bid for power in November 1917. The "Left SRs," including such figures as Marc Natanson, generally supported the new regime, but the "Right SRs" went into opposition. Chernov, always the balancer, was elected Chairman of the All-Russian Constituent Assembly, but never got the opportunity to serve in this position. On the first day that it convened, the Bolsheviks dispersed the Assembly on the ground that it no longer represented the revolutionary masses. Chernov remained in Russia until 1920, when the party was outlawed; then he again became an émigré, living in Prague and Paris for twenty years before emigrating finally to the United States at the outbreak of World War II. He died in New York in 1958.

In 1918, Socialist Revolutionary terrorism flared for the last time. A "Left SR" protesting the terms of the peace treaty with Germany gunned down the German ambassador to Russia, and "Right SRs" assassinated several Bolshevik officials, seriously wounding Lenin himself. The young woman who almost killed the Soviet leader was named Dora Kaplan; the pistol that she used in the attempt had been furnished by Boris Savinkov. Drowned in the more general violence of the Civil War, this campaign had little effect other than to provide the new regime with another reason to suppress their former allies.

Meanwhile, Savinkov, who had begun intriguing with White generals even while serving in Kerensky's cabinet, openly joined the forces attempting to overthrow the Soviet government. In 1918, in Moscow, he attempted unsuccessfully to create an underground anti-Soviet terrorist movement. In 1919, he went abroad to secure Western military aid for the White armies, and the following year, he trained Polish soldiers sent to fight against the Communists in the Soviet-Polish war. After the defeat of the Whites, Savinkov returned to Paris. For a time, he occupied himself with literature, but the early 1920s found the inveterate adventurer once again plotting with émigrés against the Russian government. In 1924, Savinkov was lured back into Russia on a sham terrorist mission actually organized by the Cheka, the Communist secret police. Arrested almost immediately, he was charged with anti-Soviet terrorism, a crime carrying the death penalty.

At his trial, Savinkov conducted his own defense. He described his life as a revolutionary terrorist, apologized for doubting the Soviet regime's legitimacy, and expressed the hope that he would be allowed to live to help build the new Russia. He was convicted and sentenced to death, but with a strong recommendation for mercy. The result was a ten-year prison sentence—merciful, perhaps, in some cases, but an intolerable burden to a barely domesticated creature like the terrorist poet. On May 7, 1925, Azef's old lieutenant ended his stormy existence by jumping headfirst from a fourth-floor window of Moscow's Lubyanka Prison.

The reader may also be interested in the fates of other of Yevno Azef's contemporaries.

Sergei Zubatov, Azef's first police supervisor, did not survive the Revolution of February 1917. After von Plehve's assassination, he had returned from exile to Moscow and was living there still when the czarist government was overthrown. The old intriguer, famous for his manipulation of revolutionary organizations, feared that he would be brought to trial by the Kerensky regime. In despair, he took his own life.

Zubatov's most distinguished successor, Aleksandr Gerasimov, was more fortunate. Although removed from his position by Kerensky, he was not prosecuted and remained in Russia until the Bolsheviks took power. Then he emigrated to Germany, where he lived in relative comfort and wrote his memoirs. Gerasimov insisted that he had placed other important agents—agents other than Azef—in the Socialist Revolutionary party and swore that he would never reveal their names. He never did. He also expressed his conviction that Azef had been for the most part a faithful police agent, compelled to play along with the SRs in order to protect himself. Gerasimov died in Berlin during World War II.

Vladimir Burtzev, the journalist who exposed Azef, returned to Russia in 1915. He described himself not as a socialist or an anarchist but as an antiauthoritarian—a "bombist." After the February Revolution, he began attacking the Bolsheviks in print, charging that the Germans had financed their efforts to take Russia out of the war. When Lenin's party took power, he continued to oppose them publicly and was briefly imprisoned, after which he moved his newspaper, *Common Cause,* to Paris. In 1921, Burtzev participated in the creation of an émigré organization intended to unite all enemies of the Soviet state and devoted himself for the next several years to exposing Soviet agents in this movement. Poverty-stricken and disappointed, he died in Paris during the Nazi occupation.

Lubov Grigorievna Azef had played a leading role in the community of SR émigrés in Paris, but although she appears to have been entirely ignorant of her husband's double life, his exposure as a police agent undermined her position in that tight little community. She left Paris with her two children shortly before the outbreak of World War I and moved to New York City, where she changed her name and eventually remarried. According to all reports, Lubov lived quietly in New York until her death in 1958. The identities and fates of her and Yevno Azef's children are unknown.

Hedwig Klopfer remained in Berlin after Azef's death. It is not known when she died, but she was still living there in the 1920s and talking willingly to Russian journalists and scholars about her late "husband." She had always loved Azef, she said, and would do so always. The historian Boris I. Nikolaevsky, who interviewed her in 1927, wrote, "My general and firm impression from conversations with Madame N—— (her real last name was Klopfer) is this: she, undoubtedly, forgot much, and there was much she didn't understand at the time. . . . But she never consciously lied."

Notes on Sources

Although little of recent note has been published about Azef's life, three older sources are indispensable. They reflect, respectively, the revolutionaries' point of view, the government's perspective, and an attempt to strike a balance between the two.

Shortly after Azef's exposure, his chief lieutenant, Boris Savinkov, published his *Memoirs of a Terrorist* (New York: Albert & Charles Boni, 1931, translated by Joseph Shaplen), a dramatic, detailed account of Azef's career as a terrorist from the point at which Savinkov met him (August 1903) until his flight from Paris early in 1909. The book contains a good deal of information that is unavailable elsewhere, although it naturally obscures certain matters that could have been dangerous to Savinkov (e.g., his precise role in eliminating Nikolai Tatarov). It is also very well written, although one suspects that Savinkov's reconstructions of past conversations owe as much to his novelist's imagination as to his powers of memory. Boris Savinkov is also the author of two other relevant works: a novel about terrorism called *Pale Horse* (New York: Alfred A. Knopf, 1919) and *What Never Happened* (New York: Alfred A. Knopf, 1917), a bitter novella influenced by the Azef Affair.

A Russian government official's perspective on Azef and the Socialist Revolutionary party is offered by Aleksandr I. Spiridovich in his *Histoire du Terrorisme Russe, 1886–1917,* originally published in 1930 and reprinted with an introduction by Paul Wilkinson (Millwood, New York: Kraus Reprint Co., 1983). Spiridovich was the czarist intelligence officer, bodyguard of Nicholas II, and, ultimately, general of gendarmes who protected Azef at the time of the Tomsk raid and later helped to expose Nikitenko's "Conspiracy against the Czar." In this memoir, he may not have revealed all that he knew of Azef's role as a police agent, but considering his former position, his is a remarkably objective and detached study. It is also a rich source of documents and biographical information about the SRs.

The outstanding biography of Azef is by Boris Nikolaevsky (also spelled Nikolajewsky), *Aseff the Spy: Russian Terrorist and Police Stool,* published in Berlin in 1932 and in the United States in 1934 (Garden City, New York: Doubleday, Doran & Company, translated by George Reavey). Nikolaevsky is also the author of the monograph *Konets Azefa (The Last Days of Azef)* (Berlin: Petropolis, 1931), based largely on interviews with Hedy Klopfer and materials supplied by her. When the Bolsheviks took power in Russia in October 1917, this old revolutionary, then aligned with the Mensheviks, gained access to the files of the Extraordinary Commission appointed by the Kerensky government in 1917 to investigate the Azef Affair. He went on to interview numerous participants in the drama, both SRs and government officials, and was given permission by Hedy to read Azef's private letters and prison notebooks.

Nikolaevsky's judicious but unsympathetic biography has long been considered the standard source on Azef. More recently, it has come under attack for insisting too strongly upon the importance of Azef's role as a terrorist. According to Dr. Anna Geifman, for example, Nikolaevsky was too much inclined to accept the SRs' version of events rather than the interpretation of figures like Aleksandr Gerasimov, who viewed Azef as a police agent forced from time to time to play along with the terrorists. See Geifman's doctoral dissertation, "Political Parties and Revolutionary Terrorism in Russia, 1900–1917" (Harvard University, 1990); and Gerasimov's memoir, *Na lezvii s terroristami,* originally published in 1934 in Berlin (Paris: YMCA Press, 1985). In my view, however, Nikolaevsky's book remains the most balanced and accurate source of information about the facts of Azef's career.

What robs *Aseff the Spy* of greater depth is its lack of psychological (or psycho-political) insight. Nikolaevsky's obvious detestation of his subject leads him to ascribe Azef's activities as a double agent primarily to his desire for money, and, secondarily, to his hedonistic tastes and alleged physical cowardice. For reasons explored in my text, none of these explanations is satisfactory. Moreover, the biographer tells us very little about Azef's personal relationships, business affairs, or family life. One learns more about the terrorist-spy's personality by reading Vladimir Zenzinov's memoirs (*Sovremennie Zapiski,* Paris, 1934), or Roman Goul's historical novel of 1930, *Azef* (Garden City, N.Y.: Doubleday, 1962, translated by Mirra Ginsburg). But the best source of insight into the psychology of the double agent is a book having nothing directly to do with Azef: John le Carré's brilliant novel, *A Perfect Spy* (New York: Alfred A. Knopf, 1986).

Other sources of information about Azef and his time are noted in the brief chapter-by-chapter references that follow. Four outstanding books on the period, however, deserve more prominent mention. W. Bruce Lincoln's dramatic history, *In War's Dark Shadow: The Russians before the Great War* (New York: Dial Press, 1983), is an accurate and moving account of social and political developments in Russia from the 1890s until 1914. Jacques Baynac's *Les Socialistes-révolutionnaires de mars 1881 à mars 1917* (Paris: Éditions Robert Laffont, 1979) is a fine history of the SRs that pays special attention to the Azef Affair. Oliver H. Radkey, *The Agrarian Foes of Bolshevism: Promise and Default of the Russian Socialist Revolutionaries February to October 1917* (New York: Columbia University Press, 1958), remains an indispensable source on the philosophy and practices of the SRs. And Roman Goul's novel, *Azef*, repays reading, although it collapses and transposes events for dramatic effect and tells us more about Boris Savinkov's personality and motives than about Azef's.

CHAPTER 1

The primary source of information about Azef's family and childhood is Boris I. Nikolaevsky, *Aseff the Spy*. Azef's mother's name, which is not mentioned in this biography, may be found in the Nikolaevsky Collection, Hoover Institution Archives (Hoover Institution on War, Peace, and Revolution, Box 12, Folder 5, Deposition of V. M. Chernov, 2 February 1910). My summary of Russia's anti-Jewish legislation and my description of conditions in the Pale of Settlement are based largely on Ismar Elbogen, *A Century of Jewish Life* (Philadelphia: Jewish Publication Society of America, 1944), supplemented by Paul Johnson, *A History of the Jews* (New York: Perennial Library, 1987), and W. Bruce Lincoln, *In War's Dark Shadow*. The quotation from Alexander II's decree on the Jews is from Elbogen, p. 58. My outline of Russia's social and economic development draws heavily upon Lincoln's book, and the discussion of cultural trends owes much to James H. Billington, *The Icon and the Axe: An Interpretive History of Russian Culture* (New York: Alfred A. Knopf, 1966). My account of the assassination of Alexander II relies on Lincoln and on Albert Parry, *Terrorism: From Robespierre to Arafat* (New York: Vanguard Press, 1976).

The portrait of Azef as a young man and the account of his activities in Rostov is based largely on Nikolaevsky. For the political thinking of the youth of this period, I relied on W. Bruce Lincoln and on James H. Billington's *Fire in the Minds of Men: Origins of the Revolutionary Faith* (New York: Basic Books, 1980). The undocumented stories that Azef left the *gymnasium* after the sixth

grade and that he was caught in a provocation while still a Rostov schoolboy
are to be found in an article entitled *"K biografii Azefa"* ("Towards a Biography
of Azef") in the newspaper *Rech'*, 24 January 1909. The same article alleges
that Azef embezzled money not from a butter-and-egg merchant but from
the office of the Rostov Factory Commission, from which he also stole a
gymnasium diploma. These stories are repeated by V. K. Agafonov in his book
The Overseas Okhranka (Petrograd, 1918), but by no other author.

Azef's activities in Germany, the quotations from his correspondence
with the Secret Police, and the police report on his "covetousness" are drawn
from Nikolaevsky's *Aseff the Spy*, pp. 25–26. The politics of the SRs during
this period are summarized by Baynac, *Les Socialistes-révolutionnaires,* and by
Radkey, *Agrarian Foes of Bolshevism*. The descriptions of Azef's individualism
and of his dreams of playing a unique role in Russian politics are extrapolations
of my own, based partly on materials contained in other sources and partly
on my own study of terrorist thinking, *Alchemists of Revolution: Terrorism in
the Modern World* (New York: Basic Books, 1987). The quotation about
Azef's letters to Lubov is drawn from Nikolaevsky, p. 30. Lenin's views on
terrorism are expressed in *What Is to Be Done? Burning Questions of Our
Movement* (New York: International Publishers, 1981, translated by J. Fineberg
and G. Hanna). Leon Trotsky's may be found in *Against Individual Terrorism*
(New York: Pathfinder Press, 1974).

CHAPTER 2

The descriptions of the Khodynka Field tragedy and of the changes
occurring in Russia at the turn of the century are based on W. Bruce Lincoln,
In War's Dark Shadow, and Richard Pipes, *Russia Under the Old Regime* (New
York: Charles Scribner's Sons, 1974). Lincoln also provides an excellent description of Sergei Zubatov's methods and career. The description of Zubatov
is based on Roman Goul's novel, *Azef,* and the overall outline of Azef's
relationship with Zubatov is based on Nikolaevsky, but the account of their
first meeting is for the most part an imaginative reconstruction based on
analyses of "Zubatovism" by Lincoln, Pipes, Spiridovich, and others. The
quotations from Zubatov and the report that Azef concluded this meeting by
demanding a salary increase and an advance are from Nikolaevsky, pp. 35–
36. Similarly, while Nikolaevsky briefly mentions Azef's defense of Mikhailovsky's philosophy at the *salon* of E. A. Neimchinova, I have summarized
the argument that a Socialist Revolutionary would probably have made against
the Social Democrats, using materials drawn from Oliver H. Radkey, *Agrarian
Foes of Bolshevism,* and from Richard Henry Eiter's doctoral dissertation,
"Organizational Growth and Revolutionary Tactics: Unity and Discord in the
Socialist Revolutionary Party, 1901–1907" (University of Pittsburgh, 1978).

Azef's relations with the Moscow Union leading to the Tomsk raid are described by Nikolaevsky. The quotations from Alexei Argunov and the quotation from *Revolutionary Russia* praising the assassination of Bogolepov are drawn from Aleksandr Spiridovich's *Histoire du Terrorisme Russe*, pp. 72 and 103. I have assumed, without knowing the date of Azef and Lubov's son's birth, that he was born shortly after their return to Russia. The information that the Azefs had two children, an older boy and younger girl, I owe to Dr. Sadi Mase of Washington, D.C. No writer, to my knowledge, tells us anything about these children, although in his novel, *Azef,* Roman Goul calls Azef and Lubov's son "Mischa."

CHAPTER 3

The description of Sipyagin's assassination by Balmashev is an imaginative reconstruction based on facts supplied by Nikolaevsky and Spiridovich. The quotations from the SR leaflet are from Spiridovich, p. 153; Gershuni's remarks ("It is only the beginning. . . .") and his quotation of the Lenzevich poem are from Nikolaevsky, pp. 50–51. The source of the story of the "contest" to establish the Fighting Organization is *Aseff the Spy,* and my discussion of the SRs' attitude toward terrorism is based on Oliver Radkey's and Richard Henry Eiter's studies. Azef's reports to the Secret Police protecting Gershuni are described by Nikolaevsky; the personal aspects of their relationship are based on my own sense of the bonds that united them, supplemented by Isaac Steinberg, *Spiridonova: Revolutionary Terrorist* (Freeport, N.Y.: Books for Libraries Press, 1935, translated by Gwenda David and Eric Mosbacher).

The story of the attempted assassination of Prince Obolensky is told by Spiridovich. Azef's letter to Zubatov asking to be recalled to Russia is quoted by Nikolaevsky, p. 55. Zubatov's later history, from the triumphant workers' march of 1902 until his dismissal by von Plehve, is based on W. Bruce Lincoln's *In War's Dark Shadow*. Nikolaevsky describes the betrayal of Melnikov and Kraft, and Spiridovich catalogs the results of the raids on SR headquarters in the winter of 1902–1903. The quotations from Kristianinov and his informant are from Nikolaevsky, pp. 59, 61, and 62. My descriptions of the Ufa strike and the assassination of Bogdanovich are based largely on Spiridovich.

My account of the events leading up to the Kishinev Massacre and the Massacre itself relies on W. Bruce Lincoln and on Ismar Elbogen, *A Century of Jewish Life*. Lincoln also documents the anti-Semitism of Zubatov and Lopukhin. The alleged plot by Witte against the czar is based on an interview of Lopukhin by Nikolaevsky and on Lopukhin's *Memoirs*. The description of Gershuni's capture by the police is based on facts supplied by Nikolaevsky and Spiridovich.

CHAPTER 4

My description of Boris Savinkov owes a good deal to Roman Goul's novel, *Azef*. The remainder of this chapter is based for the most part on Savinkov's *Memoirs of a Terrorist*. Savinkov's description of Azef is from his *Memoirs*, p. 11, as is the account of his tongue-lashing by Azef in Moscow (p. 21). The descriptions of Azef's recruiting methods and of his new methods of "scientific" terrorism are drawn from several sources, including Nikolaevsky, Goul, Edward Hyams, *Terrorists and Terrorism* (New York: St. Martin's Press, 1974); Albert Parry, *Terrorism: From Robespierre to Arafat* (New York: Vanguard Press, 1976); and Walter Laqueur, *Terrorism* (Boston: Little, Brown, 1977). The backgrounds of the terrorists who met at the Merchants Club are provided by Spiridovich; I have relied on Savinkov for descriptions of their personalities. See also W. S. Woytinsky, *Stormy Passage: A Personal History through Two Russian Revolutions to Democracy and Freedom 1905–1960* (New York: Vanguard Press, 1961). The account of Ratayev's character and of Azef's relationship with him is based on Nikolaevsky's study, as is the story of the betrayal of the Klichoglu group. See also Leonid A. Ratayev, *Provokator: Vospominaniia i documenty o rezoblacheniom Azef* (edited by P. E. Shchegolov, Moscow: 1929). The failed campaign against von Plehve is described in Boris Savinkov's *Memoirs*, pp. 26–30.

CHAPTER 5

Savinkov's *Memoirs* provide the bulk of our information about the two attempts to assassinate von Plehve, but I have also incorporated elements of Nikolaevsky's account, as well as certain facts provided by Spiridovich. The quotations from Azef on continuing the campaign are from Savinkov, pp. 35–36. The interpretation of Azef's motives in establishing the "menage" at 31 Zhukovsky Street is my own. The quotations from Azef ("When I kissed Sazonov . . .") and from Ivanovskaya are from Nikolaevksy (p. 87). The assassination itself and Sazonov's letter are described by Savinkov, and Azef's reaction to these events in Warsaw by Nikolaevsky. Savinkov quotes Kaliayev's "suicide" proposal (p. 48), Sazonov's pre-assassination remarks (p. 49), and Sazonov's prison letter (pp. 63–64). Spiridovich (p. 185) is the source of the quotation from *Revolutionary Russia*. The quotations from "N——" and from Gotz are from Nikolaevsky, pp. 88 and 90–91.

In Anna Geifman's view ("Political Parties and Revolutionary Terrorism in Russia," pp. 76–78), Azef sincerely attempted to prevent von Plehve's assassination while attempting at the same time to preserve his own personal safety. Dr. Geifman shares Aleksandr Gerasimov's opinion that the real organizer of the von Plehve operation and de facto leader of the Organization was not Azef, who remained a faithful police agent, but Boris Savinkov. In my opinion (reflected in the text), this perspective, which rests on discrediting the testimony of former revolutionaries while crediting that of former czarist officials, does not do justice to the available evidence. If Azef had wanted to expose the conspiracy (as he exposed so many later plots), he could have done so without jeopardizing his own security.

CHAPTER 6

My account of the debate among the SRs about the status of the Organization is based principally on Spiridovich's *Histoire* and Baynac's *Les Socialistes-révolutionnaires*. The unflattering description of Grand Duke Sergei is from W. Bruce Lincoln, p. 291, as are the references to the Russo-Japanese War. The brief catalog of terrorist incidents is drawn from Spiridovich. Boris Nikolaevsky, p. 95, is the source of the quotation from Stolypin, as well as of the description of Azef's attempt to throw suspicion on Sletov and Seliuk. The description of the campaign against Sergei is based for the most part on Savinkov's *Memoirs of a Terrorist*. The story of Bloody Sunday is based largely on Lincoln's account, and on Edward Crankshaw, *The Shadow of the Winter Palace: Russia's Drift to Revolution, 1825–1917* (New York: Viking Press, 1976), but the new worker's song is quoted by Nikolaevsky, p. 105. Savinkov's version of Kaliayev's refusal to attack the children is from his *Memoirs*, pp. 99–100. The account of the encounter between Kaliayev and the Grand Duchess is from the same source, pp. 107–10, as are the quotations from Kaliayev's prison speech (p. 116) and his last letter (p. 111). Kaliayev's recollection of the assassination is from Spiridovich, p. 241.

CHAPTER 7

The quotations from stories about the assassination of Sergei by European newspapers are from Roman Goul's *Azef,* p. 167. Nikolaevsky describes Ivanovskaya's conversation with Lubov in Paris and is the source of most of the information about Rachkovsky, but I have extrapolated the causes of Azef's depression from the available facts. The *John Crafton* fiasco is described both by Savinkov and Spiridovich. Azef's maneuvers leading to the betrayal of Vedenyapin and Troyitzky are based on material in Nikolaevsky's biography. Schweitzer's plots against the czar and Minister of Justice Muraviev are described by Savinkov. The details concerning the explosion that ended Schweitzer's life are supplied by Spiridovich, pp. 244–45. The March 1905 arrests of the SRs are detailed by Nikolaevsky, Spiridovich, and Baynac. The ratiocination that led Azef to suspect that Rachkovsky had planted an agent other than himself in the party is my own construction, based on existing facts.

CHAPTER 8

Nikolaevsky reports that Azef had difficulty convincing Ratayev to sanction his Russian trip; I have supplied the arguments that might have been used to convince him. The description of Savinkov's ill-fated campaign against Kleigels is based on his *Memoirs of a Terrorist*. The Anna Yakimova affair is based on facts supplied by Nikolaevsky, but I have imagined the conversation between Azef and Yakimova at Filipov's restaurant, and the reasoning that would have led Azef to suspect the involvement of Rachkovsky's spy.

The description of the SRs' war on the police is drawn from Spiridovich. See also Geifman, "Political Parties and Revolutionary Terrorism in Russia," pp. 103–21. The details of Azef's meeting with Rachkovsky are imagined, although Nikolaevsky makes it clear that the result of the meeting was the agent's decision to betray Savinkov, Breshkovskaya, and others. The account of Azef's immediate reaction to the Menchikov letter is from Nikolaevsky (p. 123), but I have constructed the thought processes that would have led him to retire temporarily from police work. Most of the material on Tatarov's background and the campaign to kill him is based on Savinkov's *Memoirs of a Terrorist*. The interrogation by Chernov is excerpted from the *Memoirs*, pp. 159–62, and the concluding quotations from Nazarov are also from Savinkov, p. 229. The information about Tatarov's pay I owe to Nikolaevsky.

CHAPTER 9

I have drawn my description of the Revolution of 1905 from several sources, including the works of Lincoln, Crankshaw, and Pipes previously cited; Sidney Harcave, *Years of the Golden Cockerel: The Last Romanov Tsars, 1814–1917* (New York: Macmillan, 1968); and Leon Trotsky, *1905* (New York: Random House, 1971, translated by Anya Bostock). The debate on suspending terrorism among the SRs and Azef's position on that question is described by both Nikolaevsky and Savinkov, and the description of the military committee's activities is based on Savinkov's *Memoirs* and on Spiridovich's *Histoire*. Nikolaevsky gives us the story of Azef's encounter with the Black Hundreds. The 1906 Imatra conference of the SRs is analyzed by Spiridovich and Radkey.

Boris Savinkov describes the campaign against Durnovo and Azef's declaration that he was considering ending his work as a terrorist (p. 200). The story of Father Gapon and his assassination is based largely on Savinkov's *Memoirs* (pp. 240–48), supplemented by Nikolaevsky and Lincoln. The quotation from Gapon ("You can't cut a tree down") is from Nikolaevsky, pp. 146–47. The account of Azef's arrest and of his meetings with Gerasimov and Rachkovsky derive principally from Nikolaevsky (see pp. 151–54), but I have imagined Azef's emotional and mental processes in the Secret Police's jail. Gerasimov's own version of these events is contained in his memoirs, *Na lezvii s terroristami* (Paris, 1985).

CHAPTER 10

The campaign against Dubasov is based on the accounts of Savinkov and Nikolaevsky, supplemented by Spiridovich. (Azef's reasoning in making the decision to assist in this campaign is my own extrapolation.) The quotations from the official report of the incident, Boris Vnorovsky's letter, and the SR proclamation are from Savinkov's *Memoirs of a Terrorist*, pp. 216–17 and 221. Azef's subsequent meeting with Rachkovsky and Gerasimov is described by Nikolaevsky (p. 162), and the affair of Savinkov's capture and escape is drawn from Savinkov's book. Savinkov's and Suliatitsky's conversation is from the *Memoirs* (p. 267), and the announcement of the escape and Savinkov's letter to Nepluyev are from the same source (pp. 269 and 276). The sources for Azef's relationship with Gerasimov include Nikolaevsky and Gerasimov (see *Aseff the Spy*, pp. 175–76). Nikolaevsky and Spiridovich are the primary sources for the betrayals of Zilberberg and Suliatitsky and of Nikitenko's "Conspiracy against the Czar." Savinkov (p. 297) describes the last days of Zilberberg and Suliatitsky. Spiridovich (p. 421) quotes the party decisions reached at Tampere.

CHAPTER 11

The opening quotation from Nicholas II is from W. Bruce Lincoln, *In War's Dark Shadow*, p. 328. The betrayal of Trauberg and the Flying Detachment is based on Nikolaevsky's and Spiridovich's accounts. The meditation on Azef's psychology and his motives for betraying fellow terrorists is my own, inspired to some extent by John le Carré's *A Perfect Spy*. The description of Hedy Klopfer's career and character is based largely on Nikolaevsky's monograph, *The Last Days of Azef*. This author nowhere mentions Hedy's last name, but it is to be found in a letter of Nikolaevsky to Aleksandr M. Gurzich dated 25 November 1927 in the Boris I. Nikolaevsky Collection, Hoover Institution Archives (Hoover Institution on War, Peace, and Revolution, Box 206, Folder 7). The interpretation of Azef's relationship with Hedy is my own, based partly on facts supplied by Nikolaevsky and conversations imagined by Roman Goul.

The betrayal of the two plots against the czar and the affair of the Charjui "expropriation" are described by Nikolaevsky and Spiridovich, supplemented by Gerasimov. The campaign to assassinate the czar on board the *Rurik* is based on Savinkov's memoirs, supplemented by the account of Nikolaevsky. The quotations from Avdeyev are from the *Memoirs* (pp. 303–4). Spiridovich's view is to be found at p. 531 of his *Histoire*. Geifman minimizes Azef's participation in this attempted regicide, remarking that even if he were involved, he had already terminated his activities as a police agent and was not obliged to report to Gerasimov. Still, the episode is clearly inconsistent with the "revisionist" view of Azef as a faithful servant of the monarchy.

CHAPTER 12

My account of the trial of Burtzev/Azef is based, in part, on Savinkov's *Memoirs,* but Spiridovich is also an important source. Savinkov's testimonial to Azef is from his *Memoirs* (p. 317). Azef's letter may be found in Spiridovich (pp. 546–47) and in Goul's *Azef* (p. 279). Goul is the source for Burtzev's open letter (p. 278). Savinkov's speech is excerpted in Nikolaevsky (p. 272), and Figner's statement is drawn from the same source (*ibid.*). Burtzev's own version of these events may be found in several articles, e.g., "Azeff's Career, Told by Vladimir Bourtzeff," *New York Tribune,* 31 August 1912; "Police Provocation in Russia: Azef, the *Tsarist Spy,*" *Slavonic and East European Review,* VI: 246–60, December 1927. My account of Burtzev's interview with Lopukhin aboard the Cologne Express derives from Nikolaevsky (pp. 4–5 and 20–21), as does the description of Argunov's interview with him in St. Petersburg (p. 277). Geifman speculates that Burtzev and his associates may have terrorized Lopukhin into cooperating with the SRs. The quotations from Lopatin and from Azef's second letter are from Savinkov (pp. 300 and 333–34). Chernov's interrogation of Azef is recalled by Savinkov (pp. 343–48), and Azef's flight is described both by Savinkov and by Nikolaevsky. The last exchange between Chernov and Azef is from Goul (p. 306).

CHAPTER 13

The notice published by the SR Central Committee is quoted by Spiridovich (p. 556). Herman Rosenthal's article on the Azef Affair, "A Phase of the Russian Spy System," appeared in *The American Review of Reviews,* 39:463–65, April 1909. Other press commentaries on Azef's exposure and flight include "Career of a Police Spy," *The Spectator,* 102:120–22, 23 January 1909, and "Russian Police Mystery," 102:212–13, 6 February 1909; "Police and Reds Both Hunt Azeff," *New York Times,* 7 February 1909; "Azeff's Treason Puzzles Terrorists," *New York Times,* 22 February 1909; "The Double-Dyed Infamy of Azef," *The North American Review,* 189:632–34, April 1909; and David Soskice, "The Story of Eugene Azeff: Unmasking of Russia's Secret Police System," *McClure's Magazine,* 34:282–99, January 1910. The material on the consequences of Azef's exposure (including the Petrov case) is based on Nikolaevsky, Spiridovich, and Radkey. Spiridovich supplies the quotation from Zenzinov (p. 569) and the accounts of subsequent terrorist acts by the SRs and by Bogrov. (See also "Terrorists Again Active," *New York Times,* 19

September 1911.) Nikolaevsky (p. 287) is the source of the observation that terrorism had become "both politically and psychologically impossible."

The story of Azef's last days, including his flight with Hedy, their resettlement in Berlin, and the interview with Burtzev in Frankfurt, is based on materials found in Nikolaevsky's biography and in his *Last Days of Azef*. Azef's "weighing" of his deeds is from *Aseff the Spy,* pp. 293–94. The interpretation of Azef's reaction to Burtzev's "stare of incomprehension" is my own. The description of Azef's arrest and imprisonment, the quotations from his prison letters to Hedy, and the accounts of his death and burial are drawn from *Last Days of Azef*. The information about the rosebush I owe to the postscript to Roman Goul's *Azef*.

Index

AZEFF'S TREASON PUZZLES TERRORISTS

Russian Revolutionists Unable to Account for His Revelations to the Police.

GAVE THEM LITTLE OF VALUE

Many Here Think Leader in the Russian Movement May Have Thought to Hoodwink Government.

The sensational unmasking of Eugene Azeff, a member of the Fighting Organization of the Russian revolutionists, as a Government spy, has aroused the greatest interest on the east side of New York, which has been a liberal supporter of the many attempts to disrobe autocracy from the Russian Empire.

they turned over to Azeff all credentials and affiliations.

"At that time there was not one iota of evidence of his having given any information to the Government.

"Azeff organized, together with Gerehuni, from December, 1901, to the Summer of 1902, the plan to institute terror in Russia, which would begin with the assassination of Sipiagine. The attack on Sipiagine was successful, and there was still no evidence of disloyalty on the part of Azeff.

"Azeff worked from the Summer of 1902 until the Summer of 1903 in St. Petersburg with the group in that city. He planned the contraband transportation of literature through Finland, became Gershuni's closest companion, and took part in the deliberations relating to the overthrow of Obolensky and Bogdanovich, and the attack on Bogdanovich was successful. From this date we obtain the first glimpses of his relations with the police. He saw Durnovo, Minister of the Interior, and received 5,000 rubles, which he was to contribute to the party fund on the one condition that the money should not be given to the Fighting Organization. He went to Durnovo to sell his services and informed him that he could be of assistance to the Government, but he did not reveal the important fact that he himself was a member of the Central Committee, which might have raised the price of his services at once.

"He did not even disclose the fact that he had become a member of the party. He said simply that he was not a member of the party. His chief boast was that he knew Gershuni. This is an important point, which throws light on the beginning of his spy work ..."

N ASSASSIN'S STO

ssful Outcome of Plot der Von Plehve Told by One of the Anarchists Who Took Part.

Eugene Azeff.

SUNDAY, JULY 10, 1910.

HE DEATH OF VON PLEHVE

ail of the Attempts on the Life of the nd of Which Was Successful.

ASSASSIN OF GRAND DUKE SERGIUS

B. Savinkov Writes a Dramatic Story of the Long Watch of the Conspirators and the Final Hurling of the Bomb That Killed the Powerful Uncle of the Czar.

Grand Duke Sergius.

By B. Savinkov.

Translated for THE SUNDAY TIMES by Herman Bernstein.

T the Geneva Conference of the Fighting Organization, in September, 1905, I was intrusted with the plot to assassinate the Governor General of Moscow, Grand Duke Sergius Alexandrovich.

Dora Brilliant, Ivan Kalayev, and Opanas were to go with me to Moscow. I had the right to enlarge the organization by one member only. Azeff recommended an old worker, named X, concerning ...

solved in their own ways. Kalayev preferred to meet me in his sled, although it was quite uncomfortable to talk that way and the frost permitted no lengthy meetings. Sometimes Kalayev, having prepared an excuse at the coachmen's inn, would meet me on Sundays in Bakstov's tavern. These meetings were a treat to us. We spent two or three hours together, discussing the details and working out plans for the future.

Opanas rarely met me in the street. Since he kept aloof from his colleagues, he would don his Sunday coat and come to meet me in the tavern or in the circus ...

Ivan Kal Taken

Kalayev Approaching "I think the right He could emotion. risk he w rare occa